Work Orientations

Work orientations and work attitudes have to do with the productive capacities in society. Insofar as individuals are positively oriented towards contributing their labour, we can expect a great amount of work to be done and to be carried out efficiently, carefully and responsibly. These subjective factors are thus very vital in modern working life.

Work Orientations: Theoretical Perspectives and Empirical Findings offers up-to-date research on people's commitment to work and employment and job satisfaction in economically advanced countries. It will also analyse changes that have taken place in these respects over the last decades.

Among the key issues in *Work Orientations* are questions about whether patterns of work centrality and employment commitment tend to remain stable or have changed across time in various countries. Moreover, we assume that the circumstances under which people participate in the social division of labour colour their subjective relationships to their jobs and to employment in general. A major aim of the book is to explore the impact of factors such as occupation, education, age and gender on work orientations and work attitudes.

Work Orientations will be invaluable for researchers and scholars in the fields or organizational studies, the sociology of work, employee engagement and related disciplines.

Bengt Furåker is Professor at the Department of Sociology and Work Science, University of Gothenburg.

Kristina Håkansson is Professor at the Department of Sociology and Work Science, University of Gothenburg.

Routledge Studies in Management, Organizations and Society

This series presents innovative work grounded in new realities, addressing issues crucial to an understanding of the contemporary world. This is the world of organised societies, where boundaries between formal and informal, public and private, local and global organizations have been displaced or have vanished, along with other nineteenth century dichotomies and oppositions. Management, apart from becoming a specialized profession for a growing number of people, is an everyday activity for most members of modern societies.

Similarly, at the level of enquiry, culture and technology, and literature and economics, can no longer be conceived as isolated intellectual fields; conventional canons and established mainstreams are contested. **Management, Organizations and Society** addresses these contemporary dynamics of transformation in a manner that transcends disciplinary boundaries, with books that will appeal to researchers, students and practitioners alike.

Recent titles in this series include:

For a full list of titles in this series, please visit www.routledge.com

Work Orientations
Theoretical Perspectives
and Empirical Findings

**Edited by Bengt Furåker
and Kristina Håkansson**

Routledge
Taylor & Francis Group

NEW YORK AND LONDON

First published 2020
by Routledge
605 Third Avenue, New York, NY 10017

and by Routledge
2 Park Square, Milton Park, Abingdon, Oxon, OX14 4RN

First issued in paperback 2021

Routledge is an imprint of the Taylor & Francis Group, an informa business

Library of Congress Cataloging-in-Publication Data
Names: Furaker, Bengt, 1943– editor. | Hakansson, Kristina,
    1959– editor.
Title: Work orientations : theoretical perspectives and empirical
    findings / edited by Bengt Furaker and Kristina Hakansson.
Description: New York, NY : Routledge, 2020. | Series:
    Routledge studies in management, organizations and society |
    Includes index.
Identifiers: LCCN 2019019657 | ISBN 9780815383291
    (hardback) | ISBN 9781351121149 (ebook)
Subjects: LCSH: Work ethic. | Work—Psychological aspects. | Job
    satisfaction. | Employees—Attitudes.
Classification: LCC HD4905 .W66 2020 | DDC 306.3/613—dc23
LC record available at https://lccn.loc.gov/2019019657

ISBN 13: 978-0-367-78534-5 (pbk)
ISBN 13: 978-0-8153-8329-1 (hbk)

Typeset in Sabon
by Apex CoVantage, LLC

Contents

1 Introduction

Bengt Furåker and Kristina Håkansson

The point of departure for this book is the need to consider people's subjective relationships to various aspects of their jobs and to work in general. These relationships are important and can be seen as part of a society's productive capacities. Insofar as individuals are positive with respect to contributing their energy, skills and effort in the production of goods and services, we can expect a large amount of work to be done and to be done efficiently, carefully and responsibly. Of course, the circumstances under which human beings participate in various activities colour their subjective relationships to those activities. It may appear that work orientations refer to something that people bring to their jobs, whereas, for example, job satisfaction seems to flow in the opposite direction—as something derived from work. We should, however, be aware of the interaction that is taking place. People enter working life with various mind-sets and expectations, but their outlook is influenced or reshaped by the conditions under which work takes place. Another formative element consists of the alternative opportunities available to make a living. We want to deepen our understanding of different aspects of these opportunities. The book aims to describe and explain the development of work orientations in the last decades. It covers a period during which significant changes have occurred in contemporary societies and labour markets. The overall guiding question is, What has happened to people's work orientations in a changing working life?

Modern societies are all work societies in the sense that a great amount of labour is continuously being carried out. In spite of the fact that some parts of the population are outside the labour force (they may be young, retired, staying at home with small children, attending universities, etc.) and others are temporarily absent from work, large numbers of people go to their jobs day after day, week after week, year after year, to take care of various tasks, which more or less contribute to maintain or improve the population's quality of life. Although the distribution of income and capital is very unequal in the economically advanced world, in historical comparison the majority of the populations enjoy an impressively high standard of living.

We do not deal with all types of socioeconomic systems but focus on contemporary developed capitalist societies, in which private ownership of the means of production, wage labour, competition and profit-making are principal features. They are also characterized by a significant public and/or non-profit service sector. The labour markets in modern societies are supposed to be 'free' in that people are not forced into specific jobs, but can choose whatever job they want to have. This freedom is vital, as people's performances are likely to be affected by whether their contributions are voluntary or not. It can be debated to what extent work in modern societies is voluntary. Without much property other than their labour power, people have rather little opportunity entirely to escape the economic necessity to work for a living.

This last statement also applies to societies with generous welfare state arrangements. The general rule in these systems is that working-age individuals have to offer their capacity for work in the labour market; they are exempted only under specific circumstances such as childbearing, sickness and disability. Still, there are significant cross-national variations regarding who is under pressure to participate. A major task for the architects of contemporary welfare states is to define the circumstances under which people should be allowed public financial support and accordingly be able to refrain from taking on employment or stay home from work. It is a task associated with an incessant debate on the principles and norms with respect to benefit entitlements, the size of benefits relative to wage levels, how much resources should be spent on various programs and how cheating can be prevented.

In this book the concept of work refers to gainful employment, in principle as identified in the developed countries' labour force statistics. This is not to deny that there is a lot of unpaid work in society, but our approach permits us to benefit from the fact that available datasets and statistics from different countries are based on the same or similar definitions of gainful employment. The key concept is thus here plainly understood as an activity in exchange for income. Hence we avoid the debate that appears from time to time concerning the question how to define work (Engelstad 1984; Eyerman 1985; Daniels 1987; Karlsson 2004, 2017).

Although employers in principle have the power to organize the work process, wage labour requires a certain degree of consent on the part of the workers. The reason is that the labour contract cannot entirely specify how employees' assignments should be performed. Employers' knowledge of the details of the work process—what is to be done and how it is to be done—is often limited and incomplete (Furåker 2005: 74–85). Employees may actually be the ones to have the best knowledge and understanding of how to carry out various tasks. This gives them an advantage in relation to their employer. The scope of freedom for workers certainly varies from one job to another, and it is of great interest to make comparisons of attitudes related to different kinds of work.

An illustration of the aspects we are interested in can be found in the classical writings by Max Weber (1930: 58–60) on the contrast between 'traditionalism' and the 'spirit of capitalism'. In one of his examples, a farm worker was offered a higher rate per acre for mowing, but instead of working more or doing the same as before (and thus still earn more money) he chose to earn the same by mowing less land. In other words, the worker had not adopted the attitude of striving for as much as possible; he just did what was required to satisfy his customary needs. He may very well have had an instrumental attitude to work—as work was a means to make a living—but within this framework there are at least two different options: to maintain a certain level of living or to increase it. For the development of capitalism, it is obvious that the attitude entailing willingness to work more in order to earn more was most appropriate.

Actually, the issue outlined above is still present under developed capitalism. In the economics literature on labour supply it is referred to as the substitution and income effects and there is the idea of a backward-bending supply curve of labour (e.g., Buchanan 1971; Sloman 2010: 229–230). On the one hand, when wages are raised work becomes more attractive as every hour spent at work is better remunerated or, to put it another way, leisure time becomes more expensive. This could hence make us expect an increase of the supply of labour. On the other hand, with higher hourly wages employees can afford to refrain from increasing their supply of labour as their income increases anyway. They can even lower their quantity of work and keep the same level of living.

We should keep in mind that people cannot simply choose how much they want to work, as flexibility in this respect is far from unlimited. One thing is how much leisure workers can afford to have and another thing is what employers allow. In many cases, nobody will be hired unless he or she accepts full-time commitment, but there are also jobs in which part-time is taken for granted. Anyhow, to some extent, people have a choice between working more, with increased earnings as the result, and working less, thus instead having more leisure. In this connection their attitudes are likely to play a significant role.

Work—A Key Sociological Category

A main point of departure for the book is that paid work is a key sociological category. It is a crucial organizing principle in society, to a large extent affecting not only people's lives but also institutions, values and discourses. We find it necessary to emphasize the importance of work in social analysis, because many authors have tried to detract from it. One of the most well-known attempts of the kind was made by Claus Offe (1985) in an analysis first published in German. The author claimed that, for a long time, work had been treated as the *key* sociological concept, but that, at least by the early 1980s, this position had become obsolete. He presented two main arguments in favour of his thesis. The first is that work had become much more differentiated due to the increased division of labour and the expansion of services. This was supposed to lead to a situation in which people experience their jobs very differently. Work is 'no longer the focus of collective meaning and social and political division' and, therefore, 'with respect to their objective and subjective contents of experience, many wage-earning activities have hardly more in common than the name "work" '(Offe 1985: 136). We find this way of reasoning untenable; it is like saying that 'food' is no longer a relevant concept because there are now so many different dishes.

The second argument refers to an alleged decline in regard of the work ethic (Offe 1985: 140–148). As the claim will be further scrutinized in Chapter 2, we can leave it out here. It is sufficient to take notice of the principal deduction involved: Offe's whole analysis implies that work must abdicate from its privileged position in sociological analysis. Our position is very different; in contrast, we assume that work is *one* major sociological category and that it will remain that way in the foreseeable future. This conclusion is not undermined by the fact that sociological studies rest on several other crucial concepts. The significance of each concept is dependent on the topic under scrutiny. Whether or not work is generally the most important category is a question which it is a waste of time to pay attention to.

There exists a perception of work as a necessary evil, as primarily associated with coercion of the individual. For those who make such an interpretation it lies close at hand to try to minimize the scope of work. In that vein we find proposals on shortening of working hours, paid sabbatical years and what is usually referred to as a citizens' wage or basic income. We should note that there are several shades within such a work-negative approach. For example, it is one thing to be in favour of shorter working hours and another to advocate a basic income or a citizens' wage–that is, an income to live on independent of one's contribution in terms of labour. Those who active represent the latter position make up a relatively small group of scholars and activists, but they can be found in many countries (e.g., Ackerman, Alstott and Van Parijs 2005; Birnbaum 2012; Gorz 1999; Offe 1996; Standing 2013, 2014; Wright 2017: 426–428).

One argument for a basic income is that work is soon about to end or at least to be significantly reduced. Through the years, we have repeatedly encountered publications making such assumptions (e.g., Aronowitz 2005; Gorz 1985; Matthes 1983; Rifkin 1995). Technical development is often supposed to lead to continuous job losses and increasing unemployment. Artificial intelligence and digitalization are the most recent dynamics to trigger these kinds of thoughts. There is, however, very little empirical support for the end-of-work thesis (Furåker 2005: 217–221, 2009; Therborn 1987). While rationalization has transformed and shrunk employment in agriculture and industry, the service sector has expanded. Moreover, the production of material products still requires a great deal of labour, and some jobs in manufacturing are not really gone, but have been moved from high-wage to low-wage countries. With respect to services, it is certainly possible with further rationalizations (a lot has already been done), but when it comes to human services such as childcare, elderly care and healthcare there are obvious difficulties.

Because the total work effort is fundamental for the level of living in society, high proportions of both the male and the female population need to work and perform well. We should, however, qualify this argument a bit by adding a few comments. First, it matters not only how much people work and how well they perform but also what they do. There is an ecological or environmental dimension to take into account; some of the work done may lead to global warming, increased pollution and other harmful consequences. As a result, the effects on the standard of living are sometimes dubious or directly negative. Additionally, we must not shut our eyes to the risks that people work too much, irrespective of the underlying reasons—whether they are forced to do it because the income is badly needed or whether they are (too) deeply engaged in their job responsibilities, their patients, their clients, etc. There are no doubt great health risks with heavy workloads; many individuals become physically injured because they are too tired to handle their own and others' safety properly and others get mental health problems because of stress and feelings of inadequacy when facing difficult-to-solve or unsolvable tasks (e.g., Dunham 2001; Karasek and Theorell 1990; Tausig 2013). Another essential aspect is the puzzle of combining extensive employment duties with family life, which is also identified as a source of stress (e.g., Bianchi, Casper and Berkowitz King 2005; Frone, Russell and Cooper 1997). We do not want to create the impression that we consider pro-work attitudes something exclusively positive. Such attitudes may be positive for the production of goods and services in society, but they may also hit back by causing problems in other respects.

Second, we should also be aware of the home- or leisure-based production outside the formal economy, including childcare, cooking, cleaning, washing, gardening, hunting and fishing, as well as work in voluntary associations and the like. It is generally difficult, if not impossible, to accurately estimate the scope of such activities in the informal sector, but there should be no doubt that they contribute substantially to the wealth of individuals, particularly in certain regions. We must emphasize that the two comments we have brought up here do not falsify—but just modify—the conclusion that the amount of paid work is crucial in contemporary developed capitalism.

Changes in Society, Changes in Work Orientations?

Changes in the labour market may impinge on work orientations. In the last decades, the development of technology, globalization, flexibilization and individualization has had a significant impact on working life. Another development is the changing composition of the workforce. The requirements for higher education levels have delayed young people's entry into the labour market and some categories of the employed postpone retirement. As a consequence, there are indications pointing to an aging workforce, but there is not so much knowledge about how such changes affect work orientations.

The development of 'postindustrialism', as described by Daniel Bell (1976), involves an expansion of service jobs which are to a large extent a matter of so-called human services. Such services imply a specific relationship between employees and patients, clients, etc. ('a game between persons'), and most are likely very important for work attitudes. Postindustrialism is also associated with a growth of highly qualified jobs, and such a transformation is significant because these jobs are often associated with certain attitudinal configurations. John Goldthorpe (1982, 2000: Chapter 10; Erikson and Goldthorpe 1993: 41–44) has developed a distinction between service and labour employment relationships, admitting that there are mixed forms as well. The former ideal type refers to employees exercising 'delegated authority or specialized knowledge and expertise', while employees on a labour contract are involved in 'a relatively short-term exchange and specific exchange of money for effort' (Erikson and Goldthorpe 1993: 41–42; italics removed). A service employment relationship means that a great deal of autonomy and discretion must be left to employees. This is in turn likely to affect work orientations and work attitudes. Erik Olin Wright (1997: 24–26) has dealt with service employment relationships in a similar way, although tying them to exploitation, antagonistic interests and domination. Furthermore, he emphasizes the distinction between authority and expertise: authority is linked to a 'loyalty rent' for managers, and expertise is associated with a 'skill rent'.

In this context we should also consider the development of information and communication technologies and the role of knowledge, already dealt with by Bell (1976). For some, contemporary societies are more than anything else knowledge societies. There are even analyses—although of the more shallow kind—in which it is argued that capitalism is being replaced (Drucker 1993). In contrast, Manuel Castells (1996) prefers to talk about informational capitalism, which stands for a system in which information and communication technologies have achieved a key role but without doing away with its capitalist basis. A similar but more critical perspective on these issues is provided by Frank Webster (2006), who has underscored the continuity and consolidation of existing social and economic structures. The implication of an expansion of information and knowledge is that working life will require more specific education and skills for jobs with a more individualistic character, which may be reflected in work orientations and work attitudes.

We need to be aware that work in the so-called new economy is often not that different from what is known about the old economy. In an interview and survey study of several workplaces in two employment sectors based on information and knowledge—namely, call centres and software companies—Chris Baldry and his collaborators (2007) did not find the patterns regarding the meaning of work to differ very much from what studies of other sectors have shown. Work was generally conceived of as a matter of exchange of effort for money. Organizational control in the female-dominated call centres was rather traditional, whereas there was more autonomy for the software developers, most of whom were male, but they were far from free-floating knowledge workers. In both cases, work was rated lower than both family (first) and leisure (second). Nevertheless, new technology provides new ways of controlling workers, such as via camera or GPS surveillance.

Technology in some cases also changes the employment relations and can potentially affect work orientations. In the so-called platform economy, as illustrated by Uber, people can use a common platform for temporary assignments without any employing organization. The consequences of this arrangement are double-edged: these platforms can on the one hand create entrepreneurship possibilities, thus releasing workers from oppressive work schedules, and on the other hand force individuals into an insecure position where they themselves have to find jobs ('gigs') every day (Kenney and Zysman 2016).

Globalization and increased market competition have been accompanied by flexibility demands from employers. There is a pressure on staffing strategies to adapt to variations in demand, which may involve just-in-time and lean production. Flexibility can be achieved through the use of temporary employment contracts. It implies a division of workers into different labour market positions with different negotiation power (Barbieri 2009; Berglund et al. 2017; Kalleberg 2009). Having temporary employment no doubt signifies job insecurity in an objective sense, although feelings of insecurity differ between individuals due to the kind of temporary contract they have. Their personal situation is also a crucial factor. It is not surprising that the available research on the temporary workers' commitment to work shows mixed results (e.g., De Cuyper and De Witte 2008; Furåker and Berglund 2014).

Some of these insecure employment contracts, such as on-call work and contracts based on hourly work imply low chances to get an open-ended contract. The individual becomes responsible for staying or making him- or herself employable but runs the risk of being trapped in a precarious employment situation (Berglund et al. 2017). This suggests is a kind of individualization similar to the 'image of the individual as the autonomous entrepreneur of her own career' (Keune 2015: 49).

Flexibility in staffing can also be achieved by the use of temporary agency workers, who are employed by the agency but are assigned to different client organizations. A large number of studies show that these employees experience lower job security than workers in other types of employment (Aletraris 2010: 1144; De Cuyper, Notelaers and De Witte 2009; De Graaf-Zijl 2012; Forde and Slater 2005; Håkansson and Isidorsson 2015, 2019). Perceived insecurity is of course related to the opportunities to get an open-ended contract, which is possible in some countries but far from all (OECD 2013). Most investigations of agency workers' commitments do not separate between different kinds of contingent work, resulting in ambiguous conclusions (Connelly and Gallagher 2004: 962).

Motives for the Book and the Chapters to Follow

This book is a continuation and partly an update of a previous publication—*Commitment to Work and Job Satisfaction: Studies on Work Orientations*—edited by Bengt Furåker and Kristina Håkansson together with Jan Karlsson and published by Routledge in 2012 (Furåker et al. 2012). What, then, is the reason we are publishing a new volume? There are several justifications for it. First, as pointed out above, contemporary societies have undergone and continue to undergo many changes with significant consequences for working life. It is therefore relevant to examine more recent empirical data on people's subjective relationships to work. Second, comparisons of countries are of great interest because countries are affected in different ways by the changes and trends outlined above. In this new volume, some further cross-national analyses of data are included. Third, this book also brings up aspects of work orientations that were not treated in the previous publication. Among these we can mention work as a calling and as having existential meaning, cross-national differences in organizational commitment, dignity and alienation in the workplace, the role of skill utilization and skill development for young people's job satisfaction, and how matching of work values and job qualities affects job satisfaction.

In Chapter 2, Bengt Furåker deals with key concepts and theoretical perspectives with relevance for the book. To begin with, attention is devoted to the concepts of work orientation, work attitude and job satisfaction. Given the role these notions play in the analyses to come, their respective meaning needs to be spelled out and clarified. Similarly, several related concepts are considered: employment commitment—or, rather, non-financial employment commitment—instrumentalism or instrumental work attitudes, organizational commitment, work ethic and work centrality, to name a few. The task of conceptual clarification is framed by a more general theoretical discussion on the reasons why people work, what factors affect how much effort they put in and how well they perform and what role work plays in their lives.

As in the previous volume, Chapter 3 is about work centrality. It is co-authored by Tómas Bjarnason and Kristina Håkansson. The alleged decline of work centrality has been the focus of numerous studies in the past decades. In recent years, the entry of the Millennials (a generation born two decades prior to the millennium) into the labour market has been at the centre of attention. The popular literature has made strong claims about their lack of work ethic, but the results from research have been somewhat inconclusive and seem to vary between countries. In their inquiry, the authors examine absolute and relative work centrality for five countries (Germany, Japan, Spain, Sweden and the United States) over a period of 16 years (1995–2011) covering four generations: 'Silent Generation', 'Baby Boomers', 'Generation X' and 'Millennials'. Using data from the World Values Survey, the study finds sizeable country variations in the levels of both absolute and relative work centrality. While no successive downward trend could be established between the three survey waves, the levels of the two dimensions were higher in 1995 than in the two consecutive waves. Moreover, in a comparison of three age groups in 2011 with the same age groups 16 year earlier it turned out that relative work centrality had decreased in most cases. This trend was not limited to Millennials but was found also for Generation X and Baby Boomers.

Mattias Bengtsson and Marita Flisbäck are the authors of Chapter 4. They aim at deepening our understanding of the existential dimensions of work, focusing on 'calling' as an example of existential work orientation. The empirical basis consists of qualitative interviews conducted in 2014–2015 with Swedish employees from different occupations, both before and after retirement. The retirement process is taken to be a so-called existential imperative that can make visible meaning dimensions in relation to work. A group of respondents showed great dedication to work, associating it with a broader purpose, and their work orientation is defined as a calling. Five main components of calling are identified: (1) work appears as an external summons; (2) the purpose of the work activity is to serve a higher cause; (3) work is carried out with personality as a tool; (4) work involves self-sacrifice; and (5) work gives rise to elevation. There is finally a discussion of how retirement is experienced as an external force that 'de-calls' the life task.

Chapter 5 is a follow-up from a previous analysis in the forerunner to this book (Furåker 2012). This time Bengt Furåker analyzes survey data from both 2005 and 2015 on non-financial employment commitments (willingness to have a job irrespective of the pecuniary remunerations) in Nordic and Anglo-Saxon countries. The overall results of the previous study remain. Non-financial employment commitments are rather greater in the Nordic countries with their relatively generous welfare state arrangements than in the Anglo-Saxon nations with their more limited welfare systems. People in the Nordic countries also tend to have employment to a higher degree. However, in terms of how much people work (referred to as work mobilization rates), the Anglo-Saxon cluster surpasses the Nordic, and non-financial employment commitments are negatively linked to this indicator. At the same time, the Anglo-Saxon nations have larger proportions that prefer to work and earn more, and this goes hand in hand with higher work mobilization rates. In the Nordic welfare systems, it is helpful to have a job, not least because it may be required to qualify for benefits or as high of benefits as possible. Nevertheless, there is little wish to work as much as in the Anglo-Saxon world, where people are more heavily dependent on a paid job and consumption relies to a greater degree on having purchasing power in the market.

Bengt Furåker and Kristina Håkansson are in charge of Chapter 6, which deals with organizational commitment—that is, employees' dedication and loyalty to the organization they work for. One question raised is whether cross-national differences in this regard are mainly due to work-related factors. There are many studies on how organizational commitment is linked to working conditions, but they often differ a great deal as to the work-related characteristics included. The chapter attempts to specify better which factors are important. Moreover, it brings in some issues that have not been explored very much before. They have to do with people's overall labour market situation: worries for a job loss and perceived opportunities to find another equally good job. To throw light on these issues the authors make use of survey data from 2005 and 2015, including 17 countries that participated both years. When work-related factors were controlled for, national differences were to some extent reduced, but they did not disappear. In other words, there must also be other essential factors, perhaps partly cultural in nature, to consider. As expected, it turned out that various indicators of job quality, job satisfaction and employee-management relations are strongly associated with respondents' backing of their employing organization. Also, the general labour market situation appears to have a role to play. For example, being optimistic about other job possibilities tends to lower organizational commitment.

In Chapter 7, Kristina Håkansson and Tommy Isidorsson compare affective organizational commitment among regular employees and temporary agency workers in the same workplace. The latter have a situation characterized by a triangular relationship, including both the employing agency and the client organization. Kristina Håkansson and Isidorsson's analysis reveals somewhat different patterns for the two groups of employees. Previous research has shown that job characteristics are principal antecedents to commitment, which is here confirmed for client organization employees. This kind of explanation is weaker for agency workers whose commitment is instead very much related to expectations of a possible future employment contract with the client organization. A couple of other observations can be mentioned. Commitment is strong among those client organization employees who are positive to agency workers as well as among those who think they should have better opportunities for development than agency workers. Both these attitudes are in line with the idea of using temporary agency workers as a buffer in case of cutbacks.

Ann Bergman and Jan Karlsson wrote Chapter 8, presenting an interview study of female Swedish cabin attendants who have spent many years in their job. The authors use a model based on the concepts of dignity and alienation. Several dimensions are outlined (with the dignity endpoint mentioned first): autonomy–powerlessness, meaningful work–meaningless work, respect–disrespect, flourishing–self-estrangement and high work-life quality–low work-life quality. In all dimensions, there has been a clear movement from a sense of subjective dignity towards subjective alienation, although the strength of this development varies between them. The explanation is a drastic deterioration, from the beginning of the 21st century onwards, in the cabin attendants' working conditions and work environment. For example, the rota system was changed in such a way that it became increasingly difficult to plan one's life. Due to changes of this kind the interviewees experienced a movement from a sense of dignity to one of alienation.

Dora Scholarios, Belgin Okay-Somerville and Edward Sosu are the authors of Chapter 9. That chapter examines the role of skill use and development opportunities in shaping meaningful work and job satisfaction for young people. Given the pervasive issue of underemployment of young people across Europe, skills play a vital role in young people's work attitudes and represent a key aspect of job quality and career success. In addition, by taking into account the socioeconomic context of recession and national country characteristics represented by employment regime, the chapter extends our understanding of some of the boundary conditions influencing young workers' attitudes. Building on theoretical perspectives to work attitudes and well-being and using the European Working Conditions Surveys (2005–2015), this chapter provides an examination of job satisfaction as predicted by skill utilization, skill development and career development opportunities. Findings from multigroup path analyses highlight the role of career development opportunities and work meaningfulness for youth job satisfaction across Europe, even after the recession (although to a lesser extent in comparison to pre-recession) and for those in Liberal in comparison to Social Democratic employment regimes. Moreover, the confirmed role of meaningfulness as an explanatory mechanism demonstrates the continued applicability of job characteristics across European workers and supports the link between work which is experienced as meaningful and well-being more generally.

Well-being in the workplace is central to sustainable work lives, warranting attention to how (preferred) job qualities matter for job satisfaction. Chapter 10, by Tomas Berglund and Ingrid Esser, starts with a description of how work values, job qualities and their matching on eight central dimensions of job quality vary across the 24 member countries of the Organisation for Economic Co-operation and Development (OECD). A novel multidimensional approach to matching work values and job qualities is proposed, grounded in theoretical expectations of how individuals may prefer several job qualities. Then the independent importance of matching on job qualities for job satisfaction is assessed—that is, in addition to the direct effects of a wide range of job qualities on job satisfaction. Survey data from the International Social Survey Programme's Work Orientation Module 2015 are used. Results show how vast majorities strongly value multiple, both extrinsic and intrinsic, value dimensions, but how jobs providing multiple job qualities are generally scarcer, although countries differ greatly in this respect. Importantly, matching on job qualities plays a substantial role for job satisfaction, over and above the direct effects of job quality, and matching on intrinsic job qualities emerges as somewhat more central.

References

Ackerman, B., A. Alstott and P. Van Parijs (2005) *Redesigning Distribution: Basic Income and Stakeholder Grants as Cornerstones for an Egalitarian Capitalism.* London: Verso.

Aletraris, L. (2010) 'How Satisfied Are They and Why? A Study of Job Satisfaction, Job Rewards, Gender and Temporary Agency Work in Australia.' *Human Relations* 63(8): 1129–1155.

Aronowitz, S. (2005) *Just Around the Corner. The Paradox of Jobless Recovery.* Philadelphia: Temple University Press.

Baldry, C., P. Bain, P. Taylor, J. Hyman, D. Scholarios, A. Mars, A. Watson, K. Gilbert, G. Gall and D. Bunzel (2007) *The Meaning of Work in the New Economy.* Houndmills, Basingstoke: Palgrave Macmillan.

Barbieri, P. (2009) 'Flexible Employment and Inequality in Europe.' *European Sociological Review* 25(6): 621–628.

Bell, D. (1976) *The Coming of Post-Industrial Society. A Venture in Social Forecasting.* New York: Basic Books.

Berglund, T., K. Håkansson, T. Isidorsson and J. Alfonsson (2017) 'Temporary Employment and the Future Labor Market Status.' *Nordic Journal of Working Life Studies* 7(2): 27–48.

Bianchi, S. M., L. M. Casper and R. Berkowitz King (eds) (2005) *Work, Family, Health and Well-Being.* Mahwah, NJ: Lawrence Erlbaum.

Birnbaum, S. (2012) *Basic Income Reconsidered: Social Justice, Liberalism, and the Demands of Equality.* New York: Palgrave Macmillan.

Buchanan, J. (1971) 'The Backbending Supply Curve of Labor: An Example of Doctrinal Retrogression?' *History of Political Economy* 3(2): 383–390.

Castells, M. (1996) *The Rise of Network Society. The Information Age: Economy, Society and Culture*, Vol. 1. Oxford: Blackwell.

Connelly, C. and D. Gallagher (2004) 'Emerging Trends in Contingent Work Research.' *Journal of Management* 30(6): 959–983.

Daniels, A. K. (1987) 'Invisible Work.' *Social Problems* 34(5): 403–415.

De Cuyper, N. and H. De Witte (2008) 'Job Insecurity and Employability Among Temporary Workers: A Theoretical Approach Based on the Psychological Contract', 88–107, in K. Näswall, J. Hellgren and M. Sverke (eds) *The Individual in the Changing Working Life*. Cambridge: Cambridge University Press.

De Cuyper, N., G. Notelaers and H. De Witte (2009) 'Job Insecurity and Employability in Fixed-Term Contractors, Agency Workers, and Permanent Workers: Associations with Job Satisfaction and Affective Organizational Commitment.' *Journal of Occupational Health Psychology* 14(2): 193–205.

De Graaf-Zijl, M. (2012) 'Job Satisfaction and Contingent Employment.' *De Economist* 160(2): 197–218.

Drucker, P. F. (1993) *Post-Capitalist Society*. London: Butterworth-Heinemann.

Dunham, J. (ed.) (2001) *Stress in the Workplace: Past, Present, Future*. London: Whurr Publishers.

Engelstad, F. (1984) *Hva mener vi med arbeid? Noen begrepsmessige refleksioner*. Oslo: Institutt for samfunnsforskning.

Erikson, R. and J. H. Goldthorpe (1993) *The Constant Flux. A Study of Class Mobility in Industrial Societies*. Oxford: Clarendon Press.

Eyerman, R. (1985) 'Work—A Contested Concept', 27–31, in B.-O. Gustavsson, J. C. Karlsson and C. Räftegård (eds) *Work in the 1980s*. Aldershot, Brookfield: Gover Publishing Company.

Forde, C. and G. Slater (2005) 'Agency Working in Britain: Character, Consequences and Regulation.' *British Journal of Industrial Relations* 43(2): 249–271.

Frone, M. R., M. Russell and M. L. Cooper (1997) 'Relation of Work-Family Conflict to Health Outcomes: A Four-Year Longitudinal Study of Employed Parents.' *Journal of Occupational and Organizational Psychology* 70(4): 325–335.

Furåker, B. (2005) *Sociological Perspectives on Labor Markets*. Houndmills, Basingstoke: Palgrave Macmillan.

Furåker, B. (2009) 'Arbetssamhällets reträtt? Samtidsdiagnoser på villovägar.' *Arbetsmarknad & Arbetsliv* 15(2): 11–26.

Furåker, B. (2012) 'Work Attitudes, Employment and Work Mobilization: A Comparison Between Anglo-Saxon and Nordic Countries', 67–85, in B. Furåker, K. Håkansson and J. C. Karlsson (eds) *Commitment to Work and Job Satisfaction*. New York, London: Routledge.

Furåker, B. and T. Berglund (2014) 'Job Insecurity and Organizational Commitment.' *Revista Internacional de Organizaciones* 13: 163–186.

Furåker, B., K. Håkansson and J. C. Karlsson (eds) (2012) *Commitment to Work and Job Satisfaction: Studies of Work Orientations*. New York: Routledge.

Goldthorpe, J. H. (1982) 'On the Service Class: Its Formation and Future', 162–185, in A. Giddens and G. MacKenzie (eds) *Social Class and the Division of Labour*. Cambridge: Cambridge University Press.

Goldthorpe, J. H. (2000) *On Sociology: Numbers, Narratives, and the Integration of Research and Theory*. Oxford: Oxford University Press.

Gorz, A. (1985) *Paths to Paradise: On the Liberation from Work*. London: Pluto Press.

Gorz, A. (1999) *Reclaiming Work: Beyond the Wage-Based Society*. Cambridge: Polity Press.

Håkansson, K. and T. Isidorsson (2015) 'Temporary Agency Workers—Precarious Workers? Perceived Job Security and Employability for Temporary Agency Workers and Client Organization Employees at a Swedish Manufacturing Plant.' *Nordic Journal of Working Life Studies* 5(4): 3–22.

Håkansson, K. and T. Isidorsson (2019) 'Job Quality for Temporary Agency Workers and Client Organization Employees at a Swedish Manufacturing Plant', 177–199, in T. Isidorsson and J. Kubisa (eds) *Job Quality in an Era of Flexibility: Experiences in a European Context*. London, New York: Routledge.

Kalleberg, A. L. (2009) 'Precarious Work, Insecure Workers: Employment Relations in Transition.' *American Sociological Review* 74(1): 1–22.

Karasek, R. and T. Theorell (1990) *Healthy Work. Stress, Productivity and the Reconstruction of Working Life*. New York: Basic Books.

Karlsson, J. C. (2004) 'The Ontology of Work: Social Relations and Doing in the Sphere of Necessity', 84–104, in S. Fleetwood and S. Ackroyd (eds) *Critical Realist Applications in Organisation and Management Studies*. London: Routledge.

Karlsson, J. C. (2017) 'Arbetsbegreppet', 33–60, in M. Bengtsson and T. Berglund (eds) *Arbetslivet*. Lund: Studentlitteratur.

Kenney, M. and J. Zysman (2016) 'The Rise of the Platform Economy.' *Issues in Science and Technology* 32(3).

Keune, M. (2015) 'Shaping the Future of Industrial Relations in the EU: Ideas, Paradoxes and Drivers of Change.' *International Labour Review* 154(1): 47–56.

Matthes, J. (ed.) (1983) *Krise der Arbeitsgesellschaft?* Frankfurt: Campus Verlag.

OECD (2013) 'Protecting Jobs, Enhancing Flexibility. A New Look at Employment Protection Legislation', 65–126, in *OECD Employment Outlook 2013*. Paris: OECD Publishing.

Offe, C. (1985) 'Work: The Key Sociological Category?' 129–150, in J. Keane (ed.) *Disorganized Capitalism. Contemporary Transformations of Work and Politics*. Cambridge: Polity Press.

Offe, C. (with U. Mückenberger and I. Ostner) (1996) 'A Basic Income Guaranteed by the State: A Need of the Moment in Social Policy', 201–221, in C. Offe (ed.) *Modernity and the State. East, West*. Cambridge, MA: MIT Press.

Rifkin, J. (1995), *End of Work: The Decline of the Global Labor Force and the Dawn of the Post-market Era*. New York: G. G. Putnam's Sons.

Sloman, J. (2010) *Economics*, 6th ed. Harlow: Pearson Education.

Standing, G. (2013) *Prekariatet. Den nya farliga klassen*. Göteborg: Daidalos.

Standing, G. (2014) *A Precariat Charter: From Denizens to Citizens*. London: Bloomsbury.

Tausig, M. (2013) 'The Sociology of Work and Well-Being', 434–455, in C. S. Aneshensel, J. Phelan and A. Bierman (eds) *Handbook of the Sociology of Mental Health*, 2nd ed. Dordrecht: Springer Netherlands.

Therborn, G. (1987) 'Tar arbetet slut? och post-fordismens problem, 109–130, in U. Björnberg. and I. Hellberg (eds) *Sociologer ser på arbete. Festskrift till Edmund Dahlström*. Stockholm: Arbetslivscentrum (Swedish Center for Working Life).

Weber, M. (1930) *The Protestant Ethic and the Spirit of Capitalism*. London: Unwin University Books.

Webster, F. (2006) *Theories of the Information Society*, 3rd ed. New York: Routledge.

Wright, E. O. (1997) *Class Counts. Comparative Studies in Class Analysis*. Cambridge: Cambridge University Press.

Wright, E. O. (2017) 'The Capitalist State and the Possibility of Socialism', 401–431, in G. Olofsson and S. Hort (eds) *Class, Sex and Revolutions: Göran Therborn—A Critical Appraisal*. Lund: Arkiv förlag.

2 Theoretical and Conceptual Considerations on Work Orientations

Bengt Furåker

Introduction

The concepts of *work orientation* and *work attitudes* refer to a subjective dimension of the relationship between a person and his/her job or employment in general. They grasp the person's conceptions, knowledge, beliefs, feelings and evaluations concerning work or various aspects of it. In addition, we find a potential behavioural element to be taken into consideration. According to the conventional notion—agreed with here—attitudes embrace three different dimensions (e.g., Rosenberg and Hovland 1960; Eagly and Chaiken 1993). The first, the cognitive, aspect has to do with beliefs, that is—conceptions and understandings of the object in question. Second, there is an affective dimension referring to feelings about and evaluations of the object. Individuals' disposition to act makes up the third, the behavioural, aspect of an attitude. It should be stressed that the three dimensions are interrelated. For example, an employer who is convinced that immigrants are just as competent as native workers and who is keen on the principle of equal opportunities can be expected at least not to discriminate against immigrants when recruiting people to vacancies. Nevertheless, there can be a mismatch between the dimensions, which in the example given might imply that the employer acts contrary to his/her beliefs and values.

In this book, work orientations and work attitudes are used more or less synonymously, although the former concept is taken to be broader; it can thus include a set of work-related attitudes. As pointed out in the introductory chapter, work orientations might appear to be something that people bring to their workplace, whereas job satisfaction might look as something that jobs confer to their incumbents. This would, however, be to simplify the issue. Individuals' work orientations are affected by their job and the experiences emanating from it, even if they are partly a function of people's expectations, too.

Job satisfaction refers to an affective dimension and in that sense it can be counted as belonging to one of the three pillars of the attitude concept (cf. the last two chapters in our volume). This does not exclude that the cognitive and behavioural aspects are also present. People may be at ease with their work because their aspirations have been fulfilled; they have obtained what they have hoped for. Satisfaction may also be due to knowing that many others in comparable positions are worse off. Accordingly, theories of social comparison are highly significant in studying job satisfaction as well as work motivation (e.g., Festinger 1954; Merton 1964: Chapters VIII–IX; Miller, Reichert and Flores 2015; Suls and Wheeler 2000). It is then decisive with whom comparisons are being made—that is, whether the reference persons have jobs in the same workplace or not, in the same occupation or not, on higher or lower levels in the occupational hierarchies, etc.

Certain analytical problems arise since satisfaction is dependent on expectations. One individual may be much happier with his/her job than another, in spite of the fact that the two have more or less identical working conditions, and the explanation may be that the former has lower expectations than the latter. Because of this peculiarity and the fact that people are sometimes satisfied with their work as it makes few demands, it has been suggested that job satisfaction is a less useful concept than *job involvement*, which refers to people's 'active interest in and enjoyment of the work' (Gallie et al. 1998: 209). Nonetheless, I believe that job satisfaction can be a helpful concept, but we must keep its premises in mind.

The subjective relationships at focus have reference not to a single object but to something more complex. One way of dealing with this complexity is to distinguish between work/employment in general and specific jobs, held by the actor himself/herself or by others. Furthermore, the concepts do not necessarily refer to jobs taken as a whole but only to certain aspects of them—for example, working conditions, work tasks, social climate at the workplace and the like. We can expect a great deal of variation across social categories (as defined by sex, age, socioeconomic category, ethnicity, etc.) regarding work orientations, attitudes to work and employment, and job satisfaction. One of the main purposes of our publication is to spell out some of the variation in these respects.

Work in general is obviously an abstraction because in working life there are just concrete activities. When people are asked about their work orientations and attitudes, it is rather likely that their own job—or some other specific job (for example, that of their partner)—will cross their minds. In other words, the abstract category tends to be conceived of through existing entities. The abstraction can also be contrasted with 'nonwork'. It is possible, in turn, to specify the latter concept in terms of alternative activities or statuses such as 'staying at home with one's children', 'going to college', or 'being retired'. Still, the question remains whether or to what extent people's orientations to work or employment in general are coloured by their experiences from their own job or some other specific job.

Studying work orientations, attitudes to work and employment, and job satisfaction, we soon run into several other concepts such as work centrality, work ethic, instrumentalism, employment commitment and other types of commitment. This chapter aims at presenting and discussing such notions and at bringing up some of the key issues associated with them. A further purpose is to see how various concepts hang together. Notably, many of the approaches presented were developed in 20th century; the more recent literature has not generated so much new but is frequently based on previous work.

The current text is structured around three topics. First, there is the issue why people work at all. Is it because they must secure their means of survival, because they want to increase their standard of living or because other wishes can be met that way? What is the role of financial and non-financial factors respectively? A second matter is about employed individuals' willingness to work a lot and to perform well. Again, are they motivated mainly by financial remunerations or by other factors? The third and final question concerns another subjective dimension—namely, the role people think that work plays in their lives. Is work perceived as a central phenomenon in their everyday existence? How does it rank in relation to other spheres of life such as family and leisure? The three sets of questions partly cover the same ground and therefore cut across each other, which in turn means that, in the following, certain issues are touched upon not only once but twice or even several times.

To Work or Not to Work

We can think of several reasons for people to engage in paid work. One crucial reason may be that it is economically necessary for them to do so. In the writings by Karl Marx (e.g., 1933/1884, 1996/1867), the capitalist mode of production is based on two main categories: owners of means of production, and individuals who own nothing but their labour power—the proletarians—and who therefore have to offer this capacity for hire in the market. The proletarians are free to work for anyone capitalist, but they are forced to do it for someone to support themselves. There is hence an economic necessity or coercion to which the property-less are subjected.

Things have unquestionably changed a great deal since the days of Marx. The standard of living in the economically advanced world has improved dramatically also for most of those at the bottom of the income hierarchy. We find more or less developed welfare state arrangements in all the matured capitalist nations, although this development has been uneven and significant differences exist between them. There are some major implications of these changes. First, today most people have more money to spend than they need for securing mere survival. The higher standard of living involves mass consumption in ways which were out of sight in the 19th century. It may be discussed whether the rise of 'consumerism' actually forces people to work; what we can say is that an increased 'normal' standard of living requires either technological progress or more work—or both. Moreover, to boost consumption continually seems to be an attractive goal or at least it appears to be desirable to 'keep up with the Joneses. Second, the modern welfare state allows people not to work under certain circumstances—if they become sick or injured, need to be on parental leave, etc. Arguably, it undermines the necessity for people to work because—as it is expressed in some accounts—it triggers a process of 'decommodification' (Esping-Andersen 1990, 1999). Although we can hardly conclude that people no longer have to work at all, the necessity for them to do this has no doubt been modified—with periods when the pressure has weakened substantially but also with periods when it has been partially restored.

The attitude associated with economic motives to work is often referred to as *instrumentalism*. This is a key concept in the 'affluent worker' study by John Goldthorpe et al. (1968). Its meaning is that work is a tool to obtain something else, normally entailing that the income from employment can be used to purchase different kinds of goods and services. Individuals with an instrumental work orientation wish to have employment because they want the money implicated. They conceive of a job as 'a means to an end, or ends, external to the work situation; that is, work is regarded as a means of acquiring the income necessary to support a valued life of which work itself is not an integral part' (Goldthorpe et al. 1968: 38–39). Thus, people look upon employment in calculative terms; there is in principle no other reason to keep the job besides the economic return it provides. Although manual workers are assumed to have an instrumental work orientation to a larger extent than others, it is emphasized 'that *all* work activity, in industrial society at least, tends to have a basically instrumental component' (Goldthorpe et al. 1968: 41; italics in original).

In case of an instrumental work attitude, it is not an issue whether people are forced or not to find employment to make ends meet; no assumption is made other than that they above all work to get paid for it. If they are after the money to survive or just to increase their consumption is another story. The idea of instrumentalism also presupposes that the intrinsic value of the job is weak and that there is a sharp division between work and nonwork. Now we may argue that the notion does not have to be, or should not be, interpreted too narrowly. It might as well be counted as instrumental to have a job for the purpose of achieving non-financial goals. For example, individuals may take a job mainly because it provides social contacts that they—for one reason or another—consider valuable. An instrumental work orientation is nonetheless commonly regarded as the opposite of non-financial employment commitment, a concept to which I will come back.

Another possibility is that people engage in employment because they feel it is a *moral obligation*. This presupposes the existence of a *work ethic* in society, implying that work is a highly valued activity and that people are subject to normative pressure to take on this kind of activity. A work ethic is associated with *meaning*. The basis can be found in religion, as in the classic study *The Protestant Ethic and the Spirit of Capitalism* by Max Weber (1930/1904–5). Seventeenth-century Christianity provided various views on work, which were more or less positive for the development of capitalism. Among other things, Weber emphasized the role of Calvinism for the advance of a suitable work ethic. It might appear strange that the Calvinist doctrine of predestination could have such a role, as it implies that what human beings do does not matter. However, Weber maintained that the doctrine took work as a sign of people's fate. Those who toiled by the sweat of their brows could consequently be expected to be predestined to salvation. I will not go deeper into these issues here, but it should be added that a work ethic is an important element also in other religions such as Islam and Buddhism (e.g., Yousef 2001; Niles 1999). Additionally, Weber emphasized that work can be a *calling*, suggesting that everyday activities are linked to an existential dimension. This theme has been further developed by later researchers (e.g., Bellah et al. 1985; Duffy and Dik 2013; Wrzesniewski, Dekas and Rosso 2013; cf. also this book's Chapter 4).

Furthermore, we should observe that more secular societies do not necessarily fall behind regarding work ethics (cf. Anthony 1977). In the contemporary, relatively secular capitalist societies, we find more or less explicit norms regarding employment. Able-bodied individuals of working age are subject to rather strong pressure to engage in paid work if they do not have sufficient means of subsistence from other sources. This can perhaps most easily be observed in the various policies of workfare and activation oriented towards putting people on welfare (back) into employment (e.g., Alcock et al. 2003; Friedlander and Burtless 1995; Lødemel and Trickey 2001).

The existence of a work ethic is linked to the fact that work is a necessity for society as a whole. Human societies would soon fall apart if many vital tasks were not carried out day after day. Even in contemporary developed capitalism, a rather moderate decline in the supply of labour would quickly damage the production of goods and services. This does not have to mean that work is a necessity for every individual. We find socially defined norms regarding who should be available for employment. The general principle is that individuals who are able-bodied and of working age should be at hand, but they are exempt if they can get their means of subsistence in certain other ways (interest from capital, speculative gains, etc.) —that is, without relying on support from the public authorities and without breaking the law.

An important aspect is that the modern welfare state requires large resources to function as intended. There is therefore normally strong pressure upon people to support themselves through paid work rather than through social benefits. The word *duty* may be somewhat obsolete in a contemporary context—but some kind of work ethic is in operation. One way—and perhaps the most adequate—of expressing the present state of things is the following: people who want to be treated as 'ordinary' or 'decent' are expected to work unless they have a due cause (such as being disabled or having small children) not to do it or have other sources through which they can get on. It is simply not easy to live on welfare without a valid reason. There are unquestionably rather strong norms as to the meaning of being a 'normal' citizen in modern society.

It has, however, been argued that the work ethic has declined in contemporary societies. Claus Offe (1985: 140–148) is one of those who has put forward such arguments. Already in the first half of the 1980s, he claimed that work was in a process of ceasing to be a duty, partly because of the decline of religious and certain other cultural traditions and because of the growth of consumer hedonism. Another of his points is that in order for work to be a duty, workers must participate 'as recognized, morally acting persons' and that with the 'Taylorization' of working life, 'processes of technical and organizational rationalization', this does not hold any longer (Offe 1985: 141). The problem is that Offe does not provide any empirical evidence in support of his argument but just takes it for granted. It must be questioned to what extent current working life developments are characterized by Taylorization. Although we discover that such processes are taking place in certain areas and that they are even expanding, this is hardly the only pattern; there are certainly many jobs which cannot easily be transformed by Tayloristic principles. Nevertheless, strategies of rationalization exist not only in manufacturing but also in the service sector—in both the public and the private service sector (e.g., Myrick 2012; Sederblad 2013; Stoney 2001).

In connection with the notion of a demise of the work ethic, we must take a number of issues into consideration. To begin with, it is not crystal clear how strong this ethic used to be; it is possible that we tend to exaggerate its strength in the past. The empirical evidence at hand is indeed limited. For one thing, there was obviously no work ethic covering all social categories to the same extent (cf. Moorhouse 1987; Rose 1985). This observation is valid even now. Actually, concerning both the past and the present—not to mention the future—we lack sufficient empirical knowledge in these respects. We should neither forget the indications that work ethics develop in new directions. In recent decades, there has been a discussion about 'workaholism' or 'heavy work investment' as a possibly growing phenomenon in certain jobs (e.g., Harpaz and Snir 2003; Andreassen 2014; Snir and Harpaz 2009a, 2009b). Workaholism may be an effect of strong job involvement, but it may also have to do with work cultures with powerful norms regarding what can be expected in terms of people's efforts.

Sociologists and other social scientists have repeatedly—and for good reasons—brought up the non-financial, 'intrinsic' job rewards and values of work (e.g., Cerasoli, Nicklin and Ford 2014; Herzberg 1966; Herzberg, Mausner and Snyderman 1959; Kalleberg 1977; Lee and Raschke 2016; Lincoln and Kalleberg 1990; Mottaz 1985; Nohria, Groysberg and Lee 2008; Wang 1996). They emphasize the significance of motivating work tasks such as various kinds of problem-solving and artistic activities. Another thing is the role of social relations—involving colleagues, customers, clients and others—that are associated with most kinds of employment. Being essentially social creatures, human beings are sometimes highly dependent on such relations.

We should also pay attention to the concept of *non-financial employment commitment*. It has often been used in research investigating how the willingness to work of unemployed individuals compares with that of the already employed (Gallie and Alm 2000; Gallie et al. 1998: Chapter 7; Gallie and Vogler 1994; Hammer and Russell 2004; Nordenmark 1999; cf. also Chapter 5 in this anthology). The concept refers to 'the importance that people attach to employment on intrinsic grounds, that is to say irrespective of the financial implications'; people can be forced to work simply because they need the money exchanged for it, but '[t]he very notion of commitment implies choice and voluntary consent' (Gallie et al. 1998: 188).

Non-financial employment commitment is in principle the opposite of instrumentalism, as the definition excludes all financial aspects. It is quite common to use the shorter expression employment commitment only, but it seems difficult to exclude the financial dimension completely, even if we reserve the term for 'choice and voluntary consent'. Individuals can very well be engaged in employment due to a need or desire for an income, although they might easily survive without it. Despite having enough money to make a living, they may still want more for 'luxurious' consumption—a larger house, yet another car, trips around the world or many other things. At the same time, we should not underestimate that work may have an intrinsic value for the employee; for example, work tasks may be so interesting for the individual that he or she is eager to perform them regardless of monetary rewards.

An important issue with respect to non-financial employment commitment is whether there are gender differences or not (e.g., Bielby and Bielby 1989; Gallie et al. 1998: 188–189; Hakim 1996, 2000, 2003; Halvorsen 1997; Warr 1982). Quite a few studies have demonstrated that men are generally more strongly committed than women, but the difference has not always turned out to be very distinct—some studies show no significant difference and others even uncover the opposite pattern. However, Catherine Hakim (1996, 2000, 2003) has insisted that men and women have different preferences as regards work and family matters. According to her 'preference theory', women care relatively more about their families and relatively less about their job, which is reflected in their larger proportion of part-time work. These conclusions have certainly been debated (e.g., Crompton and Harris 1998; Crompton 2006; Leahy and Doughney 2006). Among other things, it has been emphasized that people's choices are 'shaped (or constrained) by the context within which choice is being exercised' (Crompton 2006: 12).

Marie Jahoda (1982) has made one of the most well-known contributions to the discussion on why people work. Her argument is that work fulfils a number of latent, social-psychological functions besides the manifest economic function of providing an income. In her view, a job imposes a time structure upon the individual, it provides social contacts outside the family, it means that people can engage in activities for common purposes, it implies regular activities, and it bestows social status and identity. Jahoda has been criticized for underestimating the role of individual agency and for presenting an unacceptable functionalist perspective on work (e.g., Essy 1993; Fryer 1986; Nordenmark 1999). She tends to treat all jobs in the same way: they are all supposed to have positive effects for the individual no matter what characteristics they actually have. It is easy to agree with this criticism, but it still seems that the aspects brought up by Jahoda are worth being considered seriously; they may no doubt be of great interest in research on the role of work.

In a study of Swedish lottery winners, Anna Hedenus and I found that moderately sized or even relatively large winnings seldom made people change their work situation (Furåker and Hedenus 2009). Very few quit working, some took a shorter leave from work and others shortened their working hours, but the majority—almost two thirds—did not do anything about their employment. There are obviously also other than just the pecuniary mechanisms that tie people to working. To put it briefly, it seems that being 'normal' is an important motive for remaining in employment (Hedenus 2011). The normal thing for working-age individuals in the Swedish context is to have a job, unless they are students, have small children at home or have some other legitimate excuse for not being employed.

Determinants of Performance

A further aspect of work orientations has to do not only with people's willingness to have a job at all but to work a lot and to perform well in their jobs. Performance should be thought of in both quantitative and qualitative terms. The meaning of doing a good job may refer to various dimensions: unrelenting effort but, in addition, skilfulness, competence, accuracy, responsibility, reliability, punctuality and the like. It is a common-sense assumption that high job satisfaction goes hand in hand with organizational commitment, a willingness to remain in the job and good performance at the workplace.

The concept of *work motivation* is frequently used to grasp the strength in people's willingness to work and to perform as well as possible. In the discussion of motivating factors, it is common to bring up a large number of issues such as the role of financial incentives, conceptions of work as a moral obligation, the character of work tasks, the social climate at the workplace, and job security or insecurity (cf. Gallie et al. 1998: 15–21). There is a huge body of research and literature on these topics (e.g., Bakker and Leiter 2010; Gellerman 1963, 1998; Kleinbeck et al. 1990;Lee and Raschke 2016; Maslow 1970; McGregor 1985; Nohria, Groysberg and Lee 2008; Vroom 1964). As touched upon earlier, the 'intrinsic' job rewards and the non-financial values of work have caught the attention of many sociologists and other social scientists (in addition to the references above, see e.g., Cerasoli, Nicklin and Ford 2014; Herzberg, Mausner and Snyderman 1959; Herzberg 1966; Kalleberg 1977; Lincoln and Kalleberg 1990; Mottaz 1985; Wang 1996). The factors stimulating people to perform and perform well vary across economic and cultural systems; thus, we should not just look for a single set of driving forces for human beings but for many such sets.

A quick glance at the once 'really existing' socialism may be instructive in this connection. In the country of the October Revolution, the Soviet Union, where the use of market mechanisms was restricted, a great deal of effort was invested in finding other mechanisms that would make people work hard and conscientiously. Disciplinary labour norms, rules and legislation were ways of dealing with the problem; such measures were implemented more or less strictly and with varying success over the decades (e.g., Kaplan 1968; Luke 1985). Work was generally heroized with awards to people who made high-performance contributions. The coal miner Alexey Stakhanov is perhaps the most well-known (e.g., Siegelbaum 1988; cf. Luke 1985: 201–207). His records in coal mining from 1935 appear to go beyond the humanly possible. He was used as a role model in the propaganda and a whole Stakhanovite movement was organized with him as the front figure. This is an over-explicit example of how the absence of well-functioning material incentives for people to do their best paved the way for other measures to build up work morale and work discipline. Although perhaps sometimes having the intended effects, in the long run these other measures could not prevent poor performance, inefficiency and attitudes of work-avoidance. The concomitant stagnation of the economy played a major role in the fall of the Soviet Union and the whole Soviet bloc.

There is also the concept of *organizational commitment* (e.g., Porter et al. 1974; Mowday, Porter and Steers 1982; Lincoln and Kalleberg 1990; Meyer and Allen 1997; Mowday 1998; Gallie et al. 1998: Chapter. 9; in addition, cf. Chapter, 6 and Chapter 7 in our book). It is often taken to refer to a combination of three different attitudinal elements among employees: '(a) a strong belief in and acceptance of the organization's goals and values; (b) a willingness to exert considerable effort on behalf of the organization; and (c) a definite desire to maintain organizational membership' (Porter et al. 1974: 604). A critical issue is then whether or to what extent the values and goals under (a) above are clear, coherent and undisputed. If they are vague or contradictory, it will be difficult to use them for creating support among employees.

In an attempt to find the 'core essence' of the concept of commitment, John Meyer and Natalie Allen (1991) surveyed the literature and made a distinction between affective, continuance and normative commitment. The affective aspect has to do with employees' desire to stay with their organization, continuance refers to their need to remain with it—given the possibilities and costs of exiting—and the normative component is based on a moral belief or obligation to stay on. Meyer and Allen (1991: 67) argue that the three approaches have a common point of departure: they all treat commitment as 'a psychological state that (a) characterizes the employee's relationship with the organization, and (b) has implications for the decision to continue or discontinue membership in the organization' (cf., e.g., Meyer and Allen 1997; Meyer and Herscovitch 2001; Meyer et al. 2002).

The reasoning above should not be taken to imply that contemporary developed capitalism provides optimal mechanisms of motivation. People's engagement in their jobs is dependent on employment and working conditions, and these conditions are time and again poor in capitalist firms but frequently likewise in public sector workplaces, at least for those at the bottom of the organizational hierarchies. *Alienation* has been a concept for describing actual powerlessness, marginalization and exclusion or feelings of powerlessness, marginalization and exclusion (e.g., Blauner 1964; Israel 1971; Ollman 1976; Seeman 1959). In other words, it is a concept that has been applied to both objective and subjective phenomena. Its opposite can be said to be *dignity* (Bolton 2007, 2010; cf. Chapter 8 in this volume). Relevant work-related factors are then autonomy, job satisfaction, meaningful work, respect, and learning and development.

Given the hierarchical character of work organizations and the shortcomings many experience in their working conditions, it is not surprising that we find various forms of protests such as working-pace slow-down, working by the rule, absenteeism, boycotts and strikes. One might say that *resistance* is an essential kind of work orientation (cf. Karlsson 2012). Resistance is sometimes individual and sometimes collective, but it is above all by acting collectively that workers can really put pressure upon their counterpart. This requires that workers define the problems at hand in basically the same way and imagine similar feasible remedies. It is vital for them to develop common values and norms facilitating joint action. The key to successful resistance is the formation of a workers' collective as a counterweight to employer power. Through interviews conducted in a pulp and paper plant in the 1950s, Norwegian sociologist

Sverre Lysgaard (1961) discovered how subordinate workers developed a kind of defense organization in relation to the demands of the so-called technical-economic system—that is, the company. The emergence of a strong informal resistance body was assumed to be facilitated if workers have similar positions and characteristics, if they have possibilities to communicate with one another and if they interpret common problems in the same or similar way. In 2010 a research team, including two Swedish sociologists and a Norwegian colleague, returned to the same pulp and paper plant in Norway to see whether the workers' collective was still present (Axelsson, Karlsson and Skorstad 2019). Significant changes had taken place with respect to technology and work organization, but it could be concluded that a workers' collective continued to exist.

In addition, commitment does not have to be tied to the employing organization as such but to actors/phenomena connected with it (e.g., Fukami and Larson 1984; Meyer and Allen 1997; Reichers 1985; Wallace 1993). For example, employees can be committed to their profession or occupation rather than to their employer. It may be more important for lawyers to stick to the moral code of the profession than to be loyal to a certain law firm, and doctors may be more willing to help their patients than to follow the hospital's bureaucratic rules. Workers may besides have strong ties with unions, professional associations, the local community or other actors. There can thus be competing loyalties at a workplace, which in turn are likely to affect the overall backing of the organization's values and goals. It has been argued that we need a multiple commitments approach to handle this complexity (Reichers 1985). By way of example, in a British study of 'new economy' workplaces—carried out by Chris Baldry and his colleagues (2007: 99–103)—it turned out that employees' commitment to colleagues and to customers was largely much stronger than to the employer.

A few words should also be said about another concept—namely the '*psychological contract*' (e.g., Grant 1999; Herriot, Manning and Kidd 1997; Rousseau 1995, 2001). It is generally aimed at grasping the more informal beliefs among employers and their employees about what the two parties are supposed to give and receive respectively. Why this kind of contract should be labelled 'psychological' rather than 'social' remains an unanswered question; contracts always involve at least two actors and therefore have a 'social' character. A sociological perspective would entail some other elements, too. It would start out from the simple assumption that employers and employees normally agree on some kind of contract that can be formal (written) or informal (oral or tacit). No matter what form it takes, the agreement is crucial for the relationship between the two parties, although its contents can vary a great deal. According to Talcott Parsons and Neil Smelser (1956: 105), contracts can be analyzed either in terms of the quid pro quo (the workers' performance for the organization and the organization's compensation for that effort) or of conditioning rules that are 'socially prescribed and sanctioned'; in the latter respect there is a focus on such aspects as 'the interest of third parties' and the need for 'restrictions on fraud and coercion'. Thus, Parsons and Smelser echo what Émile Durkheim (1964/1893: 200–229) called the 'non-contractual' elements of contract.

There is still also a power aspect to take into account. In juridical terms, the contract appears as an agreement between two equal parties, but as Marx (1996/1867: 177–186) underlined, this is not the whole truth. Behind the idea that capitalists and workers voluntarily and on equal terms exchange money for the use of labour power, he saw an asymmetric relationship in which the one party dominates the other. This is a main theme in his analysis of the capitalist rule in the factory, and it was in fact recognized by Weber (1978: 729–730) as well:

> The formal right of a worker to enter into any contract whatsoever with any employer whatsoever does not in practice represent for the employment seeker even the slightest freedom in the determination of his own conditions of work, and it does not guarantee him any influence on this process. It rather means, at least primarily, that the more powerful party in the market, i.e., normally the employer, has the possibility to set the terms, to offer the job "take it or leave it", and, given the normally more pressing economic need of the worker, to impose his terms upon him.

In these accounts, there is not much room for agreements between employers and employees, although some understanding—explicit or tacit—will always be present. One might say that the less asymmetric the power relationship between the two parties is or becomes, the more space is left for employer–employee agreements.

It may be less important whether we call the informal contract between employers and their employees 'psychological' or something else. A significant observation is that both parties may have more or less articulated expectations of each other, regardless of what the formal agreement tells. Not least because of the indeterminacy incessantly associated with how work tasks are to be carried out (cf. Furåker 2005: 80–81), formal regulations and agreements must be complemented by some mutual understanding and trust. This insight might help us explain why people are sometimes doing their best in the workplace but sometimes are merely pretending to be working, are working strictly according to the rules or are going slow. It may likewise contribute to our understanding of open labour disputes and conflicts.

Work Centrality

Many sociologists and other social scientists have paid attention to the role of work in people's lives. Is it a main activity in terms of time or significance or both? A concept frequently appearing in the literature is *work centrality* (cf. Chapter 3 in our publication). In an often quoted sentence in the report from the Meaning of Work project it has been defined as 'the degree of general importance that working has in the life of an individual at any given point in time' (MOW 1987: 81; italics removed). When measuring work centrality, it is rather common to make a distinction between an absolute and a relative dimension, depending on whether work is judged without being related to something specific or by a comparison with other spheres in society such as family, leisure and religion. However, it seems likely that some comparison is embedded in the absolute case, too. Human beings hardly evaluate phenomena in the world without having some point of reference in mind. In my opinion, apart from the different ways of phrasing survey and interview questions, work centrality is essentially a matter of the *relative* significance that individuals attach to working in their life situation. It can be added that this is also the point of departure of the project by the MOW International Research Team (1987: 80).

In different ways, some authors have questioned the idea that work is a crucial element in contemporary modern societies. I will bring up a few examples. Claus Offe (1985: 141; italics in original) claims that there are two ways in which work could play a crucial role in people's lives: (a) if it is 'normatively sanctioned as a *duty*'; and (b) if it is 'a *necessity*' for physical survival. In his view, the prerequisites for this vital role have ceased to exist or at least were on their way out already in the mid-1980s. I have already touched upon some of Offe's reasoning with respect to the decline of the work ethic, but he additionally mentioned certain other processes. He argues that life is no longer organized around gainful employment the way it used to be and that job biographies show more discontinuity. The time structure and the location of work within people's biographies have become increasingly variable. For example, people are often trained for one kind of job but actually hold another. Moreover, working time has been shortened and people have more time for other activities. These descriptions are largely in line with what we know about developments in the last century, but it remains uncertain to what extent work ethics have been affected.

The second point in the quotation from Offe above is about physical survival. Yet, in his discussion, the author focuses on the general motivating effects of a wage income. He obviously believes that there is a saturation effect so that an increase of income is not accompanied by a corresponding increase in utility. With rising standards of living people become less interested in supplying the same amount of labour as before and instead look for other ways of improving the quality of their lives, including improvements of working conditions. This is Offe's version of the substitution and income effects mentioned in Chapter 1 of this book. We should not deny that there may be saturation effects, but their scope is unclear. It seems to me that Offe is too quick to dismiss people's desires for higher income and tends to overestimate the saturation effects; the evidence available is at least inconclusive.

There is also the idea that work society has been replaced by a consumer society or—in a more cautious version—perhaps will be so in some more or less distant future. This implies that people reorient themselves in several different ways. One example is given by Zygmunt Bauman (1998: 24–25, 2007: 28–29) in his discussion of the transition from 'producer' to 'consumer' society. The argument is that although both production and consumption coexist, we can speak of a transition from one type of society to another because there has been a change in the norms to which citizens are socialized. Individuals were previously supposed to become producers, but now they are above all expected to be consumers.

For the transition from producer to consumer society, two circumstances are claimed to be particularly important: the decline in industrial mass production—as a consequence of the rapid progress of technology which allows both an increase in production and a decrease in the labour required—and in the scope of the military service. These changes mean that fewer individuals are now subject to the kind of organization that the two sectors are associated with. Large-scale industry and military services are indeed institutions that train people to do monotonous, routine tasks. This type of drill has little or no room for freedom of choice and basically represents the opposite of what is anticipated in consumption markets. As consumers, people must continuously be prepared to choose between diverse goods and services for sale.

It is hence assumed that people's orientations in society have changed; individuals are now less work-oriented and more consumption-oriented. Obviously, the role as consumer has become more important over time, as the standard of living has increased compared to some decades ago. There is much more to consume, and if people buy more—and do it in a premeditated way—they must devote more attention and energy to what is offered in the markets (Bauman 1998: 25, 2007: 17–19). One aspect is simply that consumption tends to take more time. The process of purchasing things has changed people's everyday life—for example, through the expansion of shopping centres and not least the internet commerce.

There should be no doubt that consumption has got a more central place in present-day advanced capitalism, but it does not automatically follow that the producer role has been put into the shade by the consumer role. People who are not employed in large-scale industries are nonetheless supposed to work unless—as pointed out above—they have valid reasons for not working. Employees in other types of jobs are also socialized into work roles; this socialization process may be somewhat different, but it certainly takes place. The empirical evidence in support of Bauman's argument is weak and can hardly justify the far-reaching generalization that producer society has been replaced by consumer society.

A more developed analysis on the same theme is presented by Paul Ransome (2005). He classifies societies on the basis of subjective criteria—that is, on people's experiences and feelings. In work-based society, people regard paid work as their essential life interest in the sense that they ascribe the exchange from this activity greater importance than the exchange from any other field (Ransome 2005: 15). The corresponding criteria are used with respect to consumption-based society. To put it in another way, the idea is to use people's orientations for the purpose of categorizing societies. Ransome is still careful to point out that production and consumption hang closely together. All production aims at consumption—and this holds even if not everything produced is consumed—and all consumption requires some kind of production. It is thus stated that the goal of both activities is to satisfy needs.

In his analysis of work-based society, Ransome (2005: Chapter 2) focuses on what he calls its 'work-centeredness' and 'productivist' ethic. With reference to empirical research he concludes that people by and large expect work to generate material and psychological security, opportunities for creative activity and possibilities of establishing and maintaining social contacts. No alternative way of obtaining these goals seems to be within reach. Apparently, it does not matter that people are more or less forced to work. All the same, they tend to ascribe work a central role; it simply has a hegemonic position in their worldview.

The concept of consumption-based society hence requires that individuals receive greater fulfilment from consumption than from production (Ransome 2005: 61). It might be argued that there is nothing new in this, but an important observation by Ransome is that people today have greater opportunities to borrow money. This means that their liquidity can be increased rapidly allowing them to buy goods and services that otherwise would be beyond reach; they can consume now and pay later. Ransome (2005: 55–57) suggests that a postmodern mind-set here challenges the dominant productivist ethic, as loans for consumption open the door for people to spend and squander. Whether this is the most adequate description of the situation can be disputed. Loans must usually be paid back and people are then required to have the necessary money, which in turn makes income-generating employment important. It is even possible that this mechanism ties people more closely to paid work. Increased consumption may very well lead to a larger amount of work—that is, a situation in which people need to earn more in order to be able to consume more (cf. also Chapter 5). As Ransome himself points out, it has already been proposed that developments in recent decades could be characterized as a 'work-and-spend-culture' (Cross 1993: 5).

Ransome's criteria for defining different types of society are highly questionable and the lack of data makes them impossible to use. In concluding, however, he is careful to emphasize that the fully developed consumption-based society has not yet—in the beginning of the

21st century—arrived (Ransome 2005: 188–189). On the other hand, the author claims, we cannot be satisfied with the conclusion that work-based society has not been affected by the changes during the last decades. He therefore suggests a compromise implying a change in the balance between the two phenomena. Consumption has become more important and—with the increased standard of living—we must admit that pleasure and enjoyment have become permanent features of people's lives. If things continue to develop in this direction, we can expect a transformation of society to take place. Ransome's entire approach seems to imply that this scenario is likely to be realized, but as he knows that the empirical basis for it is too weak—not to say nonexistent—he is wise enough not to go all the way with it.

Closing Words

Theories and concepts should be seen as scientific tools that can help us explain phenomena in the world. It is only in their empirical application that they can prove their value for social analysis. This chapter has aimed at bringing up some theoretical and conceptual issues connected to work orientations, attitudes to work and employment, and job satisfaction. The remainder of the book consists of empirical chapters which formulate and attempt to answer various research questions. For that purpose, they make use of theoretical approaches such as those discussed here, but of course, more or less, they also aim at theoretical development.

References

Alcock, P., C. Beatty, S. Fothergill, R. Macmillan and S. Yeandle (2003) *Work to Welfare: How Men Become Detached from the Labour Market*. Cambridge: Cambridge University Press.

Andreassen, C. S. (2014) 'Workaholism: An Overview and Current Status of the Research.' *Journal of Behavioral Addictions* 3(1): 1–11.

Anthony, P. D. (1977) *The Ideology of Work*. London: Tavistock.

Axelsson, J., J. C. Karlsson and E. J. Skorstad (2019) *Collective Mobilization in Changing Conditions: On the Track of the Worker Collectivity in a Turbulent Time*. Basingstoke: Palgrave Macmillan.

Bakker, A. B. and M. P. Leiter (eds) (2010) *Work Engagement: A Handbook of Essential Theory and Research*. New York: Psychology Press.

Baldry, C., P. Bain, P. Taylor, J. Hyman, D. Scholarios, A. Mars, A. Watson, K. Gilbert, G. Gall and D. Bunzel (2007) *The Meaning of Work in the New Economy*. Houndmills, Basingstoke: Palgrave Macmillan.

Bauman, Z. (1998) *Work, Consumerism and the New Poor*. Buckingham: Open University Press.

Bauman, Z. (2007) *Consuming Life*. Cambridge: Polity Press.

Bellah, R. N., R. Madsen, W. M. Sullivan, A. Swidler and S. M. Tipton (1985) *Habits of the Heart: Individualism and Commitment in American Life*. Berkeley, CA: University of California Press.

Bielby, W. T. and D. D. Bielby (1989) 'Family Ties: Balancing Commitment to Work and Family in Dual Earner Households.' *American Sociological Review* 54(5): 776–789.

Blauner, R. (1964) *Alienation and Freedom. The Factory Worker and His Industry*. Chicago: University of Chicago Press.

Bolton, S. C. (ed.) (2007) *Dimensions of Dignity at Work*. London: Butterworth-Heinemann.

Bolton, S. C. (2010) 'Being Human: Dignity of Labor as the Foundation for the Spirit—Work Connection.' *Journal of Management, Spirituality and Religion* 7(2): 157–172.

Cerasoli, C. P, J. M. Nicklin and M. T. Ford (2014) 'Intrinsic Motivation and Extrinsic Incentives Jointly Predict Performance: A 40-Year Meta-Analysis.' *Psychological Bulletin* 140(4): 980–1008.

Crompton, R. (2006) *Employment and the Family. The Reconfiguration of Work and Family Life in Contemporary Societies*. Cambridge: Cambridge University Press.

Crompton, R. and F. Harris (1998) 'Explaining Women's Employment Patterns: "Orientations to Work" Revisited.' *British Journal of Sociology* 49(1): 118–149.

Cross, G. (1993) *Time and Money. The Making of Consumer Culture*. London: Routledge.

Duffy, R. D. and B. J. Dik (2013) 'Research on Calling: What Have We Learned and Where Are We Going?' *Journal of Vocational Behavior* 83(3): 428–436.

Durkheim, E. (1964/1893) *The Division of Labor in Society*. New York: The Free Press.

Eagly, A. H. and S. Chaiken (1993) *The Psychology of Attitudes*. Fort Worth, TX: Harcourt Brace Jovanovich.

Esping-Andersen, G. (1990) *The Three Worlds of Welfare Capitalism*. Princeton, NJ: Princeton University Press.

Esping-Andersen, G. (1999) *Social Foundations of Postindustrial Economies*. Oxford: Oxford University Press.

Essy, D. (1993) 'Unemployment and Mental Health: A Critical Review.' *Social Science and Medicine* 37(1): 41–52.

Festinger, L. (1954) 'A Theory of Social Comparison Processes.' *Human Relations* 7(2): 117–140.

Friedlander, D. and G. T. Burtless (1995) *Five Years After: The Long-term Effects of Welfare-to-Work Programs*. New York: Russell Sage Foundation.

Fryer, D. M. (1986) 'Employment Deprivation and Personal Agency During Unemployment: A Critical Discussion of Jahoda's Explanation of the Psychological Effects of Unemployment.' *Social Behaviour* 1(1): 3–23.

Fukami, C. V. and E. W. Larson (1984) 'Commitment to Company and Union: Parallel Models.' *Journal of Applied Psychology* 69(3): 367–371.

Furåker, B. (2005) *Sociological Perspectives on Labor Markets*. Houndmills, Basingstoke: Palgrave Macmillan.

Furåker, B. and A. Hedenus (2009) 'Gambling Windfall Decisions. Lottery Winners and Employment Behavior.' *UNLV Gaming Research & Review Journal* 13(2): 1–15.

Gallie, D. and S. Alm (2000) 'Unemployment, Gender and Attitudes to Work', 109–133, in D. Gallie and S. Paugam (eds) *Welfare Regimes and the Experience of Unemployment in Europe*. Oxford: Oxford University Press.

Gallie, D. and C. Vogler (1994) 'Unemployment and Attitudes to Work', 115–153, in D. Gallie, C. Marsh and C. Vogler (eds) *Social Change and the Experience of Unemployment*. Oxford: Oxford University Press.

Gallie, D., M. White, Y. Cheng and M. Tomlinson (1998) *Restructuring the Employment Relationship*. Oxford: Oxford University Press.

Gellerman, S. W. (1963) *Motivation and Productivity*. New York: American Management Association.

Gellerman, S. W. (1998) *How People Work: Psychological Approaches to Management Problems*. Westport, CT: Quorum Books.

Goldthorpe, J. H., D. Lockwood, F. Bechhofer and J. Platt (1968) *The Affluent Worker: Industrial Attitudes and Behaviour*. Cambridge: Cambridge University Press.

Grant, D. (1999) 'HRM, Rhetoric and the Psychological Contract: A Case of "easier said than done".' *International Journal of Human Resource Management* 10(2): 327–350.

Hakim, C. (1996) *Key Issues in Women's Work: Female Heterogeneity and the Polarisation of Women's Employment*. London: Athlone Press.

Hakim, C. (2000) *Work-Lifestyle Choices in the 21st Century. Preference Theory*. Oxford: Oxford University Press.

Hakim, C. (2003) *Models of the Family in Modern Societies. Ideals and Realities*. Aldershot: Ashgate.

Halvorsen, K. (1997) 'The Work Ethic Under Challenge?,' 119–149, in J. Holmer and J. C. Karlsson (eds) *Work—Quo Vadis? Re-thinking the Question of Work*. Aldershot: Ashgate.

Hammer, T. and H. Russell (2004) 'Gender Differences in Employment Commitment Among Unemployed Youth,' 81–104, in D. Gallie (ed.) *Resisting Marginalization. Unemployment Experience and Social Policy in the European Union*. Oxford: Oxford University Press.

Harpaz, I. and R. Snir (2003) 'Workaholism: Its Definition and Nature.' *Human Relations* 56(3): 291–319.

Hedenus, A. (2011) *At the End of the Rainbow. Post-winning Life Among Swedish Lottery Winners*. Gothenburg: University of Gothenburg, Department of Sociology.

Herriot, P., W. E. G. Manning and J. M. Kidd (1997) 'The Content of the Psychological Contract.' *British Journal of Management* 8(2): 151–162.

Herzberg, F. (1966) *Work and the Nature of Man*. Cleveland: World Publishing.

Herzberg, F., B. Mausner and B. B. Snyderman (1959) *The Motivation to Work*. New York: John Wiley.

Israel, J. (1971) *Alienation: From Marx to Modern Sociology: A Macrosociological Analysis*. Boston: Allyn and Bacon.

Jahoda, M. (1982) *Employment and Unemployment: A Social-Psychological Analysis*. Cambridge: Cambridge University Press.

Kalleberg, A. L. (1977) 'Work Values and Job Rewards: A Theory of Job Satisfaction.' *American Sociological Review* 42(1): 124–143.

Kaplan, F. I. (1968) *Bolshevik Ideology and the Ethics of Soviet Labor. 1917–1920: The Formative Years*. New York: Philosophical Library.

Karlsson, J. C. (2012) *Organizational Misbehaviour in the Workplace: Narratives of Dignity and Resistance*. Basingstoke: Palgrave Macmillan.

Kleinbeck, U., H.-H. Quast, H. Thierry and H. Häcker (eds) (1990) *Work Motivation*. Hillsdale, NJ: Lawrence Erlbaum.

Leahy, M. and J. Doughney (2006) 'Women, Work and Preference Formation: A Critique of Catherine Hakim's Preference Theory.' *Journal of Business Systems, Governance and Ethics* 1(1): 37–48.

Lee, M. T. and R. L. Raschke (2016) 'Understanding Employee Motivation and Organizational Performance: Arguments for a Set-Theoretic Approach.' *Journal of Innovation & Knowledge* 1(3): 162–169.

Lincoln, J. R. and A. L. Kalleberg (1990) *Culture, Control, and Commitment. A Study of Work Organization and Work Attitudes in the United States and Japan.* Cambridge: Cambridge University Press.

Lødemel, I. and H. Trickey (eds) (2001) *'An Offer You Can't Refuse': Workfare in International Perspective.* Bristol: Policy Press.

Luke, T. W. (1985) *Ideology and Soviet Industrialization.* Westport, CT: Greenwood Press.

Lysgaard, S. (1961) *Arbeiderkollektivet. En studie i de underordnedes sosiologi.* Oslo: Universitetsforlaget.

Marx, K. (1933/1884) *Wage-Labour and Capital.* New York: International Publishers.

Marx, K. (1996/1867) *Capital. A Critique of Political Economy* (volume I), in K. Marx and F. Engels *Collected Works* 35. London: Lawrence & Wishart.

Maslow, A. H. (1970) *Motivation and Personality.* New York: McGraw-Hill.

McGregor, D. (1985) *The Human Side of Enterprise.* New York: Harper & Row.

Merton, R. K. (1964) *Social Theory and Social Structure.* Revised and enlarged ed. Toronto: Collier-Macmillan.

Meyer, J. P. and N. J. Allen (1991) 'A Three-Component Conceptualization of Organizational Commitment.' *Human Resource Management Review* 1: 61–89.

Meyer, J. P. and N. J. Allen (1997) *Commitment in the Workplace: Theory, Research, and Application.* Thousand Oaks, CA: Sage.

Meyer, J. P. and L. Herscovitch (2001) 'Commitment in the Workplace: Toward a General Model.' *Human Resource Management Review* 11: 299–326.

Meyer, J. P., D. J. Stanley, L. Herscovitch and L. Topolnytsky (2002) 'Affective, Continuance, and Normative Commitment to the Organization: A Meta-Analysis of Antecedents, Correlates, and Consequences.' *Journal of Vocational Behavior* 61(1): 20–52.

Miller, M. K., J. Reichert and D. Flores (2015) *Social Comparison Theory.* New York: John Wiley & Sons.

Moorhouse, H. F. (1987) 'The "work" Ethic and "leisure" Activity: The Hot Rod in Post-war America', 237–257, in P. Joyce (ed.) *The Historical Meanings of Work.* Cambridge: Cambridge University Press.

Mottaz, C. J. (1985) 'The Relative Importance of Intrinsic and Extrinsic Rewards as Determinants of Work Satisfaction.' *Sociological Quarterly* 26(3): 365–385.

MOW International Research Team (1987) *The Meaning of Work.* London: Academic Press.

Mowday, R. T. (1998) 'Reflections on the Study and Relevance of Organizational Commitment.' *Human Resource Management Review* 8(4): 387–401.

Mowday, R. T., L. M. Porter and R. M. Steers (1982) *Employee-Organization Linkages: The Psychology of Commitment, Absenteeism and Turnover.* New York: Academic Press.

Myrick, D. (2012) 'Frederick Taylor as a Contributor to Public Administration.' *Mediterranean Journal of Social Sciences* 3(12): 10–20.

Niles, F. S. (1999) 'Towards a Cross-Cultural Understanding of Work-Related Beliefs.' *Human Relations* 52(7): 855–867.

Nohria, N., B. Groysberg and L.-E. Lee (2008) 'Employee Motivation: A Powerful New Model.' *Harvard Business Review* 86(7/8): 78–83.

Nordenmark, M. (1999) *Unemployment, Employment Commitment and Well-Being: The Psychosocial Meaing of (Un)employment Among Women and Men.* Umeå: Umeå University, Department of Sociology.

Offe, C. (1985) 'Work: The Key Sociological Category?' 129–150, in C. Offe (ed. by J. Keane) *Disorganized Capitalism: Contemporary Transformations of Work and Politics.* Cambridge: Polity Press.

Ollman, B. (1976) *Alienation: Marx's Conception of Man in Capitalist Society*, 2nd ed. London: Cambridge University Press.

Parsons, T. and N. J. Smelser (1956) *Economy and Society: A Study in the Integration of Economic and Social Theory.* London: Routledge & Kegan Paul.

Porter, L. W., R. M. Steers, R. T. Mowday and P. V. Boulian (1974) 'Organizational Commitment, Job Satisfaction, and Turnover Among Psychiatric Technicians.' *Journal of Applied Psychology* 59(5): 603–609.

Ransome, P. (2005) *Work, Consumption and Culture: Affluence and Social Change in the Twenty-first Century.* London: Sage.

Reichers, A. E. (1985) 'A Review and Reconceptualization of Organizational Commitment.' *Academy of Management Review* 10(3): 465–476.

Rose, M. (1985) *Re-Working the Work Ethic.* London: Batsford.

Rosenberg, M. J. and C. I. Hovland (1960) 'Cognitive, Affective and Behavioral Components of Attitudes,' 1–14, in M. J. Rosenberg, C. I. Hovland, W. J. McGuire, R. P. Abelson and J. W. Brehm (eds) *Attitude Organization and Change: An Analysis of Consistency Among Attitude Components.* New Haven, CT: Yale University Press.

Rousseau, D. M. (1995) *Psychological Contracts in Organizations. Understanding Written and Unwritten Agreements.* Thousand Oaks, CA: Sage.

Rousseau, D. M. (2001) 'Schema, Promise and Mutuality: The Building Blocks of the Psychological Contract.' *Journal of Occupational and Organizational Psychology* 74(4): 511–541.

Sederblad, P. (ed.) (2013) *Lean i arbetslivet.* Stockholm: Liber.

Seeman, M. (1959) 'On the Meaning of Alienation.' *American Sociological Review* 24(6): 783–791.

Siegelbaum, L. H. (1988) *Stakhanovism and the Politics of Productivity in the USSR, 1935–1941.* Cambridge: Cambridge University Press.

Snir, R. and I. Harpaz (2009a) 'Cross-Cultural Differences Concerning Heavy Work Investment.' *Cross-Cultural Research* 43(4): 309–319.

Snir, R. and I. Harpaz (2009b) 'Workaholism from a Cross-cultural Perspective.' *Cross-Cultural Research* 43(4): 303–308.

Stoney, C. (2001) 'Strategic Management or Strategic Taylorism?: A Case Study into Change Within a UK Local Authority.' *International Journal of Public Sector Management* 14(1): 27–42.

Suls, J. and L. Wheeler (2000) *Handbook of Social Comparison. Theory and Research.* New York: Kluwer Academia/Plenum Publishers.

Vroom, V. (1964) *Work and Motivation.* New York: Wiley.

Wallace, J. E. (1993) 'Professional and Organizational Commitment: Compatible or Incompatible?' *Journal of Vocational Behavior* 42(3): 333–349.

Wang, G. T. (1996) *A Comparative Study of Extrinsic and Intrinsic Work Values of Employees in the United States and Japan.* New York: Edwin Mellen Press.

Warr, P. (1982) 'A National Study of Non-Financial Employment Commitment.' *Journal of Occupational Psychology* 55: 297–312.

Weber, M. (1930/1904–5) *The Protestant Ethic and the Spirit of Capitalism.* London: Allen & Unwin.

Weber, M. (1978) *Economy and Society: An Outline of Interpretive Sociology* (ed. by G. Roth and C. Wittich), Vol. 2. Berkeley: University of California Press.

Wrzesniewski, A., K. Dekas and B. Rosso (2013) 'Calling,' 115–118, in S. J. Lopez (ed.) *The Encyclopedia of Positive Psychology.* Malden, MA: Wiley-Blackwell.

Yousef, D. A. (2001) 'Islamic Work Ethic: A Moderator Between Organizational Commitment and Job Satisfaction in a Cross-Cultural Context.' *Personnel Review* 30(2): 152–169.

3   Declining Work Centrality Among Millennials—Myth or Reality?

Tómas Bjarnason and Kristina Håkansson

Introduction

There has been a long and lively debate in sociology and psychology about the alleged decline in work centrality (Hikspoors, Bjarnason and Håkansson 2012). This is a part of a larger discussion of the alleged decline in the work ethic more generally and of its possible negative effects on work behaviour, such as declining work performance, declining work involvement, increasing absenteeism, and increasing turnover (Quintanilla and Wilpert 1991; Miller 2002; Sharabi and Harpaz 2007). Other concerns are related to, for example, whether people will stop working when opportunities for alternative means of subsistence are available (Arvey, Harpaz and Liao 2004), decreasing willingness to continue working instead of retiring (Shacklock and Brunetto 2011), and increasing acceptance of being unemployed (see review by Furnham 1984).

Work has remained a key dimension of most people's lives, although the end of work has been repeatedly predicted in past decades (Furåker 2012a and Chapter 2 in this volume). The importance of work to one's life is called 'work centrality' and can be considered in both absolute and relative terms. In this chapter we examine work centrality and how it has changed between generations in several countries in recent decades.

The recent focus on changes in work centrality, and in work attitudes more generally, has particularly concerned the arrival of the millennial generation (i.e., people born in the two decades before the millennium) in the labour market. Claims are made that this generation has fundamentally different views of work from those of previous generations. The popular literature has decried the work ethic of the Millennials, regarded as a generation characterized by narcissistic personality traits, fame obsession, laziness and entitlement (e.g., Stein 2013). Some have exaggerated the results of studies of the Millennials' work ethic, as this quotation illustrates:

> [The Millennial generation,] is self-absorbed to the point of narcissism, consumed by fame and fortune, plagued by a sense of entitlement. . . . When they do show up in the workplace, [they are]

notoriously tough to manage. They dress like slobs, question authority, shrug off criticism and impatiently wonder why, if they start in the mailroom on Monday, they're not on their way to being vice president by Friday.

(Navarrette 2008)

More systematic studies and comparisons have been less definitive: some studies have found that Millennials differ somewhat from previous generations (Twenge and Campbell 2012), and consequently that work centrality is in decline (Twenge et al. 2010), whereas others have downplayed the changes in attitudes between generations (Trzesniewsk and Donnellan 2010; Hikspoors, Bjarnason and Håkansson 2012; Pyöriä et al. 2017).

If work centrality is changing, it could be due to factors other than the arrival of the Millennials, such as a changing economic environment, higher educational levels, technological change, changing labour markets and welfare systems, weakening of families and religion, and a changing social fabric in general. The effects of these factors on work centrality are by no means straightforward. For example, the deep recession of 2008–2009 had severe consequences for employment levels in many countries and thus on living standards and quality of life. The recession affected not only Millennials who faced difficulties in entering the labour market, but also people of previous generations—for example, through declining pay levels and welfare cuts. However, knowledge of the possible effects of the crisis on work centrality is lacking. We need to know who have mainly been affected and how.

This chapter aims to describe and explain the development of work centrality over time in several countries, with a particular focus on similarities and differences between and within generations. It is guided by the following research questions:

- How has work centrality developed from 1995 to 2011 in selected countries? If work centrality has changed, how can these changes be explained?
- Do the data reveal an effect of the crisis, which began at the end of 2008? If so, what effect did the crisis have?
- What effect did the arrival of the Millennials have? Is work less important to them than to other generations and, if so, why?

Work Centrality

Discussion of the importance of work in people's lives dates to Max Weber's seminal work on the Protestant work ethic. For Weber (1976 [1904–1905]), this ethic existed in the form of a moral and religious obligation to work, forming part of the foundation on which capitalism was built. Weber argued that under Protestantism the work ethic became a moral and religious obligation, a calling, with work being seen as an end in itself, not as a means to an end. This obligation referred to 'the valuation of the fulfilment of duty in worldly affairs as the highest form which the moral activity of the individual could assume' (Weber 1976: 80; see also Chapter 4 in this book).

Work came to be experienced as a moral obligation, and those with a stronger work ethic placed a greater emphasis on 'hard work, autonomy, fairness, wise and efficient use of time, delay of gratification and the intrinsic value of work' (Miller, Woehr and Hudspeth 2002: 4). Further developments of the concept have separated different dimensions of the work ethic, with work centrality being one dimension (Hirschfeld and Feild 2000; Miller, Woehr and Hudspeth 2002).

Work centrality has been defined as 'the degree of general importance that working has in one's life at any given time' (MOW 1987: 8; cf. Arvey, Harpaz and Liao 2004). Similar definitions have been proposed by others (Paullay, Alliger and Stone-Romero 1994), although the operationalization of the concept differs between scholars. The concept has been studied as both an absolute and a relative phenomenon (England and Misumi 1986; Harpaz, Honig and Coetsier 2002). In absolute terms, work centrality concerns how important work is in one's life, while the relative measure concerns how important it is relative to other dimensions of life, such as family, leisure and religion.

The concept says nothing about the motives for considering work important—for example, whether people find work important for 'intrinsic' or 'extrinsic' reasons, or whether people find work important because they feel it is their obligation to work or because they need money for survival. It differs from concepts such as 'employment commitment', which refers to individuals' non-financial commitment to paid work (Warr 1982; see also Chapter 2 and Chapter 5 in this book). Moreover, the concept of work centrality is unrelated to any specific job or workplace, although past work experience or the availability and quality of work at any given time may play a role in determining an individual's attachment to work (Hikspoors, Bjarnason and Håkansson 2012). 'Work centrality' is distinguished from concepts such as 'organizational commitment', with the former referring to the importance of work more generally and the latter to emotional connection to the current organizational membership (Hirschfeld and Feild 2000; see also Chapter 2 and Chapter 6 in this book). Furthermore, concepts such as 'job involvement' (Paullay, Alliger and Stone-Romero 1994) and 'employee engagement' (Fenzel 2013) concern preoccupation with and engagement in the *current* job, while work centrality is the degree of importance work has in the lives of people more generally.

In sum, work centrality is a general attitude towards the importance of work. It is formed by, for example, family, culture, economic situation, education and early work experiences and likely predicts current work attitudes and behaviours, although it is not necessarily unaffected by these.

Defining Generations

A generation is a cohort; it refers to people born at a similar time in history—within a similar sociohistorical context—experiencing the same historical events and encountering similar social movements, ideas, morals, barriers and opportunities. This shared experience provides a generation with, at least to some degree, a shared worldview, affecting individuals' perceptions and interpretations of their current life situation and thus their values, motives, longing, aspirations and behaviours (Mannheim 1952; Ng, Lyons and Schweitzer 2012). So, each generation brings a new perspective to the world, to society and its institutions, and upholds new traditions, attitudes and values, and for each generation we may have both high hopes and doubts.

Theory assumes that values are shaped in the 'formative years' of individuals, through socialization in the family, in school and in early work experiences, and are for the most part fixed by the time the individual reaches adulthood. Value change happens because of changes in economic, social and political circumstances during individuals' formative years, creating somewhat distinct values for each generation. Through generational studies, it is possible to study value changes, as these happen largely through generational shifts. Evidence strongly suggests a generational trend in values, shifting from materialism towards post-materialism, and that each generation mostly keeps its outlook throughout its life cycle (Inglehart 1990; Inglehart and Baker 2000; Inglehart 2008; Welzel and Inglehart 2010).

Four generations are usually distinguished in the current literature: the Silent Generation, or the Traditionalists, born 1928–1944; the Baby Boomers, or simply the Boomers, born 1945–1960; Generation X, or the Gen Xers, born 1961–1979; and the Millennials, also referred to as GenMe, GenY, or Echo Boomers, born 1980–1999. These generational demarcations differ somewhat between scholars, though there is a fair degree of agreement as to their definitions (Smola and Sutton 2002). Three of these generations are currently major players in the labour market: the Boomers, Gen Xers and Millennials, each comprising about one fifth to one quarter of the population of the countries studied here.

The context of each generation defines its worldview. Some contexts influence all generations and all countries to some degree, though the strength of the effect differs; such contexts include events such as the Great Depression and the world wars. We will focus on some important contexts that we assume affect people's lives and needs and thus their attitudes towards work during the period under examination across the studied countries. Extensive social and economic changes happened in the early 21st century, affecting the contexts of most people. One was the financial crisis starting in late 2008, which had a major impact on the economies of most countries. Another was the rise of information technology, of social media, software platforms and automation. While this development has affected all generations, it created a distinct experience in the formative years of the Millennials, who are defined as 'digital natives', people who grew up surrounded by and using digital technology (Prensky 2001).

There are also less dramatic changes that have created distinct experiences for the generations, influencing their life choices, lifestyles and quality of life. These trends have been identified as important in the American context, but we assume that they also apply to the countries examined here. These include increasing educational attainment and simultaneously decreasing economic opportunities for those with less education, changing rates of family formation, increasing employment of women, declining fertility, young adults increasingly living with parents, increasing temporary work and widening income disparities (Levenson 2010).

Some of these changes, along with increased longevity and improved health, have created a new reality, not only for the Millennials but also for middle-aged people. The 'three-stage life' that we have become used to is inevitably giving way to more complex lifestyles and to career choices that continue much further into old age (Gratton and Scott 2016).

In addition, it should be noted that we may now be facing the most serious human crisis in modern history: the coming of an environmental catastrophe due to global warming and its manifold consequences for our ways of life. How this threat, which has become very obvious in recent years, will influence how people think about work, what they think work should be like, and their demands on workplaces and managers remains to be seen. The same questions also apply to the growth of social media and increasing automation at work, but that is outside the scope of this chapter, too.

Declining Work Centrality?

There is no shortage of claims of a decline in work centrality and in the work ethic generally, often related to the arrival of the Millennials in the labour market (Myers and Sadaghiani 2010). Drawing sound conclusions from results in this field is complicated, mainly due to methodological and conceptual variations between studies (Ng, Lyons and Schweitzer 2012). The definition and operationalization of work centrality varies. Quantitative studies tend to differ in their methodological design—for example, concerning whether the research is longitudinal (studying the same individuals at different points in time), whether it involves the comparison of cohorts at different points in time (time-lag studies), or whether conclusions are drawn from comparing age groups (defined as generations) at a single point in time (single cross-sectional studies). Single cross-sectional studies cannot separate age and generation effects, and the effects discovered might either be due to generational differences (i.e., effects that remain stable despite the aging of individuals) or be differences caused by the position of the individual in the life cycle (i.e., effects that change as the individual ages) (Parry and Urwin 2011).

Moreover, there are variations in the data examined depending on whether they derive from studies of workplaces and schools or whether nationally representative samples are used. Values are expected to change slowly over long periods through generational shifts (Inglehart 1990), so nationally representative samples followed over long periods of time are best suited for detecting such changes. Finally, there are some variations in the definition or demarcation of generations between studies, even though such variations are not the biggest concern, as they are generally small. It should be noted that some researchers problematize these differences, as illustrated by claims that the generational demarcations apply specifically to the United States and not necessarily to other countries or cultures (Parry and Urwin 2011; Zabel et al. 2017).

The focus here is on 'time-lag' studies, which can separate age and generation effects—that is, studies including at least two measurements over a period long enough to allow comparison of at least two generations of the same age when data are collected. Despite the popularity of the topic of declining work centrality, only a handful of such studies have been published (Kowske, Rasch and Wiley 2010; Twenge 2010; Twenge et al. 2010).

The main evidence for the decline in work centrality comes from the United States, where some investigations are based on student samples, while others rely on adult samples. Summarizing this research, Jean M. Twenge and Stacy M. Campbell (2012) argued that there has been a consistent decline in work centrality and the work ethic over generations. Based on nationally representative samples, they report that between the 1970s and 2000s, fewer people stated that they would continue working if they had enough money to live as comfortably as they liked for the rest of their lives. In addition, nationally representative samples of high school students have shown an increase over time in those agreeing that 'work is just making a living' and those saying that 'they prefer a job with enough vacation time' (Twenge and Campbell 2012: 9).

A much-cited time-lag study of declining work centrality between generations was conducted by Karen Wey Smola and Charlotte D. Sutton (2002). They used data gathered from a large survey conducted in 53 companies in the United States in 1974 and repeated several of the items in a much smaller study of MBA students in 1999. Based on this comparison, they concluded that Gen Xers' work values 'are significantly different from those of the Baby Boomers' (Smola and Sutton 2002: 378), with Gen Xers being less likely to report that work should be an important part of their life than did Boomers, while in contrast, Gen Xers felt more strongly than did Boomers that working hard was an indication of their worth. Smola and Sutton (2002) concluded that respondents in 1999 were less likely to believe that work should be an important part of their life than did respondents of the same age in 1974.

Twenge et al. (2010) studied a nationally representative sample of high school seniors in the United States at three points in time, finding that work centrality decreased over time. The study compared Boomers, Gen Xers and Millennials when at the same age. A clear decline in work centrality was discovered between the measurement points, with respondents being less willing to work overtime, expecting work to be less central to their lives, and being more supportive of the idea that work is 'nothing more than making a living' (Twenge et al. 2010: 12). In all cases, the Millennials exhibited the lowest work centrality scores. The authors concluded that Millennials valued leisure time more and placed a greater emphasis on extrinsic work rewards than did either Boomers or Gen Xers. The importance of the intrinsic value of work had declined over the generations, suggesting that any intrinsic meaning of work was less relevant to younger generations.

Jean M. Twenge and Tim Kasser's (2013) investigation of three generations (i.e., Boomers, Gen Xers and Millennials) of high school students in the United States concluded that materialistic values had increased considerably among Gen Xers and Millennials relative to Boomers, while being strongest among the Gen Xers. Contrary to what could be expected, the authors discovered decreasing work centrality accompanying this increasing materialism. Hence, materialism as such does not necessarily translate into work centrality, though as work is one of the main ways in which individuals can earn money, we might assume that materialism and work centrality are positively related to each other. The lack of such a relationship may indicate an inclination towards entitlement (i.e., having rights but no obligations), narcissism, inflated views of one's own talents and, consequently, unrealistic expectations of success, fame and fortune. Research has confirmed such a development in personality and found Millennials to differ from previous generations at the same age in terms of self-esteem, assertiveness and narcissism (Deal, Altman and Rogelberg 2010).

Not all studies, however, find that the Millennials have the weakest work ethic. A study of data on business students collected over a 12-year period found that Baby Boomers scored significantly higher than did either Gen Xers or Millennials on all seven measured work ethic dimensions, and that Gen Xers had the weakest work ethic across the three cohorts studied (Meriac, Woehr and Banister 2010). These researchers accordingly argued that the study does not support the existence of a linear downward trend in the work ethic.

In contrast, some doubt the decline in the work ethic and in work centrality (Deal, Altman and Rogelberg 2010). These scholars report that results indicate 'modest' differences at most, and that studies do not support fundamentally different work behaviours—for example, that Millennials work fewer hours than Gen Xers did at the same age. Similarly, others claim that 'there is little solid empirical evidence supporting generationally based differences and almost no theory behind why such differences should even exist' (Costanza and Finkelstein 2015: 308).

Studies done outside the American context have found considerable stability in work values between generations (e.g., Pyöriä et al. 2017; Breitsohl and Ruhle 2012; Sharabi and Harpaz 2007). Examining work centrality based on Finland's Quality of Work Life Surveys over two decades, it was discovered that leisure and family life had increased in importance, and that this did not apply solely to Millennials but also to previous generations. Pyöriä et al.'s (2017: 1) main conclusion was that their investigation did not support the argument that 'the Millennials are less work-oriented than older generations'. Similarly, a study of changes in work attitudes between German Millennials and Gen Xers revealed considerable stability in work attitudes between generations when controlling for age (Breitsohl and Ruhle 2012). Also, a longitudinal study of the Israeli Jewish labour force, which started in 1981 with interviews with nearly 1,000 subjects, of whom nearly 600 were re-interviewed in 1993, found relative stability in responses between the investigations. Respondents were asked to distribute 100 points between several areas of their life—for example, work, leisure, family and religion. Although there was an increase in the importance attributed to both leisure and work, the researchers concluded that no generational effect appeared in the data (Sharabi and Harpaz 2007).

Multinational studies support the existence of diverging trends in work centrality between countries. For example, Hikspoors, Bjarnason and Håkansson (2012) uncovered no conclusive trend in work centrality in their study of 11 Western countries. Although leisure had tended to increase in value relative to work in most of the countries, the trend in absolute terms was more mixed: the importance of work had increased in some countries, decreased in others and remained at the same level in others.

To sum up, there is no consensus in previous research regarding the alleged decline in work centrality, and national variations are found between studies, not the least when it comes to the Millennials. There is clearly a need for further studies of the development of work centrality that search for different explanations.

The Aims of the Chapter

In this chapter, we will investigate, with three aims, the development of work centrality from 1995 to 2011 in selected countries. Our first aim is to examine how work centrality has developed over time in different countries and in different institutional, cultural and economic contexts. We will examine whether there are similar or divergent trends in work centrality in the five surveyed countries between 1995 and 2011 and, if so, how such changes can be explained.

Past research indicates that people's work orientations differ between countries, employment statuses and economic states as measured by employment levels (Hikspoors, Bjarnason and Håkansson 2012). We have selected five countries from different parts of the Western world—Germany, Japan, Spain, Sweden and the United States—having different welfare models, household employment strategies and cultures.

Three of these countries have come to be regarded as the prototypes of three distinct welfare models (Esping-Andersen 1990; Arts and Gelissen 2010): Sweden, exemplifying the *Nordic* welfare model; Germany, exemplifying both the *conservative* (Esping-Andersen 1990) and *corporatist* welfare models (Korpi and Palme 1998); and the United States, exemplifying the *liberal* (Esping-Andersen 1990) or *basic security* model (Korpi and Palme 1998). In addition, Japan is classified by some as *conservative* and by others as *corporatist* like Germany or even *liberal* like the United States. Finally, Spain exemplifies the *southern* or *Latin Rim* welfare state model (Arts and Gelissen 2002).

Assumptions or predictions about how these different welfare models and cultures affect work centrality are not straightforward. While the negative effects of generous welfare systems can be assumed, studies have not established that a generous welfare system makes people less inclined to work, partly because welfare state arrangements in these countries (e.g., sick pay and unemployment benefits) are often tied to past employment (Esser 2009; Furåker 2012b; see also Chapter 5 in this book). In contrast, weak welfare states, such as the Anglo-Saxon states, may induce higher dependence on work for survival and thus higher work centrality.

Another way to understand the differences between these countries is through their cultural heritages. Some researchers argue that the world can be divided into cultural zones that have persisted for centuries. They order nations culturally according to the two value dimensions 'traditional vs. secular-rational values' and 'survival vs. self-expression values' (Inglehart and Baker 2000: 24). The former dimension ranges from respect for authority, the homeland, and the family to more secular values. The latter dimension ranges from the importance of economic and physical security, through fear of foreigners, ethnic diversity and cultural change, to the upholding of 'trust, tolerance, subjective well-being, political activism and self-expression' (Inglehart and Baker 2000: 25). In this typology, the United States is classified as 'English speaking', scoring high on the survival vs. self-expression dimension but below average on the traditional vs. secular dimension; West Germany and Sweden are classified as 'Protestant Europe', scoring high on both dimensions; Spain is classified as 'Catholic Europe', with average scores on both dimensions; and Japan is classified as 'Confucian', scoring high on the traditional vs. secular dimension but average on the survival vs. self-expression dimension.

Predictions regarding the levels and development of work centrality based on cultural heritage are not straightforward, and more affluent societies—scoring high in self-expressive values—might hold work to be of high importance because of its intrinsic value. In contrast, the importance of work might also decline due to a shift to post-materialistic values as countries move away from survival values towards self-expressive ones.

The latter possibility was supported by Warr (2008), who demonstrated that work centrality was higher in the historically catholic and the post-communist countries than in the historically protestant ones. Also, in our previous study (Hikspoors, Bjarnason and Håkansson 2012), we particularly found that, between 1990 and 2008, the importance of work relative to leisure had declined in the historically protestant countries, such as Norway, Sweden, Denmark and Britain, while remaining the same or even increasing in importance in some of the historically Catholic countries, such as Italy and France.

These results indicate that there could be a divide between the levels of self-expressive values in Protestant Europe and the English-speaking world, and the social and economic circumstances in which people live. Ronald Inglehart (2008) pointed out that the socioeconomic environment has not continued to improve in recent decades, as it did before. Instead, the socioeconomic environment has become more volatile, through welfare cutbacks, growing income inequality and unemployment.

If the population increasingly values personal autonomy, self-expression and well-being (Welzel and Inglehart 2010), then, given the general participation of the population in working life, work must partly be the locus where these values are realized. If not, there is increasing conflict between what people desire from life and their experience at work. Individual responses to such circumstances could explain the decreasing importance of work and the increasing importance of leisure, especially if leisure can satisfy these values better than work can. Trends in work centrality are not easy to foresee, so we will approach the question in an explorative spirit.

Our second aim is to examine whether the economic crisis, starting in 2008, left any pattern in the data. Past research indicates that work centrality is affected by the supply of work: abundance of work means that leisure becomes more important, and vice versa (Hikspoors, Bjarnason and Håkansson 2012). We want to examine whether the crisis had any effect on work centrality through examining employment and unemployment levels, with a special focus on Spain and Germany. Accordingly, we will test whether work centrality increased in Spain and decreased in

Germany after the crisis, due to low unemployment and high employment levels.

The 2008–2009 economic crisis hit all countries in the Western world, but was more severe in some countries than others. Employment levels rose in Germany after the crisis (between 2005 and 2010), while they declined in Spain and the United States and remained fairly stable in Sweden and Japan. Similarly, unemployment rates increased markedly in Spain after 2008, peaking at 26% in 2013. In contrast, unemployment levels declined in Germany and remained at similar levels in Japan. Unemployment also increased in the United States and Sweden after the crisis, though not nearly as much as in Spain. There was considerable decline in employment levels in the youngest age group after the crisis in Spain, the United States and Sweden and this development probably meant increased difficulties for young people entering employment in these countries (OECD 2019).

Although observing a general shift with succeeding generations—from materialistic values emphasizing economic and physical security to post-materialistic values—Inglehart (1990) noted that short-term fluctuations towards increasing materialism may also occur due to economic decline. This is called the 'scarcity hypothesis', which holds that 'one places the greatest subjective value on those things that are in relatively short supply' (Inglehart 1990: 68). During times of economic hardship, people therefore place more importance on material things, work and wages and worry more about unemployment than they do during periods of prosperity (Inglehart 2008; Welzel and Inglehart 2010).

The impact of economic fluctuations on individuals' attitudes and behaviours might be mitigated by the type of welfare state, with more marginal and fragmented welfare states being more likely to induce behavioural and attitude changes during economic recessions, as individuals would be less protected from market forces. This would apply to countries such as Spain and the United States, whereas less impact on attitudes would be expected in countries such as Sweden.

The importance of work scarcity for work attitudes has been postulated in several studies. In their study of 11 European countries, Hikspoors, Bjarnason and Håkansson (2012) discovered a negative correlation between work centrality and employment rates, suggesting that work is more important in countries with low employment rates. They proposed that scarcity of employment affects the importance attributed to work and that scarcity of leisure affects the importance attributed to leisure. In the Finnish study mentioned above, it turned out that the value attributed to work follows the cyclical movement of the economy: when times are good, 'the value attached to employment falls, and vice versa' (Pyöriä et al. 2017: 8). Similarly, an increase in work centrality in Israel between 1981 and 1993 was attributed to economic decline, mass redundancies and growing unemployment, which peaked in 1992

(Sharabi and Harpaz 2007). It therefore seems important to consider economic fluctuations and changes in employment levels when studying work centrality.

Our third aim is to examine generational changes in work centrality, specifically, the impact of the arrival of the Millennials. As argued above, changes in work centrality may have various causes related to changing contexts. An important but gradual change is that of 'delay of adulthood' (Gratton and Scott 2016). Associated with this trend is that of declining family stability and declining fertility; other aspects are population ageing, increasing life expectancy and declining morbidity.

Accordingly, recent decades have seen a reverse trend towards declining employment among the oldest age categories. Between 1995 and 2010, which is approximately the time frame of this study, employment increased for those aged 60–64 years in Germany (23 percentage points), Sweden (14 percentage points), the United States (8 percentage points) and Spain (7 percentage points), with the smallest increase found in Japan (4 percentage points) (OECD 2019). In line with the conclusions of our previous research, in which we found that higher employment rates go hand in hand with declining work centrality, we might actually expect to find declining work centrality in the oldest generations examined in this study.

One hypothesis drawn from the higher life expectancy and decline in morbidity is that people should make more future-oriented decisions today than people of the same age did decades ago when life expectancy was lower, morbidity higher and prosperity lower. People should simply start preparing earlier and more sensibly for a longer and healthier life. An alternative hypothesis is that younger people—and perhaps people generally—might be less inclined to make future-oriented decisions now, as they assume a longer lifespan in which to solve current and future problems. In addition, with relatively well-off parents and generally a much larger ratio of adults to children than previously,[1] young people might have become more accustomed to more attention and greater material well-being than were previous generations. As a result, Millennials' parents have been described as 'over-involved' and as engaging in 'helicopter parenting' (Nicholas 2009). This situation would result in less future orientation and less inclination to delay gratification in favour of future benefits, as Millennials would have more resources to fall back on than did previous generations.

The latter interpretation fits well with studies of trends in personality traits in the United States, which found an increase in narcissistic personality traits, 'characterized by overconfidence and an inflated sense of self' (Twenge and Campbell 2012: 5), and in materialism accompanied by less work centrality. This indicates increasing 'entitlement' and a loss in understanding of the relationship between material acquisition and hard work and of the obligation norms associated with work. Early work experiences are the key to the development of work centrality, and delayed adulthood and more fragmented work experience could weaken its foundations (Harpaz, Honig and Coetsier 2002).

Consequently, we will examine generational changes in the data with a specific emphasis on the arrival of the Millennials and try to explain changes in work centrality between generations. We will also specifically test whether elements related to the delay of adulthood, such as living with parents and integration into family life (i.e., having children and marital status), influence work centrality.

Studies have found work centrality to be related to employment status and labour market position (Warr 2008; Hikspoors, Bjarnason and Håkansson 2012), so employment status needs to be considered when studying work centrality. In a previous study, we demonstrated that work centrality was related to employment status when the full-time employed had the highest centrality scores (Hikspoors, Bjarnason and Håkansson 2012). Somewhat contradicting this, we also discovered that work centrality was higher in countries with lower employment, indicating that scarcity of employment likely increases work centrality. Hence, being employed full time increases work centrality, but so does living in a society where work is scarce.

While studies have found gender differences in work centrality (Warr 2008), these differences tend to be small, and tend to weaken or disappear in more recent data when controlling for labour market involvement (Hikspoors, Bjarnason and Håkansson 2012). As we examine historical data, we expect gender still to be an issue regarding work centrality because it is an indicator of both structural and cultural factors that affect preferences and attitudes regarding work.

Method and Data

The analysis is based on data from the World Values Survey. We limit the study to three of the six waves conducted and to five countries (i.e., Germany, Japan, Spain, Sweden and the United States). Data were collected in three waves: 1995–1997, 2005–2007 and 2010–2013. The numbers of respondents in each wave were 6,010, 6,274 and 9,001, for a total of 21,285 individuals overall. The sample size for each generation is shown in Table 3.1.

As seen in Table 3.1, the generations can be studied in two ways. First, three generations (i.e., the Silent Generation, Baby Boomers and Gen Xers) can be studied at three points in time and the Millennials at two points in time (as they were only partly included in wave 5, but not at all in wave 3).

Second, three generations (i.e., Millennials, Gen Xers and Baby Boomers) measured in wave 6 can be compared with the same age groups in wave 3: the Millennials in wave 6 can be matched with the same age

Table 3.1 Description of the data sets

	Silent Generation, born 1928–1944	Baby Boomers, born 1945–1960	Gen X, born 1961–1979	Millennials, born 1980–1999
Age in 1995*– wave 3	51–67 years	35–50 years	18–34 years	–
Age in 2006**– wave 5	62–78 years	46–61 years	27–45 years	18–26 years
Age in 2011***– wave 6	67–83 years	51–66 years	32–50 years	18–31 years
Total sample size	4,788	6,546	7,324	2,627
Germany	1,344	1,660	2,123	686
Japan	1,126	1,532	1,426	418
Spain	711	817	1,258	482
Sweden	681	924	1,008	447
United States	926	1,613	1,509	594

* Data were collected in 1995 for Japan, Spain and the United States but in 1996 for Sweden and in 1997 for Germany.
** Date were collected in 2006 for Germany, Sweden and the United States, but in 2005 in Japan and 2007 in Spain
*** Data were collected for in 2011 for Spain, Sweden and the United States, but in 2010 for Japan and 2013 in Germany.

group in wave 3, which roughly corresponds to the Gen Xers (dark grey cells); the Gen Xers in wave 6 can be matched with the same age group in wave 3, which roughly corresponds to the Baby Boomers (light grey cells); and the Boomers in wave 6 can be matched with the Silent Generation in wave 3 (dark grey cells).

Work centrality is measured by the following item in the World Values Survey: 'For each of the following aspects, please indicate how important it is in your life'. The response to this item as concerns the work dimension is used as an indicator of absolute work centrality, as has been done in some previous studies (Warr 2008; Hikspoors, Bjarnason and Håkansson 2012).

To measure the importance of work relative to other domains of life, the same item is used, with respondents rating the importance of leisure and the differences between the leisure and work dimensions being calculated. Similar methods have been used by other scholars to measure work centrality (Quintanilla and Wilpert 1991; Harpaz, Honig and Coetsier 2002).

To sum up, we will study the development of work centrality from 1995 to 2011 in five countries across the three waves. First, we examine mean differences in the scores for absolute and relative work centrality over time for each country. Second, to explore whether the crisis, starting in 2008, left any pattern in the data, we look at differences in the mean values of absolute and relative work centrality between waves. The crucial question is whether work centrality was differently affected in the country most severely hit by the crisis (Spain) than in country least affected by the crisis (Germany). Third, we examine generational changes in absolute and relative work centrality; specifically, the impact of the arrival of the Millennials. We study generational differences in two ways. First, we compare each generation over time–that is, we compare the most recent work centrality score of each generation with the scores from 5 and 16 years earlier. Then we compare each generation with the same age group 16 years earlier. The main question is whether there is a general generational decline in work centrality and, specifically, whether the Millennials score lower on work centrality than did the same age group 16 years before. In addition, to better understand the impact of different contexts on work centrality, we study the impact of several of our variables simultaneously in a regression analysis, testing the effects of waves, countries, living with parents, presence of children, marital status and employment status.

Results

To analyse work centrality, means were calculated from responses to the question 'How important is work in your life?', with the four response alternatives recoded as 'very important' (4); 'rather important' (3); 'not very important' (2); and 'not at all important' (1). A little more than half of the respondents' rated work as 'very important', while only 4% rated work as 'not at all important' (Table 3.2).

The relative measure of work centrality was calculated in comparison with the rated importance of leisure by subtracting the individual's rating of leisure from that of work. If an individual attributes more value to work than leisure, the relative work centrality variable has a positive value ranging from +1 to +3. If the individual rates leisure as of higher importance than work, then the relative work centrality variable has a

Table 3.2 Distribution regarding the importance of work and leisure, percentages

Please say, for each of the following, how important it is in your life:	Very important	Rather important	Not very important	Not at all important	Total	Sample size (n)
Work	51	36	9	4	100	20,723
Leisure	40	50	9	1	100	21,053

negative value of –1 to –3. If the individual rates work and leisure as of equal importance, the relative work centrality variable is zero (0), independent of whether the scores are low or high.

Our calculations indicate that most respondents rated leisure and work as equal in importance (45%), translating into a value of zero (0) for the relative work centrality variable. Roughly 1% rated leisure as 'very important' and work as 'not at all important', for a value of –3, and less than .5% rated work as 'very important' and leisure as 'not at all important', for a value of +3. More people rated work as of higher value than leisure, than the reverse. Thus, a total of 31% of respondents attributed more value to work than leisure (for a positive value on the relative work centrality variable), while 25% attributed more value to leisure than work (for a negative value of the relative work centrality variable). This variable has many positive characteristics. First, it eliminates cultural differences in behaviour as the value of one question (work) is subtracted from the value of another question (leisure). Second, it has a distribution much closer to normality than the absolute work centrality score.

To explain the development and levels of work centrality, we will study differences in work centrality between five countries, three waves, four generations, four age groups, gender and employment status, depending on whether the respondent is living with parents, has children, or is married or cohabitating. Table 3.3 presents means and correlations between the dependent and independent variables. These results are based on approximately 21,000 responses.

The highest correlation with work centrality is for the employment status variable, with not being in the labour market (e.g., retirees, students and homemakers) being negatively correlated with work centrality (–.28); this variable also has the highest correlation with relative work centrality (–.17). Likewise, there is a notable negative correlation between the oldest age group (67–83 years of age) and work centrality (–.20).

It should be noted that the sample sizes in the study are not weighted to reflect the population sizes. For example, there are about as many responses from Sweden as from Japan, whose population is about 13 times larger. Also, the data have been limited to the generations and age groups of interest, which means that the focus will be on trends for each country, generation and age group rather than on total means for the whole sample.

Development of Work Centrality

Regarding our first aim, we start by examining trends in work centrality between waves for each country. Analysis of variance (ANOVA) was conducted by testing mean differences between waves for each country.

Table 3.3 Means and correlations regarding the variables in the study

Variables	Percent (%)	Correlation with absolute work centrality	Correlation with relative work centrality
Age groups			
Age 18–31	23	.02**	−.03***
Age 32–50	36	.14***	.09***
Age 51–66	28	−.02**	.01
Age 67–83	13	−.20***	−.10***
Generations			
Silent Generation, born 1928–1944	22	−.14***	−.05***
Baby boomers, born 1945–1960	31	.04***	.04***
Gen Xers, born 1961–1979	34	.08***	.02**
Millennials, born 1980–1999	12	.01	−.03***
Waves			
Wave 3 (1994–1998)	28	.10***	.10***
Wave 5 (2005–2009)	29	−.04***	−.02**
Wave 6 (2010–2014)	42	−.06***	−.07***
Countries			
Germany	27	−.04***	.05***
Japan	21	.05***	.02*
Spain	15	.06***	.05***
Sweden	14	.07***	−.02**
United States	22	−.12***	−.10***
Employment status			
Employed	58	.24***	.13***
Not in the labour market	34	−.28***	−.17***
Unemployed	7	.05***	.06**
Other variables			
Living with parents	17	.04***	−.01
Have children	71	.00	.06***
Married or cohabiting	66	.03***	.06***
Sex-males	48	.04***	.04***

N = 21,285

*** p < .001; ** p < .01; * p < .05

Table 3.4 shows the values of absolute and relative work centrality for all countries and waves in the study.

To make the waves comparable, we limited parts of the study to the first three age groups, aged 18–66 years, as the Silent Generation is mostly absent from the labor market in waves 5 and 6. The mean age of the respondents in wave 3 is lower (41 years) than in waves 5 and 6 (43 years). Nearly 48% are employed full time and roughly 64% are employed to any extent. About 1 in 10 is a homemaker, and somewhat fewer are retired (8%) or unemployed (8%). Overall, 26% are not in the labour market.

Table 3.4 Means for absolute and relative work centrality by waves and countries, age 18–66 years

Country	Absolute work centrality					Relative work centrality				
	Wave 3 1994–1998	Wave 5 2005–2009	Wave 6 2010–2014	Total	Sample size (n)	Wave 3 1994–1998	Wave 5 2005–2009	Wave 6 2010–2014	Total	Sample size (n)
Germany	3.38	3.38	3.33	3.36	4,904	.18	.24	.10	.17	4,886
Japan	3.46	3.40	3.50	3.46	3,718	.11	.02	.09	.08	3,685
Spain	3.51	3.45	3.56	3.51	2,899	.37	.06	.14	.19	2,888
Sweden	3.63	3.45	3.42	3.50	2,649	.16	-.05	-.11	.00	2,646
United States	3.45	3.10	3.14	3.22	4,087	.13	-.16	-.19	-.09	4,070
Total	3.47	3.35	3.37	3.39	18,257	.19	.04	.00	.07	18,175

Looking first at the absolute work centrality scores, we find that the United States has the lowest total scores, significantly below those of the other countries (*p* < .001). Germany has lower figures than do Spain, Sweden and Japan (*p* < .001), which are all similar in terms of means. Wave 3 has the highest work centrality scores and higher scores than both wave 5 and 6 (*p* < .001), while differences between waves 5 and 6 are not significant.

We see diverging trends between countries in absolute work centrality. Three main patterns are detected: one for Germany, another for Japan and Spain, and the third for Sweden and the United States. No significant change can be verified in the German data between any of the waves. Japan (*p* < .01) and Spain (*p* < .01) display significant increases between wave 5, in which the means are the lowest, and wave 6, in which the means are the highest. For Sweden and the United States, there is a significant decline between wave 3, in which the scores are the highest, and waves 5 and 6 (*p* < .001), but not between waves 5 and 6, which exhibit similar means. It should be noted that the period between waves 3 and 5 is about twice as long (11 years) as that between waves 5 and 6 (5 years), so larger changes should be expected in the first case.

As with absolute work centrality, the mean score for relative work centrality is the lowest in the United States (−.09), where it is significantly lower than in the other countries (*p* < .01). Negative numbers indicate that people more often said leisure was more important than work. The highest mean score is in Spain (+.19), being significantly higher (*p* < .001) than in all the other countries except Germany. Positive numbers indicate that, on average, more people responded that work was more important than leisure than vice versa. The mean scores in wave 3 are higher than in waves 5 and 6, while the difference between waves 5 and 6 is not significant.

There are additional diverging trends in relative work centrality between countries. Although most of the countries display a declining trend from wave 3 to either wave 5 or 6 or both, no significant trend is found in Japan. A negative trend appears in Germany between waves 5 and 6 (*p* < .001) and between waves 3 and 6 (*p* < .05). In Sweden, Spain and the United States, we can observe negative trends between waves 3 and 5 (*p* < .001) and between waves 3 and 6 (*p* < .001), but not between waves 5 and 6.

Overall, the trend is for a decline in relative work centrality from wave 3 to waves 5 and 6. The same trend is found in three of the five countries studied. No trend can be detected in Japan, and the decline is apparent only in wave 6 in Germany. The trend in absolute work centrality is more mixed. While a significant decline emerges between wave 3 and waves 5 (*p* < .001) and 6 (*p* < .001), a positive trend is found between waves 5 and 6 in two countries and no change is visible between waves in one country.

Relative Work Centrality and Employment Status

Knowing from previous results that employment status is one of the strongest predictors of work centrality, we studied relative work centrality scores for those employed and those not in the labour market for countries and waves. In both cases, the effect of employment status on relative work centrality is significant and stronger than that of wave or country.

Examining relative work centrality by employment status, we continue to see divergent trends between the countries (Table 3.5). Those not in the labour market display a progressive decline in relative work centrality between waves ($p < .001$). The United States has significantly lower means than do the other countries ($p < .001$). Spain, in contrast, has the highest score, significantly higher than those of all the other countries ($p < .001$). Sweden, Germany and Japan exhibit similar means.

Studying only those employed, we find wave 3 to have significantly higher mean scores for relative work centrality than does either wave 5 ($p < .001$) or 6 ($p < .001$), while no difference is detected between waves 5 and 6. Germany turns out to have the highest overall means of all the countries ($p < .001$) across waves, while the United States and Sweden have significantly lower mean scores than do Germany, Japan and Spain ($p < .01$).

We note three different trends between countries among the employed. In Germany, wave 5 is significantly higher than waves 3 and 6 ($p < .05$), while no difference is evident between waves 3 and 6. In the United States, Sweden and Spain, we find relative work centrality to be significantly higher in wave 3 than in waves 5 and 6 ($p < .01$), though in Japan we again observe no trend in relative work centrality. Country trends among the employed are largely similar to those in the overall sample, although differences between waves are somewhat smaller than when studying the overall sample.

Comparing those not in the labour market with those employed, two things are notable: first, the large differences in the level of work centrality between the groups and, second, the large and increasing divergence in work centrality between those employed and those not in the labour market between waves.

The Impact of the Crisis

Coming to our second aim, we look at the diverging trends between Spain and Germany to establish whether the crisis left any mark on the results. Germany, where employment grew in the period between the waves, was stable in absolute work centrality and no significant trends can be found between the waves. The development of work centrality in Spain, the country worst hit by the crisis, differs from that in most of the countries, following a pattern similar to that in Japan, with the highest

Table 3.5 Means for relative work centrality by waves, countries and employment status, age 18–66 years

Country	Employed					Not in the labour market				
	Wave 3 1994–1998	Wave 5 2005–2009	Wave 6 2010–2014	Total	Sample size (n)	Wave 3 1994–1998	Wave 5 2005–2009	Wave 6 2010–2014	Total	Sample size (n)
Germany	.26	.37	.24	.28	3,029	-.08	-.03	-.33	-.14	1,301
Japan	.15	.10	.15	.14	2,707	-.01	-.22	-.16	-.13	810
Spain	.37	.08	.18	.20	1,492	.33	-.03	-.18	.09	958
Sweden	.19	-.02	-.05	.04	2,003	.04	-.18	-.34	-.17	513
US	.24	-.06	-.07	.03	2,688	-.22	-.42	-.56	-.44	1,044
Total	.23	.11	.09	.14	11,919	.03	-.16	-.34	-.16	4,626

levels of absolute work centrality in wave 6. Regarding relative work centrality, a negative trend is found in Germany between waves 5 and 6, while in Spain, no change appears between waves 5 and 6.

To test whether the development of work centrality differs between Spain and Germany, separate analyses of variance were conducted for the two countries and the two waves (i.e., waves 5 and 6) for both absolute and relative work centrality. In both cases, the direct effects of country are significant ($p < .05$) and the interaction effects between waves and country for absolute and relative work centrality are significant ($p < .001$), also indicating a diverging pattern of the development of work centrality between the two countries between waves 5 and 6. We therefore conclude that these different patterns are due to the different contexts in Spain and Germany caused by the crisis.

Generation, Age and Period Effects

Our third aim is to examine generational differences in work centrality in the data. For simplification, the focus will be on trends in relative work centrality. Generational changes are difficult to isolate because they are 'confounded with changes due to ageing, experience, life stage and career stage' (Cennamo and Gardner 2008: 892). To grasp generational differences, it is necessary to compare the same age groups of different generations in different periods, in what is called a time-lag study. However, the simultaneous study of cohort, age and period poses a particular methodological problem: these three variables cannot be simultaneously present in a traditional multivariate analysis. Therefore, we will instead view the trends by examining the means for age groups and generations over time, holding one variable constant at a time.

As previously discussed, a generation is a cohort sharing certain important experiences, providing it with a common frame of reference affecting its perceptions and interpretations of the current life situation. In contrast, age is a proxy for circumstances related to where one is in the life cycle–circumstances that can be expected to affect one's behaviours and attitudes. At the same age, most of us face similar choices–for example, with respect to education, career, starting a family, selecting a place to live and deciding on retirement. Last, period effects measure the effects of events and of social and economic situations and developments at particular moments; they measure changing contexts and factors that may affect needs, attitudes, or motivations for certain behaviours. These situations and developments are factors such as interest rates, job supply and housing costs that affect our decisions at particular times.

Same Generations Studied at Three Points in Time

We will start by examining changes in relative work centrality for each generation. Figure 3.1 shows the trends for the four generations–that

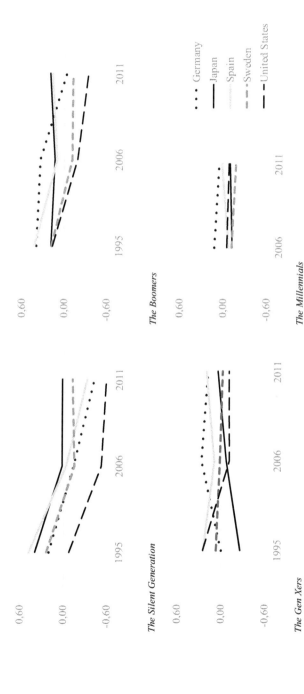

Figure 3.1 Same generation studied at three points in time: means of relative work centrality scores

is, the Silent Generation, Boomers, Gen Xers and Millennials–at three points in time: waves 3 (1995), 5 (2006) and 6 (2011). It should be noted that the Millennials can only be studied at two points in time: 2006 and 2011. In this analysis, we therefore examine the effects of age (life cycle effects) and time while holding generations constant.

Differences in means were tested using analysis of variance. First testing the overall direct and indirect effects, we find significant differences between generations ($p < .001$) and between waves ($p < .001$). There are also significant interaction effects between waves and generations ($p < .001$), indicating that the effect of the period studied (waves) varies between generations.

Table 3.6 presents an overview of the trend in relative work centrality between the three waves. The Silent Generation was 51–67 years of age in 1995 and 67–83 years of age in wave 6. The data indicate a significantly declining trend in relative work centrality as this generation ages ($p < .001$). In wave 3, this generation has the highest relative work centrality scores, along with the Boomers ($p < .001$). In contrast, in waves 5 ($p < .05$) and 6 ($p < .001$), the Silent Generation has the lowest relative work centrality scores of the generations studied.

In wave 3, about 37% of the Silent Generation had already retired, while in wave 6, about 60% of them had done so. Still, about 12% of the Silent Generation were employed in 2011.

Figure 3.1 separately shows the trends in relative work centrality over the three waves for each country and each generation. For the Silent Generation, there is a clear decline in relative work centrality between waves 3 and 6 ($p < .01$) and 3 and 5 ($p < .001$) in all the countries. The decline between waves 5 and 6 is significant in two of the five countries: Spain ($p < .05$) and Germany ($p < .01$).

For the Boomers, born 1945–1960, we similarly see a declining trend in relative work centrality between all waves ($p < .001$). In wave 3, they

Table 3.6 Means for relative work centrality for generations by waves, age 18–83 years

	Wave 3 1994–1998	Wave 5 2005–2009	Wave 6 2010–2014	Total	Sample size (n)
Silent Generation, born 1928–1944	.23	–.16	–.26	–.05	4,401
Baby boomers, born 1945–1960	.27	.08	–.04	.10	6,396
Gen X, born 1961–1979	.07	.06	.06	.06	723
Millennials, born 1980–1999	–	–.03	–.05	–.05	2,587
Total	.19	.01	–.05	.04	20,614

have the highest scores along with the Silent Generation, but in waves 5 and 6 their scores are not significantly different from those of the Millennials. This downward trend between waves 3 and 6 is noted for all the countries ($p < .01$) except Japan. For Germany, we detect a drop between waves 5 and 6 ($p < .001$); we likewise detect a drop between waves 3 and 5 in Spain and the United States ($p < .001$). It should be observed that some of the Boomers were approaching retirement in 2011, but a negligible proportion had retired in 1995 and roughly 20% had retired by 2011.

No overall trend is seen in the relative work centrality scores for the Gen Xers, born 1961–1979. However, we see diverging trends between countries. There is a positive development for Germany and Japan between waves 3 and 6 ($p < .001$), but no significant differences for Spain and Sweden and deterioration for the United States ($p < .001$). There are significant changes as well between waves 3 and 5: positive changes for Germany ($p < .001$) and Japan ($p < .05$) and negative ones for Spain ($p < .05$) and the United States ($p < .001$). No significant changes are detected between waves 5 and 6. In both waves, a negligible portion of the Gen Xers was retired (less than 1% in both waves).

The Millennials are only 18–26 years of age in wave 5, constituting a relatively small group in the dataset. No significant trend appears between waves 5 and 6 for the Millennials and no significant differences between them and the other generations can be detected in wave 5. In wave 6, they are found to have higher relative work centrality scores than the Silent Generation ($p < .001$), lower scores than the Gen Xers ($p < .01$), and similar scores to the Boomers.

Generations Compared With the Same Age Group 16 Years Earlier

We will now examine relative work centrality for three generations in 2011, comparing each of them with the same age group in 1995. We are therefore studying the impact of context (i.e., period) and generation by holding age constant.

Differences in means were tested using analysis of variance, through which both direct and indirect effects were studied. We find a significant age effect ($p < .001$), significant differences between the waves ($p < .001$), and significant interaction effects between waves and age ($p < .001$). Significant interaction effects indicate that the effect of wave varies between age groups. Overall, for both waves studied, the youngest age group has the lowest relative work centrality ($p < .001$). The highest scores are exhibited by the middle group aged 32–50 years, which has higher scores than both the youngest ($p < .001$) and oldest age groups ($p < .001$).

Figure 3.2 compares each generation with the same age group 16 years earlier. Looking first at the Millennials and comparing them with the

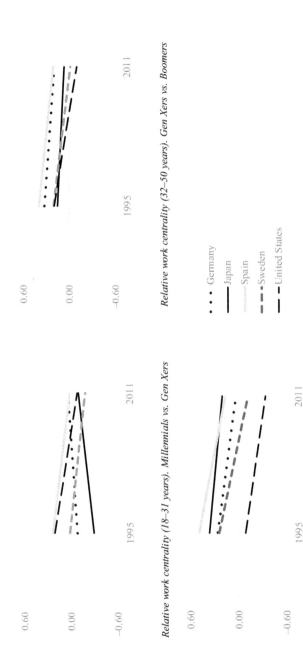

Figure 3.2 Generations compared with the same age group 16 years earlier: means of relative work centrality scores

same age group in 1995 (which roughly corresponds to the Gen Xers), we find diverging trends between the countries. Positive changes are noted in Japan (+.20, $p < .05$), while negative trends are noted in Spain (–.22, $p < .01$), Sweden (–.20, $p < .01$) and the United States (–.29, $p < .001$). No change is evident in the German data.

Comparing the Gen Xers with the same age group in 1995 (which approximately corresponds to the Boomers), we see an overall decline in relative work centrality in four out of the five countries: Germany (–.14, $p < .01$), Sweden (–.23, $p < .001$), Spain (–.20, $p < .01$) and the United States (–.30, $p < .001$). The change in Japan is non-significant.

Finally, the Boomers are compared with the same age group in 1995 (which roughly corresponds to the Silent Generation). Here we discover a general declining trend in relative work centrality for all countries. The largest decrease is found in Sweden (–.37, $p < .001$) and the smallest in Japan (–.16, $p < .01$), although both are significant.

Regression Analysis

Next we study the simultaneous effects of age, countries, waves, employment status, living with parents, marital status and having children. As discussed earlier, the variables age, period and generation are intertwined. Consequently, they cannot all be included in the type of regression conducted here. All the independent variables were tested for collinearity using the variance inflation factor (VIF) coefficient. The VIF was lower than 5 in all cases and between 1 and 3 in most cases—far below 10, the rule of thumb for detecting multicollinearity (Robinson and Schumacker 2009).

Marital status, living with parents and having children are included to test the impact of delayed adulthood and family integration on relative work centrality. Living with parents lessens the burden on individuals to provide for themselves, as costs of housing and food are shared. We would expect being married or cohabiting and having children to represent integrating mechanisms in society, and that their absence would lessen the burden on individuals and their obligation to work.

We also include gender in the regression. In our previous study, we found that the effect of gender was reduced in latter waves compared with the earlier ones (Hikspoors, Bjarnason and Håkansson 2012). There are numerous reasons to expect smaller gender effects on work centrality than before: increased labour participation of women, decreased pay inequality between men and women, decreased inequality in educational levels and decreased adherence to traditional gender roles in general (Galinsky, Aumann and Bond 2011; see also OECD 2019).

An OLS regression (hierarchical regression) was conducted in three steps (see Table 3.7) for three of the four age groups (aged 18–66 years). First, we entered gender, employment status and the three variables

Table 3.7 OLS regressions for relative work centrality, age 18–66 years, b-values

	(step 1)	(step 2)	(step 3)
(Constant)	–.31***	–.59***	–.69***
Gender (male = 1)	.07***	.06***	.06***
Employment status (ref. not in the labour market)			
Employed	.29***	.32***	.33***
Unemployed	.42***	.40***	.41***
Delayed adulthood and family integration			
Have children (yes = 1)	.06***	.06***	.06***
Living with parents (yes =1)	.01	.00	.01
Married or cohabiting (yes = 1)	.07***	.05**	.05**
Waves (ref = wave 6)			
Wave 3 (1995)		.17***	.21***
Wave 5 (2011)		.04*	.06**
Age (ref = 18–31 years)			
Age 32–50 years		.05*	.12***
Age 51–66 years		.04*	.12***
Country (ref = United States)			
Germany		.26***	.26***
Sweden		.08**	.08**
Spain		.31***	.31***
Japan		.16***	.17***
Millennials added			.15***
Adj. R2	.033	.053	.055
Adj. R2 change		.021***	.001***
VIF multicollinearity statistic	Highest VIF = 1.3	Highest VIF = 2.1	Highest VIF = 2.1

*** p < .001; ** p < .01; * p < .05

measuring delayed adulthood and integration into family life. Of the variables mentioned, employment status (i.e., being employed or unemployed) has the strongest effect, positively influencing relative work centrality, as expected. These variables explain about 3% of the variation in relative work centrality.

In the next step, we added waves 3 and 5, using wave 6 as the reference category. The outcome indicates lower work centrality in wave 6 than in waves 3 and 5. We also included two age categories in the equation, using the youngest age group as the reference category. The two age groups (i.e., 32–50 years and 51–66 years) contribute positively to relative work centrality (the oldest age group was excluded from this analysis). We also entered countries at this stage, with the reference being the United States. All other countries have positive b-values, indicating higher relative work centrality than in the reference category. Spain displays the strongest positive effect. The effects of gender, marital status, children and living at home on relative work centrality are negligible.

In the final stage, we added the Millennials—those born 1980–1999—who were found to have a positive effect on relative work centrality when controlling for all other factors. Including the Millennials in the analysis, increases the effect of age: the two older age groups have stronger positive effects in step 3 than in step 2 (as seen in the table) indicating a stronger negative effect of the youngest age group on relative work centrality. Multicollinearity statistics indicate very little collinearity between the independent variables, as shown by a low VIF factor below 3.

We also conducted a separate regression for waves 3 and 6 in step 2, finding a large decline in the *constant* (i.e., the mean score of relative work centrality when all independent variables are zero) from –.37 in wave 3 to –.65 in wave 6, indicating a downward trend in relative work centrality between 1995 and 2011 when taking account of the same variables.

Discussion

The alleged decline in the work ethic has been of interest to scholars, politicians, policy makers and employers alike for decades. This interest is partly due to the impact this decline might have on people's willingness to work and their dedication to work, and partly due to the impact it might have on economic prosperity and, in turn, the functioning of our society and welfare systems.

Despite the popularity of this theme, results have been somewhat inconclusive. Studies from the United States, often based on student samples, provide overwhelming evidence for the decline in work centrality over time. Results from other countries have instead indicated stability in work centrality. Several possible reasons exist for these inconsistent results; one is sample differences in terms of both what nations are studied and what groups (e.g., students or employed persons) are studied within those nations.

We studied levels and trends in work centrality in five countries (Germany, Japan, Spain, Sweden and the United States) over 16 years (1995–2011) and four generations (the Silent Generation, born 1928–1944; Boomers, born 1945–1960; Gen Xers, born 1961–1979; and Millennials, born 1980–1999), using approximately 21,000 responses from the World Values Survey. This chapter had three aims. The first was to examine how work centrality developed over time in different institutional settings and cultures, so work centrality was scrutinized in five countries with different cultures and welfare models. Our second aim was to see whether the economic crisis, starting in 2008, had an impact on the existing patterns. More specifically, we were interested in whether work centrality was affected differently in the country most severely hit by the crisis (Spain) versus in the country least affected by the crisis (Germany). Our third aim was to examine generational changes in work centrality—specifically, what impact the arrival of the Millennials had on work centrality.

To analyse absolute work centrality, means were calculated from responses to the question 'How important is work in your life?' To analyse relative work centrality, responses concerning the importance of work were subtracted from responses concerning the importance of leisure.

Development of Work Centrality

Regarding the first aim, we studied absolute and relative work centrality in five countries across the three waves. As this study is limited to four generations and the Silent Generation is present only in wave 3, we limited this part of our analysis to the three younger age groups (i.e., 18–31 years, 32–50 years and 51–66 years).

First, we discovered considerable country variations in the levels of both absolute and relative work centrality. The lowest overall scores—across the waves—were found for the United States, while the highest overall scores appeared for Spain and Japan. Several scholars have similarly found work to be of higher importance to the Japanese than the American labour force (England and Misumi 1986). No progressive downward trend in work centrality was established, while levels of work centrality turned out to be higher in wave 3 (1995) than in the two following waves.

Second, while the results for most of the countries indicated a declining trend in work centrality from wave 3 to either wave 5 or wave 6, a complex picture unfolded with divergent trends in different countries. With respect to relative work centrality, three out of five countries (Sweden, Spain and the United States) exhibited a trend consistent with the overall trend towards higher relative work centrality in wave 3 than in the two following waves. In contrast, no trend was found in Japan and only a negative trend was detected in the last wave (6) in Germany.

Third, trends in relative work centrality were studied in relation to employment status–that is, for those employed (i.e., full time, part time, or self-employed) and for those outside the labour market (i.e., retirees, students and homemakers). Past research has found employment status to be of importance in explaining work centrality. For example, full-time employed persons have been shown to have higher work centrality scores than other groups studied (Hikspoors, Bjarnason and Håkansson 2012), and the present analysis confirms this pattern.

Also, mean scores for work centrality were higher among the employed than in the total sample, while trends in relative work centrality were similar, although somewhat smaller in most of the countries. The same decline in relative work centrality was found between wave 3 and the two following waves in three out of five countries in both the employed and the overall sample.

Another finding from the analysis was a huge gap in relative work centrality between those employed and those not in the labour market. This gap was largest in Germany and the United States, where the employed had much higher relative work centrality than did those outside the labour market. Moreover, the analysis revealed a widening trend in relative work centrality between the employed and people not in the labour market between waves. This indicates that a small part of the negative trend from wave 3 to waves 5 and 6 is due to more negative scores among those not in the labour market, particularly in wave 6.

One possible interpretation of this widening gap is that there is increasing conflict between what people desire from work and their labour market experiences. The growth of self-actualizing values means that people increasingly seek intrinsic satisfaction from work, but if existing jobs do not supply such satisfaction or if job seekers have insufficient cultural or human capital to attain such jobs, the work ethic may be negatively affected given that people stop longing for things they cannot attain. Consequently, work might decrease in importance among those groups and leisure may become more important instead. A rudimentary analysis of the differences between these groups disclosed large educational differences between the employed and those not in the labour market, which might support this interpretation.

This large and increasing gap between the employed and those not in the labour market could also explain the divergent results between studies. Thus, studies examining employed persons would find smaller differences in work centrality between waves than those using nationally representative samples, as we do here.

The Impact of the Crisis

For the purpose of fulfilling our second aim, we looked at the diverging trends between Spain and Germany to establish whether the crisis left any mark on the results. We studied differences in relative work centrality in Germany, where employment grew in the period between the waves, and in Spain, which was the country worst hit by the crisis and where employment declined between waves 5 and 6.

Results indicated a diverging pattern in the development of relative work centrality between the two countries between waves 5 (2006) and 6 (2011). A large decline in employment was noted in this period, especially among young employees in Spain. None of the other countries experienced a similar downward trend. Variations in work centrality between the studied countries are therefore partly due to economic factors and the impact of 'scarcity' either of work or leisure at any given time.

Extrapolating from these results, high work centrality scores in Sweden in 1995 (wave 3) may have been affected by the economic crisis at that time, when unemployment was 9% versus 2% in 1990. Unemployment declined in two of countries between 1995 and 2006, mainly in Spain but also in Sweden. Accordingly, Spain exhibited the largest decline in relative work centrality of the countries between 1995 and 2006.

Generation, Age and Period Effects

Our third aim was to examine differences in work centrality between generations. First, we examined all four generations at three points in time. In this analysis, we studied the impacts of life cycle and period simultaneously. Large negative trends in relative work centrality were found in the Silent Generation and the Boomers. These trends are for the most part understandable and are partly explained by life cycle effects. A movement towards 'disengagement' from work as people approach retirement has been reported in several studies (Sharabi and Harpaz 2007; Hikspoors, Bjarnason and Håkansson 2012). Partly, these trends could be explained by 'scarcity' of leisure, due to increased employment among the oldest age groups. However, further analysis of these changes showed that much larger change is attributed to the former–that is, declining relative work centrality among those retired and others not in the labour market than those employed.

Context (or period) effects were also found, as large cross-national differences were found in the data on the degree to which workers are retired. These patterns might reflect differences in 'exit cultures' between countries regarding older workers' labour market participation (Hikspoors 2011). Three types of exit cultures are identified: 'late-exit culture', emphasizing active aging and the right and duty to participate in the labour market; 'early-exit culture', emphasizing the right to early retirement, if an individual chooses it; and 'medium-exit culture', which is situated between the two (Hikspoors 2011: 86). Thus, only 3% of the Silent Generation in Germany were employed in 2011, compared with 35% in Japan and 34% in Sweden. These figures reflect the different trends in relative work centrality among the Boomers, especially in Germany and Japan.

No trend in relative work centrality was found among the Gen Xers or Millennials, but the Silent Generation and the Boomers exhibited much higher scores in 1995 than the Gen Xers did in any of the three waves or the Millennials did in the two waves in which they are represented.

Second, we examined relative work centrality and compared the results for each generation with those for the same age group in 1995 (wave 3). In this way, we studied the impact of changing contexts (i.e., period) and generations while holding age constant. There was a negative trend for the three generations in most of the studied countries, with the same age groups exhibiting lower relative work centrality scores in 2011 than in 1995.

When comparing the Millennials (in 2011) with the same age group in wave 3 (in 1995), we detected negative trends in three out of five countries (i.e., Spain, Sweden and the United States). No change was found in the German data and a positive change was found in Japan. Comparing the Gen Xers in 2011 with the same age group in 1995, we again saw an overall decline in relative work centrality, now in four out of five countries. No significant change appeared between waves in Japan. Finally, when comparing the Boomers in 2011 with the same age group in 1995, we discovered a general declining trend in relative work centrality in all countries.

Hierarchical regression analysis was conducted to examine the simultaneous impact of the variables on relative work centrality. Variables measuring employment status, gender, delay of adulthood, integration into family life, waves, countries and age groups were included in the analysis. Employment status was found to have the strongest effect in all three steps. Being employed or unemployed had strong positive effects on relative work centrality in comparison with those not in the labour market, as expected. Likewise, integration into family life contributed positively to relative work centrality. In the data we see that there was an overall decrease in people having children and marrying, especially in the youngest age group. As these variables contribute positively to relative work centrality, declining fertility and declining family formation are two factors that have contributed to lower relative work centrality in subsequent waves. Living with parents did not negatively affect relative work centrality, contrary to expectations, but being male contributed positively to relative work centrality, as expected.

There has been an ongoing convergence of men's and women's labour market behaviours in recent decades as well as in care activities and housework (Galinsky, Aumann and Bond 2011). While these gaps have narrowed, they have not closed, and this likely negatively affects women's and positively affects men's work centrality scores.

Waves 3 and 5 contributed positively to relative work centrality compared with wave 6, indicating a decline in relative work centrality over time. All countries displayed positive work centrality effects relative to the United States, which was the reference category. The negative trends were accordingly most apparent in the United States. The inconsistent results reported in the literature are therefore partly due to the divergent patterns between countries.

Regarding age, two of the older age groups contributed positively to relative work centrality, while the youngest group, 18–31 years of age, had negative effects. Adding Millennials to the equation increased the positive impact of the two older age groups, implying that the youngest age group had a large negative effect while the Millennials had a positive effect. The Millennials actually had a positive effect on relative work centrality when controlling for all other variables.

In this chapter, we have found evidence for a general decline in relative work centrality between three generations over a period of 16 years. The decline is not limited to the Millennials; to the contrary, it is more apparent among the Gen Xers and the Boomers. While the trend is apparent to some degree in all five countries, it is more evident in the United States, Sweden and Spain and less evident in Germany and Japan. The decline is thus noticeable in three different welfare systems; the liberal model, the Nordic welfare model and the southern model, but less so in the two countries belonging to the conservative or corporatist model.

Is this decline in relative work centrality a sign of a value change or of changes in context (i.e., period effects)? We tested the effects of some of the context variables we assumed could be of importance: family building, living at home and presence of children. While these variables had significant effects, none of them was very successful in explaining the variation in relative work centrality. Employment status was, however, found to have the overall strongest effect on relative work centrality. It is therefore tempting to look for explanations for declining relative work centrality in the intersection between labour markets and society: the quality of work and the rewards we get from work and the opportunities we have for getting quality jobs. There is perhaps an increasing divide between what people want from work and what they perceive that they get from it. If their needs somehow exceed the opportunities to satisfy them at work, the work ethic is likely negatively affected. Or perhaps the trend towards having rights but no obligations describes a more general cultural shift in advanced industrial economies (Twenge and Kasser 2013).

To conclude, this study has identified declines in both absolute and relative work centrality over a 16-year period (1995–2011). Despite considerable country variations in these trends, for the most part there has been a general decline in relative work centrality in each generation compared with the same age group 16 years earlier. We argue that these changes are not specifically related to the Millennials, but are related to a more general trend in advanced industrial countries.

Note

1. In Spain, the ratio of the number of adults aged 18–64 years to children younger than 12 years increased from 2.5 adults per child in 1980 to 5.2 in 2000; this ratio was 3.6 in 1980 and 3.8 in 2010 in Sweden, and 3.9 in 1980 and 4.8 in 2000 in Germany (incl. GDR) (Eurostat 2019, own calculations).

References

Arts, W. and J. Gelissen (2002) 'Three Worlds of Welfare Capitalism or More? A State-of-the-Art Report.' *Journal of European Social Policy* 12(2): 137–158.

Arts, W. and J. Gelissen (2010) 'Models of the Welfare State.', 570–583, in F. G. Castles, S. Leibfried, J. Lewis, H. Obinger and C. Pierson (eds) *The Oxford Handbook of the Welfare State*. Oxford: Oxford University Press.

Arvey, R. D., I. Harpaz and H. Liao (2004) 'Work Centrality and Post-Award Work Behavior of Lottery Winners.' *The Journal of Psychology* 138(5): 404–420.

Breitsohl, H. and S. Ruhle (2012) 'Differences in Work-Related Attitudes Between Millennials and Generation X: Evidence from Germany', 107–129, in E. S. Ng, S. T. Lyons and L. Schweitzer (eds) *Managing the New Workforce. International Perspectives on the Millennial Generation*. Cheltenham, Northampton: Edward Elgar.

Cennamo, L. and D. Gardner (2008) 'General Differences in Work Values, Outcomes and Person-Organisation Values Fit.' *Journal of Managerial Psychology* 23(8): 891–906.

Costanza, D. and L. Finkelstein (2015) 'Generationally Based Differences in the Workplace: Is There a *There* There?' *Industrial and Organizational Psychology* 8(3): 308–323.

Deal, J., D. G. Altman and S. G. Rogelberg (2010) 'Millennials at Work: What We Know and What We Need to Do (If Anything).' *Journal of Business and Psychology* 25(2): 191–199.

England, G. and J. Misumi (1986) 'Work Centrality in Japan and the United States.' *Journal of Cross-Cultural Psychology* 17(4): 399–416.

Esping-Andersen, G. (1990) *The Three Worlds of Welfare Capitalism*. Cambridge: Polity Press.

Esser, I. (2009) Has Welfare Made Us Lazy? Employment Commitment in Different Welfare States, 79–105, in A. Park, J. Curtice, K. Thomson, M. Philips and E. Clery (eds) *British Social Attitudes*. The 25th Report. London: Sage.

Eurostat (2019) http://appsso.eurostat.ec.europa.eu/nui/show.do?dataset=demo_pjan&lang=en.

Fenzel, J. L. (2013) *Examining Generational Differences in the Workplace: Work Centrality, Narcissism, and their Relation to Employee Work Engagement*. Dissertation. Milwaukee: University of Wisconsin-Milwaukee.

Furåker, B. (2012a) 'Theoretical and Conceptual Considerations on Work Orientations', 11–25, in B. Furåker, K. Håkansson and J. C. Karlsson (eds) *Commitment to Work and Job Satisfaction Studies of Work Orientations*. New York, London: Routledge.

Furåker, B. (2012b) 'Work Attitudes, Employment and Work Mobilization A Comparison Between Anglo-Saxon and Nordic Countries,' 67–85, in B. Furåker, K. Håkansson and J. C. Karlsson (eds) *Commitment to Work and Job Satisfaction Studies of Work Orientations*. New York, London: Routledge.

Furnham, A. (1984) 'The Protestant Work Ethic: A Review of the Psychological Literature.' *European Journal of Social Psychology* 14(1): 87–104.

Galinsky, E., K. Aumann and J. T. Bond (2011) *Times are Changing. Gender and Generation at Work and at Home*. Revised ed. New York: Families and Work Institute.

Gratton, L. and A. Scott (2016) *The 100 Year Life. Living and Working in an Age of Longevity*. London, Oxford, New York, New Delhi, Sydney: Bloomsbury.

Harpaz, I., B. Honig and P. Coetsier (2002) 'A Cross-Cultural Longitudinal Analysis of the Meaning of Work and the Socialization Process of Career Starters.' *Journal of World Business* 37(4): 230–244.

Hikspoors, F. (2011) *Work Values Antecedents and Consequences.* Academisch Proefschrift. Vrije Universitet: Wink Print.

Hikspoors, F., T. Bjarnason and K. Håkansson (2012) 'Declining Work Centrality in Western Europe: Myth or Reality?' 26–46, in B. Furåker, K. Håkansson and J. C. Karlsson (eds) *Commitment to Work and Job Satisfaction Studies of Work Orientations.* New York, London: Routledge.

Hirschfeld, R. R. and H. S. Feild (2000) 'Work Centrality and Work Alienation: Distinct Aspects of a General Commitment to Work.' *Journal of Organizational Behavior* 21(7): 789–800.

Inglehart, R. (1990) *Culture Shift in Advanced Industrial Society.* Princeton: Princeton University Press.

Inglehart, R. (2008) 'Changing Values Among Western Publics from 1970 to 2006.' *West European Politics* 31(1–2): 130–146.

Inglehart, R. and W. Baker (2000) 'Modernization, Cultural Change, and the Persistence of Traditional Values.' *American Sociological Review* 65(1): 19–51.

Korpi, W. and J. Palme (1998) 'The Paradox of Redistribution and the Strategy of Equality: Welfare State Institutions, Inequality and Poverty in the Western Countries.' *American Sociological Review* 63(5): 661–687.

Kowske, B. J., R. Rasch and J. Wiley (2010) 'Millennials' (Lack of) Attitude Problem: An Empirical Examination of Generational Effects on Work Attitudes.' *Journal of Business and Psychology* 25(2): 265–279.

Levenson, A. R. (2010) 'Millennials and the World of Work: An Economist's Perspective.' *Journal of Business and Psychology* 25(2): 257–264.

Mannheim, K. (1952) 'The Problems of Generations', 276–322, in P. Kecskemeti (ed.) *Essays on the Sociology of Knowledge.* London: Routledge & Kegan Paul.

Meriac, J. P., D. J. Woehr and C. Banister (2010) 'Generational Differences in Work Ethic: An Examination of Measurement Equivalence Across Three Cohorts.' *Journal of Business and Psychology* 25(2): 315–324.

Miller, M. J., D. J. Woehr and N. Hudspeth (2002) 'The Meaning and Measurement of Work Ethic: Construction and Initial Validation of a Multidimensional Inventory.' *Journal of Vocational Behavior* 60(3): 451–489.

MOW International Research Team (1987) *The Meaning of Work.* London: Academic Press.

Myers, K. K. and K. Sadaghiani (2010) 'Millennials in the Workplace: A Communication Perspective on Millennials' Organizational Relationships and Performance.' *Journal of Business and Psychology* 25(2): 225–238.

Navarrette, R. J. (2008) 'As Teenage Work Ethic Declines, Illegal Immigrants Pick Up Slack.' http://qctimes.com/news/opinion/editorial/columnists/as-teenage-work-ethic-declines-illegal-immigrants-pick-up-slack/article_d1d3f8af-7c3b-5a81-a68e-6f2b3599a56a.html.

Ng, E. S., S. T. Lyons and L. Schweitzer (2012) 'Preface', xvii–xxiii, in E. S. Ng, S. T. Lyons and L. Schweitzer (eds) *Managing the New Workforce International Perspectives on the Millennial Generation.* Cheltenham: Edward Elgar Publishing Limited.

Nicholas, A. (2009) 'Generational Perceptions: Workers and Consumers.' *Journal of Business & Economic Research* 7(10): 47–52.

OECD (2019) Labour Force Statistics. https://stats.oecd.org/Index.aspx?Query Id=64196.

Parry, E. and P. Urwin (2011) 'Generational Differences in Work Values: A Review of Theory and Evidence.' *International Journal of Management Reviews* 13(1): 79–96.

Paullay, I. M., G. M. Alliger and E. F. Stone-Romero (1994) 'Construct Validation of Two Instruments Designed to Measure Job Involvement and Work Centrality.' *Journal of Applied Psychology* 79(2): 224–228.

Prensky, M. (2001) 'Digital Natives, Digital Immigrants Part I.' *On the Horizon* 9(5): 1–6.

Pyöriä, P., S. Ojala, T. Saari and K. M. Järvinen (2017) 'The Millennial Generation: A New Breed of Labour?' *Sage Open* 7(1): 1–14.

Quintanilla, S. A. R. and B. Wilpert (1991) 'Are Work Meanings Changing?' *European Work and Organizational Psychologist* 1(2–3): 91–109.

Robinson, C. and R. E. Schumacker (2009) 'Interaction Effects: Centering, Variance Inflation Factor, and Interpretation Issues.' *Multiple Linear Regression Viewpoints* 35(1): 6–11.

Shacklock, K. and Y. Brunetto (2011) 'A Model of Older Workers' Intentions to Continue Working.' *Personnel Review* 40(2): 252–274.

Sharabi, M. and I. Harpaz (2007) 'Changes in Work Centrality and Other Life Areas in Israel: A Longitudinal Study.' *Journal of Human Values* 13(2): 95–106.

Smola, K. W. and C. D. Sutton (2002) 'Generational Differences: Revisiting Generational Work Values for the New Millennium.' *Journal of Organizational Behavior* 23(4): 363–382.

Stein, J. (2013) 'Millennials: The Me Me Me Generation.' *Time Magazine*, May 20, 2013.

Trzesniewsk, K. H. and M. B. Donnellan (2010) 'Rethinking "Generation Me": A Study of Cohort Effects From 1976–2006.' *Perspectives on Psychological Science* 5(1) 58–75.

Twenge, J. M. (2010) A Review of the Empirical Evidence on Generational Differences in Work Attitudes.' *Journal of Business Psychology* 25: 201–210.

Twenge, J. M. and S. M. Campbell (2012) 'Who Are the Millennials? Empirical Evidence for Generational Differences in Work Values, Attitudes and Personality', 1–19, in E. S. Ng, S. T. Lyons and L. Schweitzer (eds) *Managing the New Workforce: International Perspectives on the Millennial Generation*. Cheltenham, Northampton: Edward Elgar.

Twenge, J. M., S. M. Campbell, B. J. Hoffman and C. E. Lance (2010) 'Generational Differences in Work Values: Leisure and Extrinsic Values Increasing, Social and Intrinsic Values Decreasing.' *Journal of Management* 36(5): 1117–1142.

Twenge, J. and T. Kasser (2013) 'Generational Changes in Materialism and Work Centrality, 1976–2007: Associations with Temporal Changes in Societal Insecurity and Materialistic Role Modelling.' *Personality and Social Psychology Bulletin* 37(7): 883–897.

Warr, P. (1982) 'A National Study of Non-financial Employment Commitment.' *Journal of Occupational Psychology* 55: 297–312.

Warr, P. (2008) 'Work Values: Some Demographic and Cultural Correlates.' *Journal of Occupational and Organizational Psychology* 81(4): 751–775.

Weber, M. (1976) *The Protestant Ethic and the Spirit of Capitalism*. London: George Allen and Unvin.

Welzel, C. and R. Inglehart (2010) 'Agency, Values, and Well-Being: A Human Development Model.' *Social Indicator Research* 97(1): 43–63.

Zabel, K., B. Biermeier-Hanson, B. Baltes, B. Early and A. Shepard (2017) 'Generational Differences in Work Ethic: Fact or Fiction?' *Journal of Business and Psychology* 32(3): 301–315.

4   Work as a Calling

Existential Dimensions of Individuals' Work Orientations

Mattias Bengtsson and Marita Flisbäck

Introduction

John Goldthorpe and his co-authors once stated that '*all* work activity, in industrial society at least, tends to have a basically instrumental component' (1968: 41; italics in original; cf. Chapter 2 in this book). Accordingly, whether people express more or less commitment to work, their identities are more or less associated with work activities, or their work is performed in keeping with social norms, modern capitalistic working life involves wage labourers exchanging labour power for remuneration to be able to consume and survive. One could also elaborate on this, and add that 'all work activity tends to have a basically *existential* component': everyday work practices have the potential to give us a sense of being part of broader context, and give rise to questions about the meaning of life (Weber 1965). As we will see, work can offer meaningfulness and comprehensibility (cf. Antonovsky 1987) when personal existential enigmas—what we do, who we are, and who we can be in the future—are linked to the needs of our fellow man and society (Weber 1992).

The aim of this chapter is to deepen the understanding of existential meaning dimensions of work activities by highlighting the *calling* as an example of existential work orientation.[1] Here, we follow a research tradition regarding the meaning of work that stresses that besides having a 'job' or 'career', whereby the primary aim of working is financial gain or occupational advancement, people can approach their work as a calling. This means that the work has 'meaning and value in itself', and that it 'constitutes a practical ideal of activity and character that makes a person's work morally inseparable from his or her life' (Bellah et al. 1985: 66).

In the chapter, we present five main components of work as a calling, understood as an ideal type (cf. Portis 1978: 115). These components have emerged through analyses of empirical data from a qualitative interview study of the retirement process among Swedish employees (see also Bengtsson and Flisbäck 2016, 2017a, 2017b). In the phase at which

occupational life was about to be left behind, both the absence and presence of existential meaning dimensions of work seemed to be highlighted.
A group of respondents expressed such great dedication to work, and
that work aligned with a broader sense of purpose, that we defined it as
a calling.

When we explore the calling as an existential work orientation, the
main theoretical starting point is Max Weber's approach regarding how
people struggle to find meaning in modern working life. For Weber, the
concept of the calling was a tool for analysing the individual's struggle to find and live out ultimate values or meanings in life in order
to make sense of a fragmented and seemingly meaningless everyday
life. Even though calling as a concept belongs to classical sociology of
work domains, earlier scholarship reviews testify that research on calling 'remains a young field of inquiry' (Wrzesniewski, Dekas, and Rosso
2013: 118). The existential meaning of work is a research area where
there still 'exist many opportunities for further research' (Rosso, Dekas,
and Wrzesniewski 2010: 107).

We argue that one way to study existential meaning dimensions of
work (for example, a calling) is by using empirical data, built upon
phases in the working life cycle in which the existential meaning-making
is particularly noticeable, such as entering or exiting employment. If one
of the purposes of this book is to spell out variation regarding work orientations etc. 'across social categories' (Chapter 2: 17 in this book), this
chapter additionally focuses on how work orientations are specifically
noticeable in life phases reflecting changes, endings, or new beginnings.

The retirement process can be seen as a distinct empirical case of making visible the existential meaning of work. Thus, we will discuss how
the process can make visible, or even construe, the calling as a work
orientation. However, it should be underlined that the calling was not
a conceptual starting point in our study of the retirement process—that
is, it was not assessed against predetermined items measuring a calling.
Instead, the five components we will discuss emerged through inductive
reasoning. Before we deal with these methodological themes, we start
by discussing the importance of analysing work in terms of its existential content and, thereafter, present the data and the selection of interviewees, our methodological choices, and the data analysis and coding.
The empirical analyses start with a section on how retirement acts as an
existential imperative and, thus, can make visible and enforce existential
meaning dimensions in relation to work. This is followed by a presentation of the main findings and thereafter we discuss the kind of components or aspects that could be included in approaching work as a calling.
We round off the empirical analyses with a discussion on how retirement
as an external force 'de-calling' the life task can act as both freedom and
curse. In the concluding discussion, we emphasize the main points of our
study.

Highlighting Existential Meaning Dimensions of Work

According to Brent D. Rosso, Dekas, and Wrzesniewski (2010), the existential meaning of work is an important, but often overlooked, research issue in the meaning of work literature. Sociologists, such as Jeffrey C. Alexander (2006) and Jack D. Douglas (2010), emphasize that social scientists too often exclude existential issues as these are rarely viewed as part of a modern and rational scientific project. However, the work by Weber is one exception here, providing us with a better understanding of the existential meaning dimensions of work activities. Moreover, Weber manages to connect the individual's search for meaning in his or her everyday with changes in modern working life.

The Legacy of Weber: Man's Search for Meaning in a 'Disenchanted' World

Weber is often referred to as having 'emphasized the role of Calvinism for the advance of a suitable work ethic' in modern capitalist societies—that is, the emphasis is on paid work as a moral obligation (Chapter 2: 20 in this book). Here, however, we draw on another side of Weber's writings: how individuals struggle to find, or handle a lack of, meaning in a 'disenchanted' world. Weber emphasizes ideal typical aspects of religious-ethical meaning systems to offer an understanding of how people in their human praxis strive to create coherent overall meaning in life (Weber 1965). Discussing how modern man strives to solve existential riddles of vulnerability, transience, and injustice through creating a meaningful whole, Weber points to how the Protestant ethic is one way to handle a longing for salvation from suffering and death, through directing one's actions towards the world. Of main concern was the Calvinist practice of being a 'tool' of God in the meaning of 'reshap[ing] the world in accordance with God's predestined plan' (Schroeder 1991: 67).

One of Weber's main contributions is the description of the tension between unfolding processes of rationalization in modern societies and individuals' longing for an existentially meaningful everyday life. Individual autonomy is curtailed through the bureaucratization of life, and value commitments are eroded by the diffusion of empirical scientific knowledge and the diminishing role played by religious belief systems. As a consequence, in a 'disenchanted world' a new type of human being is formed who has difficulty handling existential meaning (Schroeder 1991). However, Weber points out that in the modern world people can also seek wider (existential) meaning through a passionate devotion to a task. In this way, Weber emphasizes the calling as an ideal typical concept for unifying the profane everyday work with broader existential issues. Even though the secularized man may not regard himself as the tool of God, he often wants to show an 'inner devotion to the task', such as when a scientist serves a higher cause—that is, scientific work being 'chained to the course of progress' (Weber 2009b: 137).

Even if Weber (1992) often understood social actions in relation to a common ethic, such as the rational ethics of ascetic Protestantism, he also analysed man's 'yearning for meaning', as 'existential meaning or meaningfulness' (Segal 1999: 659). In a similar way, what we apply is a perspective that highlights how people's life paths create dilemmas and give rise to difficult questions, the answers to which often need to be framed in existential meaning systems. Regarding work as a calling and a task performed for a greater cause could be a way of handling the existential dilemma of the life path. Therefore, with inspiration from Weber, we are not one-sidedly considering calling as a response to a specific cultural context. Our focus is more on how individuals live out a calling as a response to existential enigmas and how ethical and cultural meaning systems constitute a supportive bank of ideas in this praxis (cf. Weber 1965). This means that, although Weber's starting point is Calvinist practice and our study relates to the Swedish Lutheran context, this difference is of minor importance compared to the usefulness of Weber's understanding of how the existential meaning dimensions of work are lived out and performed.

Existential Meaning at Work: Calling as Analytical Tool

In line with Weber, we use the calling as a sociological concept, thereby contributing to the understanding of how people strive to create persistence and deeper meaning in their work activities. Thus, an approach to work as a calling can be actively used by individuals as an answer to their need for existential meaning in a secular society.

Existential meaning involves the individual reflecting on his or her life course, choices, and experiences in a broader context—that is, concerning questions regarding the meaning of life. In other words, highlighting questions as existential means focusing on how the significance of life and death is always part of our choices, concerns, worries, and well-being (cf. Jackson 2005, 2011). Thus, the meaning of existential dimensions of work entails that individuals relate their tasks to these questions and place the meaning of work in a wider context. The meaning of the tasks could have an ecological, social, or ethical fundament—that is, the meaning relates to something more than simply having value for the individual's career path.

Studying existential dimensions of work can be a challenge. For Weber, calling is an ideal type for use in dealing with this difficult subject (cf. Portis 1978). 'Being called' is often associated with religious election, even though its meaning differs between Christian Protestant theology and contemporary secular views of the 'increasingly individualistic and work-related meanings of a calling'. The latter are specifically found in various disciplines within psychology (Wrzesniewski, Dekas, and Rosso 2013: 116; cf. Duffy and Dik 2013). Thus, in modern capitalist societies with a widespread diffusion of instrumental orientations, work as a calling can offer a possible answer to the existential riddles that are part of being human, as well as increase people's well-being. A research review of studies of people who perceive that they have a calling shows 'consistent links between perceiving a calling and heightened levels of career maturity, career commitment, work meaning, job satisfaction, life meaning, and life satisfaction. These links appear most robust when individuals are actually living out their calling at work' (Duffy and Dik 2013: 428; cf. Wrzesniewski 2003: 305–307; Wrzesniewski, Dekas, and Rosso 2013: 117–118).[2]

The sense of being called to a specific task has a broader meaning in organizations and working life than it would initially appear to. Knowledge about what aspects tend to limit or enable existential meaningful work may be useful in the creation of a more sustainable working life. We will return to this theme in relation to our own data, but an interesting study in this area was conducted by Ann-Kristin Eriksson (2016), who analysed fatigued individuals' work rehabilitation in Sweden and found that the loss of existential meaning could be a main factor affecting ill health at work. Another study on the same theme is a U.S. study on how individuals experience and respond to 'unanswered' occupational callings. Justin M. Berg, Grant, and Johnson (2010) show that people, in trying to pursue 'unanswered callings', employ different techniques for crafting their jobs and their leisure time in order to derive enjoyment and meaning. However, the downside of these techniques is that they also lead to 'unpleasant states of regret over forgone fulfilment of their unanswered callings and stress due to difficulties in pursuing their unanswered callings' (Berg, Grant, and Johnson 2010: 973).

The studies by Eriksson (2016) and Berg, Grant, and Johnson (2010) illuminate the complexity of (ill) health at work, and stress that it must be understood in relation to individuals' quests to understand their work in a broader existential context. However, in European working life research as well as trade union work, the concept of calling is commonly used to make visible relations of exploitation in working life. This has specifically been the case regarding women in working-class positions, whereby a work orientation being referred to as a calling often means they have not received fair remuneration for their work (Skeggs 1997; Greiff 2006). Weber's definitions, together with findings in contemporary research (e.g., Duffy and Dik 2013; Wrzesniewski, Dekas, and Rosso 2013), provide a more complex interpretation of the calling as analytical tool for capturing existential meaning in a sustainable working life. As we will show, at the same time as the calling is a burden, it can also function as a fundamental resource in an individual's life.

Methodology

The calling orientation to work specifically 'has been positioned as a key pathway to enhancing work-related well-being'. Therefore, in the past decade research on calling has become 'vibrant' (Duffy et al. 2018: 423). Still, there are methodological difficulties regarding the possibilities to study existential components of work. Capturing existential meaning-making is more difficult than measuring financial gain or steps on the career ladder. As most research on calling has assessed it through survey items, Amy Wrzesniewski, Dekas, and Rosso (2013: 118) emphasize the need for innovative research, such as qualitative interview methods 'to explore the nuances of calling'. Below, we briefly describe our research project, the design, and the empirical data that meant we had to search for a perspective that could help us analyse how the soon-to-be retirees' dedicated work orientations could be framed as a calling.

Data and Selection of Interviewees

The empirical data forming the basis of our analyses were collected within a Swedish research project on meaning-making in the retirement process. Altogether, the empirical data consist of semi-structured interviews with 43 individuals. These were conducted in Swedish by the authors of this chapter and the project leader in 2014 and 2015. Since the project focuses on the individuals' experience of the transitional nature of the retirement process, 35 of them were interviewed in two rounds, a short time before and about half a year after retirement.

In Sweden, previously there was a fixed retirement age of 65, but a more flexible system was implemented in the new century. At the time of writing, one can at the earliest take out pension at age 61 and there is no upper age limit. However, at 67 the employee will have to let go of his or her status as permanently employed but can have fixed-term employment in the labour market.[3]

There are great differences between when and to what extent workers and professionals in Sweden retire (Andersson and Öberg 2012). Therefore, one important factor in the selection of interviewees was to have a spread of occupations. Reflecting a qualitative spectrum of occupations was also important as we expected that issues such as social inequality, class, gender, and professional identity would matter in experiences of the retirement process. Thus, we have included women and men from different sectors and activities: low-skilled, manual jobs (e.g., in waste disposal, cleaning, and logistics); skilled jobs in the public sector (e.g., teachers and doctors); occupations dealing with financial means (e.g., payroll administrators and auditors); high-skilled professions mainly dealing with existential questions (e.g., priests and psychologists); and occupations within the creative industries (e.g., actors).

Methodological Choice: Studying Specific Life Phases as Existential Imperatives

Why do we focus on a group of people in the process of leaving employment for another everyday life? Why are their work orientations so interesting to analyse, even though they are about to enter a new phase in which the meaning of work activities is expected to diminish or even cease? The answer to these questions is that throughout the research project we found that the retirement process brings about new valuations of life and not least a reassessment of the meaning of work. In other words, the results indicate that the process can be seen as a critical case for understanding existential meaning. This meaning seems to emerge at the breaking points in life's various phases: when we are about to lose or leave something behind.

Anthropologists and philosophers of existentialism have often emphasized that reflections on the meaning of existence are accentuated when specific life phases cease and people enter a new everyday life (cf. Heidegger 2008; Turner 1974). The social anthropologist Michael D. Jackson (2005, 2013), who has frequently pointed out how existential aspects of meaning appear at the borders of previous practices and routines, conceptualizes these situations or events as existential imperatives—that is, critical moments in life when a particularly existential mood arises such as losing a job or a family member, when entering or leaving working life, or when we fall in love or become parents (cf. Flisbäck 2014).

The existential imperative entails the tangible feeling that one's life will one day cease, and that life seemingly consists of losses and births, endings and new beginnings (cf. Heidegger 2008).[4] We use the concept as a tool to make visible the existential meaning of work. In this context, we regard Jackson's perspective more as a methodology than a theory. According to Jackson (2013: 162), an existential imperative may present 'uncertain possibilities', leading to experiences of loss of control, due to a feeling of being under the influence of powerful external forces. A main point is that it is not the individual who enforces existential reflections and decisions. It is rather the practical situation (cf. Weber 1965) that brings forth an existential mood—for example, starvation, immigration, parenthood, or retirement.

As we will see, with calling as one's (existential) work orientation, retirement seems to represent a tension, as the calling as a life task cannot easily be limited to a specific time or place. For our respondents, questions as to which practices are meaningful and meaningless can be accentuated and articulated in a new way. According to Jackson, existential imperatives include both a loss of control and a potential for change, as well as a redefinition of former meanings, beliefs, and values. With an existential imperative, a belief may arise that life can be arranged beyond given directives and that the future is more open than it previously was. Nevertheless, this does not take form in a single moment; the existential imperative is a process, a phase. Therefore, in the research project it was necessary to use a qualitative longitudinal design to capture the process of retirement as an existential imperative that makes visible, amplifies, or reassesses meanings that the individual has previously attributed to work.

Using a Socio-Biographical Method

Longitudinal data are useful for understanding interviewees' narratives of the changing meaning of work during a specific life phase. We have used a *socio-biographical method* (cf. Douglas 2010; Flisbäck 2014). This method has similarities to both life history interviews and the life course approach; the latter has been rather dominant in ageing and development studies (cf. Alwin 2012). An advantage with the methods applied in the life course approach is that they allow an analysis of trajectories by emphasizing both contextual factors and intrapersonal development (e.g., Elder, Kirkpatrick, Johnson, and Crosnoe 2003). However, the socio-biographical method differs in its stronger focus on meaning and existential themes. One of the method's advantage is that it permits us to see how 'internal' differences in each interviewee are displayed over time and in transition between different social milieus. In this way, the socio-biographical method helps us focus on how existential orientations shift within each subject over time in various life processes (Flisbäck 2014), and regarding the calling: how the individual constructs and rethinks his or her calling during the time that passes.

Data Analysis and Coding

Our empirical point of departure is data collected within a sociological research project aiming to explore subjective experiences of the retirement process from several angles: a social inequality perspective, the influence of social norms and cultural meaning, and the impact of occupational identity and existential questions. Following this, 'calling' was not a conceptual starting point within our sociological research project; rather, various components of a calling were mainly brought forth through data processing and analysis, in line with Kathy Charmaz's (2014) constructivist grounded theory method. Thus, the data have been analysed by exploring similarities, differences, and contradictions in each person's approach to his or her profession and retirement process, as well as between the interviewees. We coded the data from empirical indicators towards higher levels of conceptual abstraction and theory integration. Through the application of stepwise coding and memo writing, several key categories emerged. In this process, we eventually moved towards Weber's approach and Jackson's methodology, which helped us both understand the existential meaning of work and highlight the relationship between this and retirement as a process.

During the coding process, we discovered that many among the interviewees embraced such a dedicated approach to their work that their orientation could be classified as a calling. However, when we discuss the calling as an existential work orientation, here we choose to focus more on certain persons within this group as illustrative examples to clarify the meaning aspects included in a calling. We should stress that the interviewees express different dimensions of a calling, and to varying degrees—our main aim is to 'carve out' an ideal typical construct. In this abductive process (cf. Charmaz 2014) the aforementioned theoretical perspectives were especially important in the analysis, contributing to conceptual development. When we present the results of this analysis process, we hope the concepts moreover, and in a broader context, can be applied and/or tested in other studies of the existential meaning of work.

Empirical Analyses

Retirement as an Existential Imperative

According to Jackson (2005), the reason why existential questions are tangible in relation to existential imperatives is that life's finiteness tends to be prominent in transitions between different states. Among our respondents, this emerged in the retirement process. In this transition, the existential meaning of work also seemed to be more palpable. As an existential imperative, retirement seemed to raise the issue that life and life situations always end. This became particularly clear in metaphors used by the respondents when describing the process. For example, the garbage collector George, with three months left until retirement at the age of 67, explains: 'Then it's, so to speak, "Finito"!' Åke, a priest in the same circumstances, jokingly uses the expression 'I'm approaching the end' and Claes, a museum director, points to how retirement reminds him of a divorce he went through earlier in life.

While the words of the respondents above explaining their experience of retiring can have a more or less serious undertone, they all denote endings and separations. However, metaphors for retiring can also suggest that life is beginning anew. Lars, a principal, compares the retirement process with 'having children, it's somehow that kind of happiness'. In a similar way, Ingmar, an organist, says the process can be compared to 'becoming a father'. The use of metaphors referring to life's ending as well as beginning when reflecting on retirement indicates that something is essentially at stake. The phase seems to constitute an existential reminder, with questions of meaning arising. In this situation, meaning is formed and re-formed.

Thus, near the end of many years of gainful employment, the meaning of work can appear with greater clarity. For Monika, an assistant nurse who will retire at 67, the process has meant a re-evaluation of work in relation to other life spheres. She is eager to continue her work at an intensive care unit, but says several people in her near surroundings, especially those who have not approached retirement age, show a lack of understanding for her wish to continue working:

> Many people say, 'Don't you think it's going to be nice to be at home?' And, 'What if it were me!?' Maybe that was what I also thought when I was in my 50s and 60s: 'How nice it'll be!' But when you get there [at the age of 67], then . . . I don't know.
>
> (Monika, assistant nurse)

The positive value of work in Monika's life has increased as she approaches retirement and, as a result, she does not experience it as wholly positive. Later we will discuss what aspects of her work Monika, like other respondents, finds valuable and does not want to be separated from. However, first we will analyse how retirement, as an existential imperative, can also create opposite feelings: of finally experiencing a specific form of freedom as a pensioner that one previously lacked as a wage labourer. A case in point is the experience of Gunilla, who like Monika has also worked as an assistant nurse. Gunilla sees retirement as something positive, a new beginning in life that stands in stark contrast to her earlier situation as employed, being set up by someone else:

> After a long professional life, you have to decide [for] yourself to make something of the day because it's not set up; because it is if you work, then every day is set up, in the way that you're going to work or do some other things, and it's not right now. . . . You can enjoy, make the most of the day, do something with it!
>
> (Gunilla, assistant nurse)

When feeling that a new everyday life is possible, people may ponder, like Gunilla, upon aspects of their work that have been less meaningful. Feelings of subordination, exploitation, and having to endure a maximization of work and being disciplined with time are examples. For instance, Olle, a former garbage collector, expresses strong relief at being a pensioner, saying the best thing about this new everyday situation is that he is released from the early rising that had been part of his job: ' . . . at the end of working life, one could feel sick of the alarm clock in the morning'. Olle describes great relief at letting go of the subordination concerning when and how work should be performed.

Whether life is described as 'set up' or controlled by an 'alarm clock', the contrast between the old and new everyday life has the same meaning:

there is something positive to being the 'master' of one's life and the fact that the new conditions are more meaningful than the former. Before retiring, at 63 years of age, Gunilla reflects on this. At this moment her thoughts and experiences are related to life's finitude and, thus, with capturing retirement as an existential imperative:

> I have both friends and former colleagues who have barely become pensioners before they get a cancer diagnosis and pass away. And I feel like 'What?' We're here briefly, here on Earth.
>
> (Gunilla, assistant nurse)

When retirement approaches, people's relationship to work and its value can be re-valued through being related to life's finitude and the uncertainties of existence. For Gunilla, it is important to seize the time beyond wage labour. She recounts how several friends and care recipients passed away shortly after retiring, a fate that she wants to avoid. Similarly, Olle measures the value of his previous work against thoughts about life's finitude. His conclusion is that the quality of life truly differs from collecting garbage. Thus, he asks himself: 'One could collapse tomorrow; should we then keep working?' When reflecting on life's finitude, Gunilla as well as Olle cannot assume that work is that which makes life meaningful. This differs significantly from the group of retirees we will discuss below, for whom the retirement process has provided insight into the deeper meaning of professional activity.

Retirement as Making Visible Work as a Calling

Above we have seen how retirement as an existential imperative can make visible and enforce meaning dimensions in relation to work. However, of main interest in this chapter is how the retirement process, among some, can make visible a highly committed orientation to work—work as a calling. In the following we discuss five components, which can be included among those with an existential work orientation in terms of a calling. In relation to the presentation, it should be noted that in our empirical data the calling could not easily be connected to specific occupations or job tasks. This has also been underlined in previous studies of the calling (e.g., Wrzesniewski et al. 1997; Wrzesniewski, Dekas, and Rosso 2013).

Moreover, we will emphasize that all respondents do not use the word 'calling' when talking about their work. Nevertheless, we have chosen to analyse the group with a dedicated approach in terms of a contemporary calling because their stories contain—particularly five— similar existential meaning dimensions. The five components we will discuss are: (1) work appears as *an external summons*; (2) the purpose of the work activity is to *serve a higher cause*; (3) work is carried out with *personality as a tool*; (4) work involves *self-sacrifice*; (5) and work gives rise to *elevation*. Before the presentation, it is important to keep in mind that work as a calling is an ideal type: an analytical construct used to understand the dedicated approaches to work. In relation to the data presented below, this means that the five components could have a different impact, significance, and strength in the various respondents' life stories.

An External Summons

When those we have categorized with calling as a work orientation looked back on their careers, they sometimes question whether their 'choice' of profession had truly been an active one; it is more described as *an external summons*. Memories of special events from childhood can arise, having staked out the direction of a future career path. For example, Birger, a full-time firefighter and commander prior to retirement, tells about a crucial event he experienced at the age of 10 that influenced his future choice of profession:

> When I was 10 years old, where we lived, there was a fire in the apartment next door. And then I became so interested in these guys who came, the firemen. And they showed me some things—they saw my interest—when they were done, of course. And it was probably then, at the age of 10, that I thought, That's what I'd like to be when I grow up! And so it was.
>
> (Birger, firefighter and commander)

After 34 years of employment with the rescue service, Birger has retired. But despite all the years that have passed, he vividly portrays his very first encounter with the firefighting occupation as a child. Ingmar, who was a professional organist, says he was aware since early childhood that he wanted to devote his life to music. Like Birger, he recounts a crucial event—a musical experience as a four-year-old:

> I had no alternative, one could say. . . . My first memory is as a four-year-old child, hearing a fantastic organist playing in the cathedral, so my first memory [in life] is an organ memory.
>
> (Ingmar, musician)

Ingmar had access to this first poignant musical memory of the organist playing in the cathedral because his father was a priest by profession. Thus, part of Ingmar's everyday life was in the vicinity of the organ. The music touched Ingmar in a special way and gave birth to a wish to become a musician, a path he describes as lacking any 'alternative'. The fact that his first memory is connected with an activity that later became his profession is important for understanding professional choice as an external summons.

It may be easy to think that Ingmar's early indication of his future life path coincides with his artistic career choice. The myth of the artist who early in life nourishes a need to make artistic mark is widespread (cf. Flisbäck 2014). However, following our respondents' stories, memories may appear from special events in which the profession as a predetermined task appears to be made visible. The use of such images is not specifically related to only those with artistic professions. When discussing her choice of profession, Anna-Britta, a children's librarian, says that 'it has just been obvious to me that it is children's librarian that should be my profession. It was obvious'. In her family of origin, an ascetic Protestantism was practiced. Culture—such as books, movies, and music—was considered a sin. But a longing to work with books arose in her after interacting with other families, mainly one for which she worked as a babysitter. She recounts that there was shelf after shelf of 'the classics' in that family's home, and she understood that books should become her life:

> I've never had enough of this with children's books. Because I didn't get—yes, you know, there's some starvation I lived with since I was little because it wasn't really in my childhood home, any books.
>
> (Anna-Britta, librarian)

When analysing five different meaning dimensions relating to a calling, we should emphasize that they are ideal typical—that is, the components' strength and extent vary from person to person. However, an external summons is prominent in the stories. We can understand this narrative of a specific work activity or occupational place to which one has been called as a way to confirm 'a stable and coherent sense of self' (Bunderson and Thompson 2009: 37). Thus, this entails that occupational performances are often seen as an extended part of the self and as an experience of authenticity. Åke recalls how his calling appeared to him during military service, where the authenticity of the calling stood in contrast to the masculinity culture in which discussion topics mostly concerned conquering women and drinking alcohol. Åke found his own space for reflection in the restroom, which led to the appearance of his calling:

> I usually say, 'I built my calling in the restroom during military service'. There was a booth, you know. . . . That was the only place I could be alone and be myself. That's how it emerged. I felt I had something to share.
>
> (Åke, priest)

Having an orientation to work as a calling means, as we have seen, that the discovery of the calling—the 'choice' of profession—is not possible to delineate to experiences in adulthood. Birger, Ingmar, and Anna-Britta date their experiences of being called to a task to early childhood. In such a way, this testifies to a view of professional performance as a life task. Åke's calling appeared in early adulthood. In other words, the calling can take shape when one is a young child, during the transition to adulthood, or later in life. Moreover, it can appear as a process, forming over time. The summons may occur by adding event to event.

In a study of young musicians, Shoshana R. Dobrow (2007), therefore, challenges the idea of '*finding* a calling' in favour of an analysis of musicians '*developing* a calling'. Among some of our respondents, it seems as if the calling sometimes needs a certain 'response' from one's fellow man or the institutions of society. For example, despite the experience of her work as 'obvious', Anna-Britta needed to 'try' her calling as a substitute for seven years before taking the step to being educated as a librarian. She said: 'I wanted to see if it really was what I wanted, and how it really was to work in a library, before I went through this education'. While Anna-Britta was 'testing' her calling, she also became the mother of two children. The ability to undergo training for the profession that had been obvious to her was made available through access to universal public childcare:

> So while I worked there [at the library] I formed a family as well. So it wasn't until they [the children] started kindergarten, which was so difficult at the time, that I started at the library college. . . . So when they started kindergarten, both of them, I applied and then I was admitted right away.
>
> (Anna-Britta, librarian)

A clear example of calling as a process, whereby it finds its form through being tried and eased by welfare institutions, is seen in the experience of Maarit, who is retiring from her duties as a principal. She recounts how since childhood she was convinced that she should engage in tasks for the common good and not let other people decide how society should be ordered. For Maarit, this conviction meant that 'it's not possible to just sit in the armchair and whine', but 'well, try to do something about it. I try this in my teaching'.

As a young woman, it was not obvious to her that this engagement for the common good should be expressed through the teaching profession. When she was 20, Maarit arrived in Sweden as a labour migrant. After working for a number of years in a textile factory, she graduated from elementary school and then high school. Set goals were followed by good study results. Maarit says that she step by step tried to convince herself to 'see if I could make it [in Sweden]. I didn't know Swedish when I moved to Sweden'. Maarit also recounts the importance for her self-confidence of encouraging, 'good' conversations and various tests through the employment agency. She was also offered a temporary position as a teacher, which allowed her to meet people who showed appreciation for her work performance. The various steps Maarit recounts ultimately resulted in her attending the teaching programme at the university, and later in a position as a principal.

Maarit's calling, consequently, was built up through a process. An early external summons to 'make a difference' found a context in a stepwise manner through the accumulation of educational capital and affirming institutional actors. Thus, similar to the findings by Dobrow (2007) on the dynamics of the calling in her longitudinal study of young musicians, an ongoing behavioural involvement in the calling domain (that is, the educational system) and social encouragement were pertinent for Maarit to be able to develop a calling orientation to work.

To Serve a Higher Cause

Above, the respondents describe the appearance of work as being called by an external summons to a life task. In this way, they recount an experience of something external or a supra-individual force calling them to a specific task (Duffy and Dik 2013: 429). This means that the calling does not belong only to the premodern, feudal society where the Lutheran teaching of a calling was a regulatory principle in Protestant Sweden (Grenholm 1988). Secularized contemporary man, while not following a religious teaching of calling, may also show a steadfast adherence to work as a life task (Wrzesniewski et al. 1997: 22; Dik and Duffy 2009: 427). From our point of view, however, it is essential to emphasize the active, existential approaches in which individuals relate their work to the meaning of life. This means that it is not the case, in either the premodern or the contemporary context, that the calling is reduced to a cultural meaning structure, which is activated in the individual. The calling is lived; the individual constructs its content in relation to her own occupational path, and as a response to the meaning and mystery of life.

In our existential sociological approach, experiencing work as a calling is 'an external summons' (Duffy and Dik 2013), whereby the called person experiences a 'sense of destiny' (Bunderson and Thompson 2009) or a 'Transcendent guiding Force' (Hagmaier and Abele 2012) in having been selected for the specific profession. This guiding force can have religious as well as social connotations. It is not especially surprising that Åke, the priest, describes his profession in terms of a calling. But even the museum director Claes, an outspoken atheist, looks upon his profession in terms of a calling: 'There is a little calling in it somehow'. Claes's calling took shape after psychological counselling. Following the psychologist's advice, he begun to study archaeology, which eventually led to work within cultural heritage and museum activities. He recounts the psychologist's words: 'It's quite obvious that you, who are interested in houses and history and the like, that you should choose archaeology, excavation'. When Claes finally embarked on this life path, he experienced having connected to a more authentic part of himself. He says: 'I can probably buy that picture now in retrospect'.

By calling, we mean that it is not enough that the professional choice is experienced as if the individual has been true to herself or that she has fulfilled the task she experiences having been called to. Additionally, the person has to serve someone—that is, the task must be of interest to someone other than oneself. Even though Ingmar has a great love for music and finds the craft developing, even as 'a *need*, like eating or drinking', he stresses his work as 'a task that needs to be performed'. And to perform the task in the best way, he believes that 'one has to listen more to others than to oneself. It's not for promoting my brand [as artist]'. This type of 'value-rational orientation' (Weber 1978: 25), 'Value-driven Behavior' expressed in serving the collective good (Hagmaier and Abele 2012), or work being 'prosocially oriented' (Duffy and Dik 2013: 429) also becomes tangible when George reflects upon his professional life: 'I've always been interested in people and people's well-being', he says and adds: 'It's not everyone who feels it as a calling. But for me it developed into a calling'. George says that collecting garbage has been necessary for the well-being of society: 'I think I've contributed to society in such a way that I've made it happen that garbage, or litter, has been cleaned away!'

In interpretations of the value of work activities one can understand that care work, teaching, or preaching can transform into passionate devotion. However, serving others and contributing to their best is also described as an important part of the activities George refers to as his calling. Irene, an accountant, also stresses a desire to make a difference—contributing to a development towards a more gender-equal society. She recounts how after graduation from high school she was uncertain of which university training to choose, but felt 'very convinced' she should choose anything 'where there was skewed gender representation'. It is somewhat difficult for her to explain the cause of this conviction, but it was in her mind when she chose to apply to a business school, where more or less all the students were men. Through this gender-atypical choice of schooling at the time, Irene's calling can be interpreted as her opposing the gender order of society. In doing so, she hoped that women after her would follow her path.

Personality as a Tool

So far, in the respondents' accounts of the work they are about to leave we have seen that they have been externally summoned to this life task, which first and foremost has been directed at serving their fellow man or society at large. But what makes a called person suitable to serve his fellow man? Often, the ability to meet human-to-human has been seen as a main characteristic, specifically in descriptions of 'the female calling'. Historically, the ability to 'act personally' has been connected with traits attributed to women's chores, both in the private sphere and in care work, and typically used to make visible relations of exploitation in working life (cf. Skeggs 1997; Kollind 2003). The personal attitude which is part of a calling has been described as more common in female-dominated professions—for instance, among nurses. Instead, the medical profession has been characterized as a more male-dominated professional culture. This may explain why even female physicians in various studies have pointed to extrinsic work values, such as pay and social status, as reasons for entering the medical profession (Greiff 2006). Meanwhile, in our study, the physician Jens stresses that he considers the essential aspect of his profession to be that of helping people have a better life. However, for Jens, in order to be able to do this, his encounters with patients must be in the form of a personal relation. He tells how important personal care is in meeting, for example, chronically ill patients:

> What we have is thus a little more, a greater patient–doctor relationship, so it's more personal. So I'm more a personal doctor for them than just a doctor.
>
> (Jens, physician)

Jens emphasizes the importance of being a 'personal doctor'—that is, acting in a personal way, which means that the person being served is never an object. Instead, there is more reciprocity concerning trust and emotional force in the relationship between the professional and his or her fellow man. Through these 'human-to-human' meetings, the called person also receives something valuable from those he or she serves, and this creates existential meaning. When talking about this topic, it could be difficult for the respondents to find words to explain this. For instance, Anna-Britta, the librarian, says: 'The energy you get from conversations with children, I can't describe the feeling!'

Our analysis shows that similar existential meaning can arise even for people who handle financial means, such as Irene, for whom customer contacts have been important in her work. As an accountant for minor family-owned businesses, she has been able to build more long-term and personal relationships. Irene says that one becomes an 'interlocutor for nearly all things related to the economy'. This work and the personal relationships made possible through the customer contacts have given her existential meaning and, thus, the power to face and endure difficulties such as losses and major separations in life. She recounts how her network of customer contacts was a main source of support during a vulnerable time in her life when she could not cope with her private matters. In this way, Irene's story can also serve to variegate interpretations of the calling as a relation of exploitation.

Through acting in personal ways, existential meaning can be formed in work. In the interpersonal meeting, the person who is served also returns this support and trust. Following Weber (2009a), a devout professional performance is in opposition to the dictates of many modern organizations, where the rational and specialized methods of bureaucracy are a means to the end goal of reaching maximum efficiency. Our analyses bear witness that a similar tension exists between the cause of the calling and the enforcement of bureaucratic forms of regulation in middle-class professions as well as working-class jobs, whereby work should be controlled, measured, and relentlessly documented and reported (cf. Power 1997). As a pensioner, the garbage collector George points to how computerization has made waste collection 'extremely supervised'. Additionally, Åke reflects on how 'organizational planning' has grown in importance, greatly contrasting the calling that once led to his choice of occupation as a priest. This topic resurfaced in conversations about his work performance with his manager:

> She [my manager] started as follows: 'What's the most important thing in your work?' And I replied quickly: 'People!' 'Yes, but—', and then she said: 'But organizational planning is important!' 'Yes, yes', I said. 'I know what you're talking about', I said, 'but I still think people are the most important'.
>
> (Åke, priest)

The respondents express frustration at the fact that interpersonal meetings, personal conduct, and their devotion to the calling give way to too many bureaucratic rules, supervision, and administrative burdens. Jens is irritated with regard to how 'the power over the job, over care, has changed' with increased financial control and documentation requirements. He describes it by saying that the professional practice is alienated 'further from my ideals'.[5]

As seen so far, the meaning of being called involves experiencing an external summons and feeling one has been chosen to serve a higher cause—for example one's fellow man or society at large. With the help of an external force, or the feeling of being in someone's service, the assigned task eventually appears as an authentic part of the self. In Weber's (2009a: 84, emphasis in original) words when discussing the calling of politics, the individual lives 'for' politics instead of barely living 'off' politics: 'He who lives "for" politics makes politics his life . . . his life has *meaning* in the service of a "cause" '. Thus, when the individual shows passionate devotion to the professional practice, life is perceived as meaningful.

The fact that there is consistency between values governing one's work and the professional practice is thus a central aspect of the existential orientation we refer to as a calling. However, there are aspects of modern working life that the respondents have experienced as threatening this consistency—for example, when professional practice is increasingly steered by the dictates of instrumental efficiency. When work cannot be performed according to the 'ideal' of the calling, the result can then be a loss of existential meaning.

Self-Sacrifice

Perhaps work as a calling is most comprehensible in activities directed towards interpersonal relationships. However, in both traditional and modern understandings of the calling, the assumption is that this orientation can be expressed in all types of work (Wrzesniewski et al. 1997; Wrzesniewski, Dekas, and Rosso 2013; Dik and Duffy 2009). As mentioned, this is a result in our study as well. Another important outcome is that the calling seems to emerge more clearly in the retirement process—a process interpreted here as an existential imperative. The phase also means that the interviewees reflect retrospectively on what they have had to choose and sacrifice during their lives because of their calling.[6]

That the calling has required self-sacrifice is a key component. George emphasizes how his strong work commitment has demanded major sacrifices. He has performed his duties with almost complete accountability, driven by the belief that the tasks are needed for the well-being of society. An example of this is when he was ill for a long time, but could not help checking to make sure the work was not suffering: 'The first months I was sick, I went down every morning to check that they were leaving, the other guys who were driving in my place'.

Even though George was absent from work due to long-term sick leave, he felt such a responsibility that he wanted to be part of the work process. This was certainly not good for his health. Furthermore, he always answered work calls in the evenings and on holidays. Kristina, who worked as a family counsellor for the elderly and disabled, also recounts how she took work calls in her spare time. She says the meaning of work and life is 'to be needed!' The meaningfulness, for Kristina, has involved 'broadening their [clients'] lives so that they are able to develop from their horizons', to help people live more independently. Although the work was existentially meaningful, Kristina says she regrets certain aspects of her professional practice: 'A person shouldn't really be available 24 hours a day'. She says, 'In retrospect, I myself feel self-critical that I didn't set that limit'.

As seen above, the existential meaning that comes from having work as a calling entails some costs. The sacrifices and the boundary-free work have not always been healthy for the individuals in question. In other words, with the calling as a life task, it seems difficult to limit professional demands. In a research review, Ryan D. Duffy and Bryan J. Dik (2013: 433) discuss this as 'the possible dark side of a calling', with negative outcomes of a calling entailing various personal sacrifices: for example, being overworked or exploited, or making sacrifices in non-work domains. Thus, an orientation to work as a calling seems to have downsides whereby one's love for serving the community and one's fellow man can lead to organizational exploitation and unhealthy investment in work—workaholism (Greiff 2006; Bunderson and Thompson 2009; Duffy et al. 2018).

For the person who feels called, the value of the practice is articulated based on the meaning the tasks may have for others and in a larger life context. What this contribution and value consist of, however, may vary among professions. When Weber (2009b) mentions the scientific profession as a calling, the core of scientific activity is a search for knowledge about the higher cause of scientific progress. According to Weber, scientific work cannot be forced but comes from lust, vision, and passion, which can mean major sacrifices in nonwork domains. For Ingmar, such a 'dark side of the calling' has been the case as he, working as an organist, has not spent as much time with his family as he would have liked:

> It hasn't been like I've thought it was boring to be home or, 'I'm so tired of the kids, so I'm going to [church to] play a little'. It hasn't! Instead I've felt like: 'Now I have this concert in front of me'. For example: 'I'm playing tomorrow at twelve, and then I have to finish it and master this and that'.
>
> (Ingmar, musician)

Following Ingmar's words, similar life priorities cannot be understood as active considerations. He believes that, despite his love for his children and grandchildren, work demands simply took over.

Elevation

We have seen how work as a calling tends to entail that professional practices dominate nonwork domains because a calling means that individuals see their efforts as difficult to replace, which has its pros and cons. However, the self-sacrifices a calling requires can lead to elevation and, thus, a way of finding a distinctive place in one's (professional) life. Following Weber (1992: 40), the Reformation's interpretation of the calling refers to a hierarchical order-making principle whereby the 'only way of living acceptably to God was . . . through the fulfilment of the obligations imposed upon the individual by his position in the world'.

Since the experience of substitutability is more common in low-status than high-status groups, in accordance with Weber (1965, 1978: 491), socially disadvantaged and negatively valued status groups can nourish their sense of honour through a belief they have been assigned a special mission. Thus, marking the indispensable, difficult aspects of work can be a way to make oneself irreplaceable. However, the more or less bound-less investment in work should not be seen as emphasizing one's own merits but rather as placing one's efforts within a larger life context—that is, attributing an existential meaning to one's work. One example is the firefighter Birger who, through his work deeds, managed to both prevent death and deliver life:

> I have saved lives. This has happened a few times. People have been taken down by windows. . . . And what makes me the most proud is that I've helped deliver a child on the kitchen floor, as an ambulance man.
>
> (Birger, firefighter and commander)

Following Birger's story, difficult work tasks can be the chores that make an individual feel indispensable. Similarly, Monika points to how the unique value of the chores she performs is that it is life-sustaining, which she partly considers to be different from other work carried out by assistant nurses:

> Then we get the patients directly from the ambulance. The infarcts and so on—those who are really bad—they go directly to the ward. We take electrocardiograms and we take samples, and one could say that we do a great deal that they may not do on other wards. Not as an assistant nurse in any case.
>
> (Monika, assistant nurse)

Sustaining life practices is perceived in the above examples as existentially meaningful. That the work is labourious and requires self-sacrifice means that it carries with it an elevation. But other types of chores can also be regarded as 'necessary' and as leading to a special elevation. Although it is not necessary for creating or saving lives, the work performed by librarian Anna-Britta can be interpreted as being significant for the welfare society's efforts to alleviate differences between resource-rich and resource-poor children, through increasing reading among the latter. A similar desire to make a difference is also prominent in the impact her work has had on the parents of these children: 'I've made them go to the libraries. Many of these parents, they've never been to the library before.' As Anna-Britta is about to retire, these are the aspects she sees as the most important ones in her work.

Leaving Work as a Calling: Freedom or Curse?

Above we have seen how calling is a work orientation that entails self-sacrifices, as well as how these sacrifices can create a sense of being irreplaceable, which can allow an individual to experience existential meaning. However, the tension resulting from the fact that the work practice causes both self-sacrifices/suffering and elevation implies that retiring has different meanings in the lives of 'the called'. For family consultant Kristina, making an effort for her fellow man and society has been a 'reason to get up in the morning'. When she retired at the age of 67, she was offered the possibility to remain in the workplace for another six months, but when this period ended, retiring was 'like a black wall'.

Kristina belongs to those whose existence as a pensioner has partly emerged as an 'existential vacuum', to use the terms of Viktor E. Frankl (1988). This entails feelings of emptiness, resulting from the loss of meaning created through leaving work as a calling, while at the same time one's existence as a 'nonworker' is not perceived as equally valuable and meaningful. 'What should I do when retirement day comes? Should I sit and look at four walls?', Kristina asks five months before retiring. She later summarizes her first days as a pensioner with the following words: 'Then came the next morning and then there was a lot of fatigue, almost apathy. . . . That was the feeling: no longer needed!' This case exemplifies how the calling created existential meaning for Kristina; her need to understand her place in a greater whole was taken away through retirement.

Kristina's case refers to the difficulty one can experience in delimiting a calling. According to Martin Kohli (1986), coming of age or retiring are examples of 'age thresholds' in the life course, resulting from linking welfare rights and obligations to age. In Kohli's view, this has resulted in individuals' unique lifestyles being homogenized and standardized. But the calling seems difficult to correct after such age thresholds. Thus, retirement can be perceived as an external force de-calling the life task. But it is not all the interviewees who regard this process of de-calling as a loss. For some, retirement offers a window of opportunity and a liberation from 'the dark side' of the calling. The organist Ingmar has always tried to do his best for the congregation he has served. However, his calling has required countless hours of exercise. Due to these sacrifices, retirement offers an opportunity for a new existence with fewer work chores and more space for close relationships. Ingmar hopes to be able to listen to a private calling: the family sphere. When reflecting on the professional life he is soon to leave, he states: 'If I had my life to live over, I hope and believe I would've taken better care of my family'.

Concluding Discussion

The aim of this chapter has been to discuss the existential dimensions of individuals' work orientations. As a concrete example, we have highlighted the calling as a way of understanding the approaches contained in the descriptions of the work our interviewees will leave behind upon retirement. Based on previous research and qualitative interviews (conducted before and after retirement), we have developed an ideal type that includes five components of 'work as a calling': (1) following *an external summons*, a life task in which the individual (2) *serves a higher cause*, his fellow man or society, by means of (3) *personality as a tool*, which demands (4) *self-sacrifice*, which in earlier research has been called 'the dark side' of the calling, which at the same time leads to (5) *elevation* at the feeling of being irreplaceable.

In the chapter, we have pointed to a sociological and secular interpretation of a calling. As we have seen, the fact that there are social forces behind the calling means that the calling can be *induced* by experts in society—for example, psychologists or job brokers. That is, the calling, as interpreted here, may be an ongoing process before an external summons appears. Consequently, our sociological perspective on the calling differs from some psychological studies, in which the pursuit of the calling 'is more oriented around self-exploration and fulfillment' (Wrzesniewski, Dekas, and Rosso 2013: 117). Among the 'called' in our study, self-development is a less prominent topic. However, elevation coming from self-sacrifice and the performance of difficult tasks can be seen as the 'bright side' of the calling. From a broader perspective, sacrifices for others can be existentially meaningful to the individual.

Following Weber, existence is meaningful when there is consistency between one's ethical values and work practices. To form such an existential foundation for the self can be the opposite of the approach to work called 'job'—that is, a means of simply earning a living (Bellah et al. 1985: 66). Work as a calling entails a personal execution of the chores that cannot be calculated or standardized in advance. Thus, as a concept, calling not only shows how individuals attribute their professional lives to a fundamental cause; it also creates an understanding of complex tensions between the individual's experience of the practice of a calling and ongoing rationalization processes in capitalistic societies. Perhaps it is the case, as Weber claims, that the bureaucratization of economic life gives prominence to routinization and immediate material gains. This counteracts a coherent 'personality', which, in interpretations of Weber's works, 'demand[s] an adherence to values which give a far-reaching aim to one's life' (Schroeder 1991: 63). For our respondents, the experience of work having developed towards more monitoring and documentation has not only resulted in a loss of meaning; for some, it has led to a longing for life as a pensioner, a topic that we, however, barely touched on in this chapter.

Our study shows how the existential meaning of work may be amplified in processes when we leave something behind to enter something new—that is, at the borders of previous practices and routines. Perhaps the calling is constructed and verbalized most clearly when we have to exit professional life—when it emerges in an existential imperative, inviting us to reflect on our life's accomplishments and shortcomings. We have also pointed to the specific meaning, possibilities, and complications of the calling in a modern welfare society. Here, retirement is interesting in relation to the calling because it can be a paradox for those who relate to their work as a life task. Is it possible to give up work conceptualized as a life task? Thus, retirement can lead to doubts as to whether one has truly succeeded in one's calling and the question of what might be as meaningful as the deeds of work. However, in the chapter we have seen that it is not everyone who regards the process of de-calling as a loss. For some, retirement offers liberation from 'the dark side' of the calling. The different experiences we have learned of in connection to 'being called' as a work orientation testify that we, as researchers, consider the complexity of the calling and its consequences, and thus must beware of demonizing as well as romanticizing work as a calling.

Notes

1. There are also other forms of existential work orientations. For instance, Marita Flisbäck (2014) shows, with examples from artistic work, how existential enigmas are problematized in what she calls an artistic life politics. This work strategy, with feminist connotations, is a way of translating experiences from the private sphere, such as personal grief, to a resource in work—for example, used as inspiration for topics in artistic work.
2. It could be mentioned here that there exist constructs such as 'meaningful work', 'intrinsic motivation', and 'sense of purpose at work' that are partly related to the concept of calling. However, specifically the 'neoclassical' perspective of calling is a wider construct, emphasizing prosocial motives and an external summons (Duffy et al. 2018: 425). Moreover, as the calling can lead to substantial sacrifices in nonwork domains, it can be related to the concept 'work centrality', defined as 'a general attitude towards the importance of work' (Chapter 3: xx in this book). However, this general attitude, which does not indicate the *reasons* for finding work important and meaningful, clearly differs from the multidimensional construct of a calling.
3. In December 2017, representatives of six political parties in Swedish Parliament presented a political agreement to raise the earliest retirement age successively from 61 to 64 years and to extend the possibility of retaining one's permanent job from 67 to 69 years. Even if our respondents are not covered by these changes to the pension system, political and media debates concerning a longer working life were highly topical at the time of our interviews.
4. The mood can also arise throughout the life course in less dramatic situations, such as when summer vacation ends and we have to return to paid employment.
5. According to Jens, the work differs from earlier times when he experienced having greater influence over it. We can relate Jens's experiences to the re-regulation of the work process of physicians in Sweden, which began in the 1990s: a re-regulation with new forms of control and supervision that usually goes by the name 'New Public Management', and that has come to threaten the autonomy of the physician profession (Bejerot and Hasselbladh 2003).
6. Being called can be interpreted as labouriously serving one's fellow man and society at large. In the calling, there is accommodated a work ethic reminiscent of Martin Luther's (1520), whereby 'it is impossible that he should take his

ease in this life, and not work for the good of his neighbours'. However, this can also mean—as the etymological meaning of the word *passion* indicates—a suffering. Serving others carries sacrifices, which Luther metaphorically described as carrying the cross of Christ (Grenholm 1988). Consequently, this downside of the calling can become apparent in relation to retirement.

References

Alexander, J. (2006) *The Civil Sphere*. New York: Oxford University Press.

Alwin, D. F. (2012) 'Integrating Varieties of Life Course Concepts.' *The Journals of Gerontology* (Series B: Psychological Sciences and Social Sciences) 67(2): 206–220.

Andersson, L. and P. Öberg (2012) 'Äldre i arbetslivet—delaktiga eller marginaliserade?', 39–63, in L. Andersson and P. Öberg (eds) *Jämlik ålderdom? I samtiden och framtiden*. Malmö: Liber.

Antonovsky, A. (1987) *Unraveling the Mystery of Health: How People Manage Stress and Stay Well*. San Francisco: Jossey-Bass.

Bejerot, E. and H. Hasselbladh (2003) 'Nya kontroll- och maktrelationer inom sjukvården.' *Arbetsmarknad & Arbetsliv* 9(2): 107–127.

Bellah, R. N., R. Madsen, W. M. Sullivan, A. Swidler and S. M. Tipton (1985) *Habits of the Heart: Individualism and Commitment in American Life*. Berkeley, CA: University of California Press.

Bengtsson, M. and M. Flisbäck (2016) 'När kallet ställs på sin spets. Pensionering ur ett existenssociologiskt perspektiv.' *Sociologisk Forskning* 53(2): 127–150.

Bengtsson, M. and M. Flisbäck (2017a) *Farväl till arbetet. Sociologiska perspektiv på meningen med att gå i pension*. Lund: Nordic Academic Press.

Bengtsson, M. and M. Flisbäck (2017b) 'On Leaving Work as a Calling: Retirement as an Existential Imperative.' *International Journal of Ageing and Later Life* 11(1): 37–67.

Berg, J. M., A. M. Grant and V. Johnson (2010) 'When Callings Are Calling: Crafting Work and Leisure in Pursuit of Unanswered Occupational Callings.' *Organization Science* 21(5): 973–994.

Bunderson, J. S. and J. A. Thompson (2009) 'The Call of the Wild: Zookeepers, Callings, and the Double-edged Sword of Deeply Meaningful Work.' *Administrative Science Quarterly* 54(1): 32–57.

Charmaz, K. (2014) *Constructing Grounded Theory*. London: Sage.

Dik, B. J. and R. D. Duffy (2009) 'Calling and Vocation at Work. Definitions and Prospects for Research and Practice.' *The Counselling Psychologist* 37(3): 424–450.

Dobrow, S. R. (2007) 'The Development of Calling: A Longitudinal Study of Musicians', in *Academy of Management Conference, 2007*, Philadelphia, USA.

Douglas, J. D. (2010) 'Existential Sociology', 3–73, in J. D. Douglas and J. M. Johnson (eds) *Existential Sociology*. Cambridge: Cambridge University Press.

Duffy, R. D. and B. J. Dik (2013) 'Research on Calling: What Have We Learned and Where Are We Going?' *Journal of Vocational Behavior* 83: 428–436.

Duffy, R. D., B. J. Dik, R. P. Douglass, J. W. England and B. L. Velez (2018) 'Work as a Calling: A Theoretical Model.' *Journal of Counseling Psychology* 65(4): 423–439.

Elder, G. H., Jr., M. Kirkpatrick Johnson and R. Crosnoe (2003) 'The Emergence and Development of Life Course Theory', 3–19, in J. T. Mortimer and M. J. Shanahan (eds) *Handbook of the Life Course*. New York: Kluwer Academic/ Plenum.

Eriksson, A.-K. (2016) *Vid utmattningens gräns: Utmattningssyndrom som existentiellt tillstånd. Vårdtagares och vårdgivarens erfarenheter av utmattningssyndrom och rehabilitering med en existentiell ansats i svensk vårdkontext.* Sundsvall: Mittuniversitetet.

Flisbäck, M. (2014) *När livet går bort, när livet kommer till: Existenssociolo-giska betraktelser av konstnärligt arbete, familjebildning och anhörigförlust.* Lund: Studentlitteratur.

Frankl, V. E. (1988) *The Will to Meaning: Foundations and Applications of Log-otherapy.* New York, NY: Plume.

Goldthorpe, J. H., D. Lockwood, F. Bechhofer and J. Platt (1968) *The Affluent Worker: Industrial Attitudes and Behaviour.* Cambridge: Cambridge University Press.

Greiff, M. (2006) 'Kall eller profession? Yrkeskulturer och skapandet av manligt och kvinnligt mellan klient och arbetsköpare', 111–136, in H. Petersson, V. Leppänen, S. Jönsson and J. Tranquist (eds) *Villkor i arbete med människor— en antologi om human servicearbete.* Stockholm: Arbetslivsinstitutet.

Grenholm, C.-H. (1988) *Arbetets mening. En analys av sex teorier om arbetets syfte och värde.* Stockholm: Almqvist & Wiksell.

Hagmaier, T. and A. E. Abele (2012) 'The Multidimensionality of Calling: Conceptualization, Measurement and a Bicultural Perspective.' *Journal of Vocational Behavior* 81: 39–51.

Heidegger, M. (2008) *Being and Time.* New York: Harper Perennial.

Jackson, M. D. (2005) *Existential Anthropology.* New York: Berghahn Books.

Jackson, M. D. (2011) *Life Within Limits: Well-Being in a World of Want.* Durham: Duke University Press.

Jackson, M. D. (2013) *Lifeworlds. Essays in Existential Anthropology.* Chicago: The University of Chicago Press.

Kohli, M. (1986) 'The World We Forgot: A Historical Review of the Life Course', 271–303, in V. W. Marshall (ed.) *Later Life: The Social Psychology of Aging.* Beverly Hills, CA: Sage.

Kollind, A.-K. (2003) 'Kvinnor och socialt arbete—vid övergången från filantropi till profession.' *Socialvetenskaplig tidskrift* 10(2–3): 172–192.

Luther, M. (1520) *Concerning Christian Liberty.* Project Gutenberg Etext.

Portis, E. B. (1978) 'Max Weber's Theory of Personality.' *Sociological Inquiry* 48(2): 113–120.

Power, M. (1997) *The Audit Society. Rituals of Verification.* Oxford: Oxford University Press.

Rosso, B. D., K. H. Dekas and A. Wrzesniewski (2010) 'On the Meaning of Work: A Theoretical Integration and Review.' *Research in Organizational Behavior* 30: 91–127.

Schroeder, R. (1991) ' "Personality" and "inner distance": The Conception of the Individual in Max Weber's Sociology.' *History of the Human Sciences* 4(1): 61–78.

Segal, R. A. (1999) 'Weber and Geertz on the Meaning of Religion.' *Religion* 29(1): 61–71.

Skeggs, B. (1997) *Formations of Class & Gender: Becoming Respectable*. London: Sage.

Turner, V. W. (1974) *Dramas, Fields, and Metaphors: Symbolic Action in Human Society*. Ithaca, London: Cornell University Press.

Weber, M. (1965) *The Sociology of Religion*. London: Methuen & Co.

Weber, M. (1978) *Economy and Society: An Outline of Interpretive Sociology*. Berkeley: University of California Press.

Weber, M. (1992) *The Protestant Ethic and the Spirit of Capitalism*. London: Routledge.

Weber, M. (2009a) 'Politics as a Vocation', 77–128, in H. H. Gerth and C. Wright Mills (eds) *From Max Weber: Essays in Sociology*. London, New York: Routledge.

Weber, M. (2009b) 'Science as a Vocation', 129–156, in H. H. Gerth and C. Wright Mills (eds) *From Max Weber. Essays in Sociology*. London, New York: Routledge.

Wrzesniewski, A. (2003) 'Finding Meaning in Work', 298–309, in K. S. Cameron, J. E. Dutton and R. E. Quinn (eds) *Positive Organizational Scholarship*. San Francisco: Berrett-Koehler.

Wrzesniewski, A., K. Dekas and B. Rosso (2013) 'Calling', 115–118, in S. J. Lopez (ed.) *The Encyclopedia of Positive Psychology*. Malden, MA: Wiley-Blackwell.

Wrzesniewski, A., C. McCauley, P. Rozin and B. Schwartz (1997) 'Jobs, Careers, and Callings: People's Relations to Their Work.' *Journal of Research in Personality* 31(1): 21–33.

5 Work Attitudes, Employment and Work Mobilization

A Comparison of Anglo-Saxon and Nordic Countries, 2005 and 2015

Bengt Furåker

Introduction

The point of departure for this chapter is the discussion and the research on the role of the welfare state for people's willingness to enter or stay in the labour market. In essence, it is about whether or not social benefits of various kinds create disincentives for labour market participation. The analysis focuses on Anglo-Saxon and Nordic countries. In research on welfare systems, these two clusters usually appear as examples of different models (e.g., Castles 1993, 2004; Gallie and Paugam 2000; Esping-Andersen 1990, Korpi and Palme 1998; Korpi 2000). Although the Nordic countries have had their share of tightening measures, cuts in public spending, deregulations and privatizations during the first decades of the 21st century, their public support systems are in the main more comprehensive and generous than those in the Anglo-Saxon countries. The discussion on the relationship between the welfare state and citizens' readiness to take on paid work seems to be incessantly ongoing. In essence, it is about whether or not social benefits of various kinds create disincentives for labour market participation. Some claim that welfare state arrangements should be limited to keep up people's will to take a job, while others find that the incentives are sufficient even when the welfare state is more openhanded (see further below).

This chapter is a follow-up of my own previous research that can be summarized as follows (Furåker 2012). By means of data from the International Social Survey Programme (ISSP) in 2005, I found that employed persons in Denmark, Norway and Sweden had comparatively high levels of non-financial employment commitment (desire to have a job even if one does not need the money). The degree of such commitment was generally higher in these Nordic nations with their comparatively generous welfare systems than in Australia, Canada, Ireland, New Zealand, the United Kingdom and the United States, with their more parsimonious welfare schemes. Moreover, the outcome on non-financial employment commitment was slightly positively associated with employment rates. It was common that people in the Nordic countries not only stated they would like to have a job regardless of the financial compensation, it was actually also common that they had jobs.

Results of this kind no doubt have bearings on the debate on the welfare state. The picture is, however, more complicated because the Nordic countries did not keep up with the Anglo-Saxon in terms of the amount of work carried out (Furåker 2012). The general pattern was that the population's potential work effort was to a larger extent made use of in the latter than in the former countries. Hence, non-financial employment commitment correlated negatively with what I called work mobilization rates.

It was thus relevant to look for other subjective indicators in the ISSP data set. The most interesting item turned out to be a question aimed at capturing people's preferences to increase or decrease their work effort and, as a consequence thereof, to get higher or lower income. The proportion willing to work more and earn more was not that big because most respondents in all the countries included in my analysis did not express any readiness to change their work situation. Largely, however, respondents in the Anglo-Saxon cluster more often preferred to work and earn more than respondents in the Nordic. This outcome went hand in hand with the higher work mobilization rates in the latter countries.

There are now more recent ISSP data available and it is possible further to explore the topics outlined above. We have access to data from the 2015 wave, through which we may see whether the conclusions from 2005 still stand. The overall purpose of this chapter, in which six Anglo-Saxon countries—Australia, New Zealand, Britain, Ireland, Canada and the United States—and four Nordic—Denmark, Finland, Norway and Sweden—are subject to comparison, is to examine the relationship between work attitudes and levels of employment and work mobilization. The exploration also has reference to theoretical and methodological issues by questioning and elaborating our analytical tools in the field.

The chapter is organized in the following way. To begin with, I consider theoretical perspectives and previous research with relevance for my research questions. This part includes a discussion of the crucial concepts. In the next section, I present the data to be used. Information from national labour force surveys for the 10 countries under scrutiny, put together by the Organisation of Economic Co-operation and Development (OECD), is supplied: employment rates, hours worked and work mobilization. This gives us a background for the analysis of attitudes. The succeeding section examines data from the ISSP 2005 and 2015 on non-financial employment commitment and their association with employment rates and work mobilization rates. Thereafter I bring in the item on preferences regarding working time and earnings. The chapter ends with a discussion of the results and of how to understand them.

Theoretical Considerations

For several decades, social scientists have paid attention to the fact that capitalist nations are not cast in the same mould. It is indispensable to account for the existing diversity when dealing with work attitudes and phenomena such as employment rates and work efforts. Although the Anglo-Saxon and the Nordic countries all have capitalist market economies, their societal models are quite different from each other. I am concerned about whether the existing differences are related to work attitudes, employment and work mobilization and, if so, how they should be interpreted. As mentioned above, the literature contains several attempts to classify welfare state models (Esping-Andersen 1990; Castles 1993, 2004; Gallie and Paugam 2000; Korpi and Palme 1998; Korpi 2000). In spite of some divergence regarding which and how many categories can be distinguished, most of these attempts seem to have one thing in common: the Anglo-Saxon and the Nordic countries end up in separate categories because they clearly differ in terms of welfare institutions and welfare generosity.

A crucial issue is whether public support systems affect people's incentives for working and, if so, how. Critics of the welfare state commonly claim that the provision of various kinds of benefits undermines recipients' inclination to take a paid job and to contribute a substantial work effort (e.g., Lindbeck 1995, 2003). The opposite argument is that the welfare state does not have such effects or, at least, that this is not a general rule. Authors sometimes even suggest that it can be the other way around because of the so-called entitlement effect (e.g., Hamermesh 1979, 1980). There are certain mechanisms in the welfare arrangements that encourage people to put up a good work record. Such a record is advantageous when individuals want to get as much as possible out of the unemployment insurance, the sickness insurance, the pension system, etc. The rules are simply to a large extent designed to make benefits dependent on previous employment and the amount of work carried out.

The two 'families of nations' also seem to differ in another respect—namely, regarding the quality of jobs. When jobs are relatively attractive or decent, we can expect people to be more motivated to have employment and to work a great deal as well. According to some studies, in comparison with their Anglo-Saxon colleagues, job incumbents in the Nordic region generally have stronger employment protection, more task discretion or autonomy and better opportunities for training and development (e.g., Dobbin and Boychuk 1999; Esser and Olsen 2012; Gallie 2007a). These differences may be interpreted in terms of a classification of 'production regimes' or of 'employment regimes' and, again, the Anglo-Saxon and the Nordic countries fall into separate categories. In the production regime approach, the Anglo-Saxon cluster belongs to the 'liberal market economies' (LMEs) and the Nordic to the 'coordinated market economies' (CMEs); LMEs make firm activities primarily depend on market relationships, whereas in CMEs these activities are much more dependent on non-market actors (Hall and Soskice 2001). Another distinction is that between 'market employment regime' and 'inclusive employment regime' (Gallie 2007b: 16–19). The Anglo-Saxon countries come under the first category and the Nordics under the second. A decisive factor is the role ascribed to markets and organized labour respectively. If, as suggested in the literature, CMEs or the inclusive employment regimes usually provide better jobs, it is likely that, all other things being equal, people in these countries be more inclined for having paid work.

Non-financial employment commitment is a crucial concept in the current chapter. It refers to how people look at having a job irrespective of the pecuniary remunerations involved (Gallie et al. 1998: 188). To be committed to employment in this sense means to be willing to work, although one does not have to for the sake of money. The opposite is instrumentalism—that is, the attitude implying that the motive for working lies more or less exclusively in the income generated by a job. Notably, measures of non-financial employment commitment have often been made use of in assessing whether unemployed individuals are willing to work or not (Gallie and Alm 2000; Gallie et al. 1998: Chapter 7; Gallie and Vogler 1994; Hammer and Russell 2004; Nordenmark 1999). In the present analysis, however, this is not an issue to be dealt with.

As 'non-financial' employment commitment is a somewhat clumsy concept, it is now and then replaced by the shorter expression 'employment commitment'. One problem with doing this is obvious; then we have no concept left for grasping the totality of relevant motives, including also financial motives. There is a need for a broad category to cover all kinds of drives that make people engage in paid work. It appears as self-evident that the concept of employment commitment should be reserved for such a comprehensive purpose, including both financial and non-financial aspects.

Another important conceptual question is the distinction between willingness to work at all and preferences with respect to how much work to perform. In other words, it makes sense to look at both employment rates and hours worked. Social researchers sometimes have a tendency to ignore people's financial motives or to treat them as secondary, but we need an inclusive approach in examining the relationship between subjective, attitudinal information and actual employment and work efforts. Non-financial employment commitment may be a useful indicator of whether people are interested in having a paid job, but it is perhaps not the best to assess the amount of work they are prepared to carry out. There may be a need for other concepts when we want to grasp people's attitudes towards working a lot.

One significant issue is whether financial motives for working should be considered voluntary or involuntary. It has been emphasized that non-financial employment commitment entails voluntariness and consent (Gallie et al. 1998: 188). Whether this is the case is certainly not always easy to determine. Without a question, millions and millions of people throughout the world are forced to work because, literally, they cannot survive without doing it. However, in the economically advanced societies treated here it is seldom physical survival that is at stake, but rather survival at a certain standard of living—typically far above the mere subsistence level. It is simply difficult to be a citizen in these societies without adjusting to a 'normal' life. Paying for common necessities such as food, clothes and housing requires a considerable income, which is in turn often hard to get unless one has a job. We might say that this kind of necessity rules over voluntariness and the coercive mechanism consists of the pressure upon people to lead a socially passable life, which requires a certain standard of living.

Nevertheless, financial motives for working may not be due as much to necessity as to a desire to increase income for consumption. For individuals who have sufficient money to live on, it can still be very appealing to have a little more to spend. Nor do people who are unambiguously rich automatically stand free from such enticements. Sayings such as 'the more you have the more you want' and 'the appetite grows with eating' might be taken to illustrate this point; individuals with plenty of money may all the same want more to expand their consumption, sometimes perhaps merely to show that they can do what they want. More than a century ago Thorstein Veblen (1899/1953) launched the concept of conspicuous consumption, and it is definitely still a relevant notion. He also called attention to leisure as another way of demonstrating wealth and we may ask whether or to what extent this holds today.

Some Previous Research

Several studies have shown that willingness to engage in employment is at least as strong—or even stronger—in Nordic countries as in Anglo-Saxon. One of them, based on data from ISSP 1997, demonstrated that employment commitment—referring to people's non-financial motivation to have paid work—was stronger particularly in Norway, but also in Sweden, than in New Zealand, the United States and Britain (Hult and Stefan Svallfors 2002). These results spring from an analysis with controls for sex, age, social class, education and working time. Parenthetically it can be mentioned that West Germany was also included, and it came right after Sweden in the ranking on employment commitment. The most interesting for us is the comparison between the two Scandinavian and the three Anglo-Saxon countries. A main conclusion in the report is 'that fears of a comparatively generous welfare state, such as in the Scandinavian countries, undermining the work ethic are exaggerated' (Hult and Svallfors 2002: 326).

Similar results have been presented by Ingrid Esser (2005) in another cross-national comparison on employment commitment, defined in the same way as in the study just mentioned and also built on data from ISSP 1997. Esser dealt with 12 countries, including four Anglo-Saxon—Britain, Canada, New Zealand and the United States—and three Scandinavian—Denmark, Norway and Sweden. Separate analyses were run for working men and working women with controls for a large number of individual-level characteristics (Esser 2005: 75–77). Among men, all the Scandinavian countries got significantly higher scores on employment commitment than Britain and Canada, whereas the advantage over New Zealand and the United States could not be verified statistically. With the same measure applied to women, Denmark, Norway and Sweden clearly outdistanced Britain, Canada and the United States, but their lead over New Zealand remained uncertain.

In a later publication, Esser (2009) came back to these issues by analyzing data from ISSP 2005—in other words, the same data as used here. Her comparison entails non-financial employment commitment, measured in the same way as in the previous study. Amid the 13 nations included, we find the six Anglo-Saxon countries to be treated in this chapter—Australia, Britain, Canada, Ireland, New Zealand and the United States—and the same three Scandinavian countries as before—Denmark, Norway and Sweden. The results are very much in line with what we have already seen. Among both men and women, employment commitment tended to be strongest in Scandinavia. Esser also used a measure of welfare regime generosity, according to which Norway, Sweden and Denmark all scored higher than each of the countries in the Anglo-Saxon cluster did. For both men and women, this measure turned out to correlate positively with employment commitment. In a separate analysis including Norway, Britain and the United States, data from 1989, 1997 and 2005 were compared to examine whether there had been changes across time. There were no signs that employment commitment had become weaker in the country with the most generous welfare state—that is, Norway. It was rather the other way around, while the data for Britain and the United States did not reveal much change. On the basis of this study it was concluded that 'work morale cannot be described as being undermined by generous welfare states today' (Esser 2009: 98).

The results briefly presented above seem to be robust. At the same time, however, we know that people in Anglo-Saxon countries perform a great deal of labour. Employment rates are generally rather high and the same can certainly also be said about annual hours worked per employed person. In a comparison some years ago of Western labour markets, I examined cross-national differences with respect to work mobilization (for definition, see below) (Furåker 2003: 249–250). The patterns were not entirely consistent, but in 2000 all five Anglo-Saxon countries in the comparison—the United States, New Zealand, Australia, Canada and the

United Kingdom—scored higher than each of the four Nordic countries included—Denmark, Finland, Norway and Sweden. I also related work mobilization rates to a 'social protection score', based on union density, employment protection legislation, social security transfers, government employment and resources spent on active labour market policy (Furåker 2003: 242–244). For the late 1990s, all the countries in the Anglo-Saxon cluster had higher work mobilization rates than any of the Nordic countries, but all the latter had higher social protection scores.

Data and Measures

This chapter makes use of several types of empirical data. A first section presents 'objective' information, derived from labour force statistics and compiled by the OECD. The presentation includes employment rates, average annual hours worked and work mobilization rates for 2005 and 2015. Employment rates are simply the percentage of a given population in employment. They are here supplied for persons aged 15–64 and for men and women separately. Thereafter I bring up annual averages of employed persons' time spent in a paid job. These data allow us to calculate an overall measure of how much of a population's work potential that is actually utilized, what I call work mobilization rates. The concept is defined as employment rates times annual hours worked per employed individual.[1] For each country, the employment rate, expressed as a number between 1 and 0, is multiplied by the number of annual hours on average worked by the employed.

The second type of information is survey data, collected through the ISSP in 2005 and 2015, on people's attitudes and preferences regarding paid work. I use data from six Anglo-Saxon countries—Australia, Canada, Ireland, New Zealand, the United Kingdom and the United States—and four Nordic—Denmark, Finland, Norway and Sweden. All 10 participated in the survey 2005, whereas for 2015 Canada and Ireland are lacking. Moreover, in some parts of the analyses, Finland cannot be included for reasons to be clarified below. The individuals included in the analysis are employed persons aged 15–64 years. The number of respondents can be read from the tables below; as shown there are fewer respondents in 2015 than in 2005 because the number of countries is lower. For details about the surveys in the different countries, see the ISSP homepage for the respective years.

A first subjective indicator is what is usually referred to as non-financial employment commitment. It is measured by a statement that respondents were requested to agree or disagree with: 'I would enjoy having a paid job even if I did not need the money'. People were asked whether they (a) strongly agree, (b) agree, (c) neither agree nor disagree, (d) disagree, or (e) strongly disagree with this statement. It is common to build an index with the help of this item and another statement (turned in the opposite direction) that is also available in the ISSP data set: 'A job is a just way of earning money—no more' (Berglund 2012; Hult and Svallfors 2002; Esser 2005, 2009). However, like Gallie and his colleagues (1998: 188–190) I just use a single item.

The ISSP data sets also contain information on a number of other issues. One item that I find particularly interesting is a question asking whether people—compared to their present situation—would want to work (a) longer hours and earn more money; (b) work the same number of hours and earn the same; or (c) work fewer hours and earn less. It explicitly focuses on the financial consequences of a change of the amount of work people want to perform. As we shall see in the coming analyses, it is clearly relevant. In addition, a number of control variables will be included in the regressions to follow.

Employment Rates, Hours Worked and Work Mobilization Rates

As a beginning of the empirical analysis, I provide an account of employment rates, hours worked and work mobilization in the 10 selected countries (Table 5.1). In the first columns of figures, we find employment rates, referring to all persons, males and females, aged 15–64 years.

We notice that employment rates were slightly higher in 2015 than in 2005 in some of the 10 countries, but lower for men almost everywhere. Increased female figures frequently compensate for the decrease of male figures. In spite of Finland being far below the other three, the Nordic quartet scores a little higher than the Anglo-Saxon sextet. This is perhaps not surprising because the latter also has an outlier: Ireland with even lower rates than Finland.

The figures for men vary between approximately 70 and 81 percent in 2005 and 69 and 80 percent in 2015. Male employment rates tend to be higher in the Anglo-Saxon than in the Nordic countries, whereas it is the other way around in regard of female rates. Among women, figures vary between about 58 and 72 percent in 2005 and 59 and 74 percent in 2015. Three Nordic countries—Denmark, Norway and Sweden—have the female top scores both years.

The next columns show average annual hours worked per person employed. Unfortunately, the OECD does not provide this information with sex breakdown. The highest figure in 2005 is found for New Zealand with 1,815 hours, but in 2015 no nation reaches the 1,800-hour level. With three exceptions—the United Kingdom, Norway and Sweden—figures are lower in 2015 than in 2005. As we can see, the Anglo-Saxon countries score clearly higher than the Nordic both years in the table. The overriding pattern is related to the fact that females commonly have a large proportion of part-time work. Figures are also a function of other factors such as how full-time jobs are defined, the occurrence of absence from work and

Table 5.1 Employment rates, annual hours worked per person in employment and work mobilization rates in Anglo-Saxon and Nordic countries, age 15–64 years, averages 2005 and 2015

Countries	Employment rates		Male employment rates		Female employment rates		Annual hours worked per employed		Work mobilization rates	
	2005	2015	2005	2015	2005	2015	2005	2015	2005	2015
Australia	71.5	72.2	78.5	77.5	64.6	66.8	1732	1690	1238.4	1220.2
Canada	72.4	72.5	76.6	75.6	68.2	69.4	1747	1711	1264.8	1240.5
Ireland	67.6	64.8	76.9	70.3	58.3	59.4	1780	1741	1203.3	1128.2
New Zealand	74.2	74.3	81.3	79.6	67.4	69.2	1815	1757	1346.7	1305.5
UK	71.8	72.7	77.8	77.6	65.9	67.9	1673	1673	1201.2	1216.3
US	71.5	68.7	77.6	74.2	65.6	63.4	1794	1785	1282.7	1226.3
Denmark	75.9	73.5	79.9	76.6	71.9	70.4	1451	1407	1101.3	1034.1
Finland	68.4	68.6	70.3	69.3	66.6	67.7	1697	1637	1160.7	1123.0
Norway	74.8	74.8	77.9	76.5	71.8	73.0	1423	1424	1064.4	1065.2
Sweden	72.3	75.5	74.3	77.0	70.2	74.0	1605	1610	1160.4	1215.6
Families of nations										
Anglo-Saxon[a]	71.5	70.9	78.1	75.8	65.0	66.0	1757	1726	1256.3	1223.7
Nordic[a]	72.9	73.1	75.6	74.9	70.1	71.3	1544	1520	1125.6	1111.1

Source: OECD

[a] Unweighted means

the existence of overtime. Denmark and Norway take turns to show by far the lowest number of hours worked per person in employment.

Finally, we arrive at the work mobilization rates that represent the most all-embracing measure in the table. In 2005, all the Anglo-Saxon countries score higher than each of the countries in the Nordic cluster does, and the same would hold for 2015 had there not been one exception—Sweden shows a higher figure than Ireland that year. Besides, Finland is rather close to the Irish level and Sweden is close to the United Kingdom. New Zealand has the highest work mobilization rate both years, followed by the United States (2005) and Canada (2015). Denmark and Norway alternately have the lowest levels of all.

To summarize, the general pattern is that employment rates are slightly higher in the Nordic region than in the Anglo-Saxon area. In terms of average number of hours worked per person and work mobilization it is contrariwise. The main explanation as to why the Nordic countries score higher on total employment rates is that women to a larger extent have jobs. At the same time, the average numbers of annual hours worked are negatively affected. Counting these numbers, several factors need to be considered: the patterns of part-time working, the length of a normal working day, the occurrence of absence from work, the prevalence of overtime, etc. Overall, with respect to work mobilization rates, the Anglo-Saxon countries outdo the Nordics. In the next step, we turn to data on attitudes, asking whether they are related to the outcomes uncovered.

Non-Financial Employment Commitment

From the two ISSP data sets, we can make a comparison of non-financial employment commitment measured as defined above. Finland is not included in this analysis, simply because its figures are so much lower than in any of the other countries that one must suspect some problem with the translation of the questionnaire.[2] Moreover, regrettably, in 2015 neither Canada nor Ireland took part in the survey, which means that we have only seven countries this year. Table 5.2 shows the results that can be used.

Respondents commonly agree (strongly agree or agree) that they would like to have a paid job even if they did not need the money. In 2005, five countries (Ireland, New Zealand and the three Nordic countries) show proportions agreeing of 70 percent or more, with Norway at the top. Among the remaining countries, there is a notably low figure for the United Kingdom. We also find a difference between the two families of nations. In 2015, scores are in most cases higher and none of them is below 70 percent. Additionally, the difference between the two country clusters is smaller.

To look more carefully at the country differences, binary logistic regressions have been run with controls for sex, age, socioeconomic category and working time (Table 5.3). With Norway as the reference category, in

Table 5.2 Proportions agreeing that they would enjoy a job even if they did not need the money ('non-financial employment commitment') in Anglo-Saxon and Nordic countries, 2005 and 2015, percentages

Countries	2005	2015
Australia	64.7	73.6
Canada	66.0	n.a.
Ireland	72.4	n.a.
New Zealand	73.6	70.1
UK	56.4	70.0
US	67.7	71.6
Denmark	77.9	74.8
Norway	80.4	81.9
Sweden	70.9	74.2
Families of nations		
Anglo-Saxon	67.2	71.3
Nordic	76.5	77.6
n	7,385	6,459

Source: ISSP

Table 5.3 Country differences regarding non-financial employment commitment. Controlled for sex, age, socioeconomic category and working time. Logistic regression, odds ratios

Countries	2005		2015	
	Model 1	Model 2	Model 1	Model 2
Australia	.41***		.71**	
Canada	.42****			
Ireland	.63***			
New Zealand	.64***		.52***	
UK	.30***		.49***	
US	.50***		.54***	
Denmark	.96		.72*	
Norway (ref.)	1		1	
Sweden	.62***		.62***	
Family of nations				
Anglo-Saxon		.56***		.71***
Nordic (ref.)		1		1
Nagelkerke R²	.07	.06	.05	.04
Constant	4.45 ***	3.73***	6.66***	5.09***
n	6,850		4,582	

Source: ISSP

Levels of significance: * = p < .05; ** = p < .01; *** = p < .001

both 2005 and 2015 all Anglo-Saxon countries have clearly lower coefficients. This is also true for Sweden both years and for Denmark in 2015. Model 2 shows that the Anglo-Saxon cluster as a whole scores distinctly below the Nordic, of course partly due to the high Norwegian figures. We should recall, though, from Table 5.2 that both Denmark and Sweden have relatively high scores.

Regarding the results on the control variables, I will not to go into the details but just mention a few things. Non-financial employment commitment is particularly salient among women and the youngest respondents. Compared to people in manual occupations this also holds for managers, professionals, semi-professionals and service workers.

In Figure 5.1, the data on non-financial employment commitment for 2005 and 2015 are plotted against one of our objective measures: employment rates. Again, unfortunately, data are not available for Finland any of the years or for Canada and Ireland in 2015. As a consequence, the first diagram includes nine countries and the second only seven. There is a positive correlation between the two variables both years, but it is weak (R^2 = .20 and .16 respectively). Still, in 2005, Denmark and Norway—together with New Zealand and if we are generous also Sweden—are located in the upper, right-hand fourth of the diagram. These four countries thus score high on both indicators. Taking into account that the scale on the Y-axis starts higher up in 2015, we see that the pattern that year is not very different, at least not with respect to the three Nordic countries. The associations between non-financial employment commitment and employment rates are certainly not very strong, but there is not much to indicate that the pattern has changed over the 10-year period between the surveys.

However, we should not mix up employment rates with the amount of work that people carry out. People may have a job but still work relatively little; they can have part-time contracts or high levels of absence due to sickness, parental leave or other circumstances. As we have seen above, in terms of work mobilization rates the Anglo-Saxon countries surpass the Nordics. For some forms of non-attendance in the workplace welfare state provisions may be highly important as much as they allow people to stay away from their job without too severe income losses.

Figure 5.2 shows scatter plots with non-financial employment commitment on the Y-axis and work mobilization rates on the X-axis. For both years, the two variables are correlated, but this time, in contrast to what the previous figures show, negatively correlated. The 2015 association is stronger than the one for 2005 (R^2 = .64 compared to .37). The Nordic countries have rather high scores on non-financial employment commitment, but their work mobilization rates do not correspond to this outcome.

Non-financial employment commitment is thus positively related to employment rates and negatively related to work mobilization rates. We

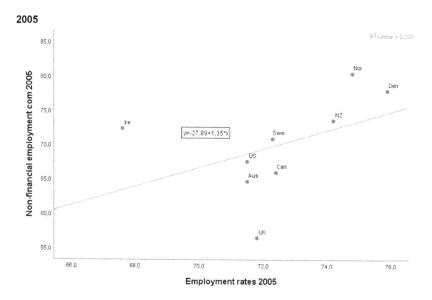

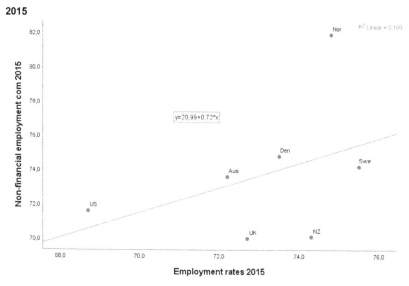

Figure 5.1 Relationship between non-financial employment commitment and employment rates in Anglo-Saxon and Nordic countries, 2005 and 2015

Sources: OECD and ISSP

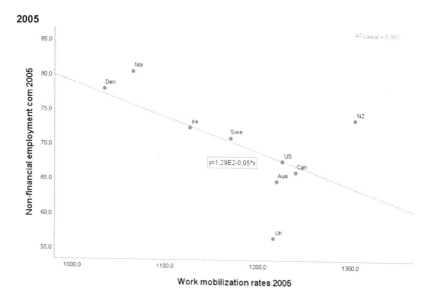

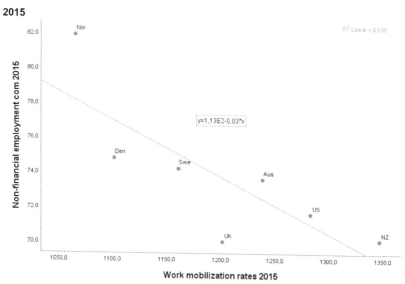

Figure 5.2 Relationship between non-financial employment commitment and work mobilization rates in Anglo-Saxon and Nordic countries, 2005 and 2015

Sources: OECD and ISSP

must ask how these outcomes can be interpreted. Evidently, a generous welfare state does not have to be an obstacle to either non-financial employment commitment or high employment rates, but substituting the latter aspect for amount of work carried out we find a different pattern.

Asking whether or to what extent people are motivated to engage in paid work, we should not merely focus on the notion of non-financial employment commitment but rather on a wider concept. Such an approach to people's willingness to work requires that financial motives are taken into account. As mentioned above, there is a question in the ISSP data sets on whether or not people prefer to change (increase or decrease) their working hours and accordingly their earnings. This item is helpful, but it could be worthwhile to develop further questions—or batteries of questions—to remedy the relative neglect of financial motives in many social science analyses. For the current inquiry, we must stick to what is available in the ISSP data sets.

Preferences about Working More/Less and Earning More/Less

As in the previous section, I start with a cross-national description of the outcome regarding one of the questions in the ISSP surveys. The item behind Table 5.4 explicitly includes the pecuniary consequences of

Table 5.4 Preferences as regards to working more/earning more and working less/earning less in Anglo-Saxon and Nordic countries, 2005 and 2015, percentages

Countries	Prefer to work more and earn more		Prefer to work less and earn less	
	2005	2015	2005	2015
Australia	23.0	26.6	10.8	7.2
Canada	22.7	n.a.	11.8	n.a.
Ireland	22.2	n.a.	9.1	n.a.
New Zealand	23.9	28.9	8.6	6.2
UK	21.7	29.0	7.6	8.9
US	32.2	38.4	5.9	4.4
Denmark	8.4	17.5	16.8	9.1
Finland	14.3	17.9	14.3	9.0
Norway	12.7	16.0	11.3	7.6
Sweden	17.2	13.8	13.9	15.6
Families of nations				
Anglo-Saxon	25.0	31.3	8.9	6.7
Nordic	12.7	16.3	14.3	10.0

Source: ISSP

Note: n = 7,673 in 2005 and 5,872 in 2015

changes in working time. This time we have access to Finnish data, which means that 10 countries are included in the first of the two surveys and eight in the second.

A majority in all the countries have answered that they want to work the same as at the time of investigation. To be sparse with numbers, this answer is excluded in the table that merely focuses on the two possibilities for change. The proportion stating that they prefer to work longer hours and earn more money is considerably higher in the Anglo-Saxon than in the Nordic countries, both in 2005 and 2015. We find the clearly highest proportions for the United States, whereas Denmark has by far the lowest score in the table (2005). The averages for the Anglo-Saxon cluster are almost twice as high as for the Nordic countries.

There are not that many respondents who want to work less and earn less. In this regard, the differences between the country clusters are also smaller than with respect to working more and earning more, but the proportions are generally higher in the Nordic countries than in the Anglo-Saxon, although the cross-national differences show some variation. I have run logistic regressions to explore whether the cross-national differences remain when we control for sex, age, socioeconomic category and working time. Table 5.5 gives the results for the countries included. In 2005, Australia, Canada, New Zealand, the United Kingdom, the

Table 5.5 Country differences regarding preference to work more and earn more. Controlled for sex, age, socioeconomic category and working time. Logistic regression, odds ratios

Countries	2005		2015	
	Model 1	Model 2	Model 1	Model 2
Australia	1.71***		1.54**	
Canada	1.81***			
Ireland	1.32			
New Zealand	1.81***		1.82***	
UK	1.50*		1.61***	
US	2.61***		2.70***	
Denmark	.60**		.97	
Finland	1.03		1.03	
Norway (ref.)	1		1	
Sweden	1.35*		.84	
Family of nations				
Anglo-Saxon		1.93***		1.99***
Nordic (ref.)		1		1
Nagelkerke R^2	.12	.11	.13	.12
Constant	.14***	.13***	.15***	.16***
n	7,114		4,989	

Source: ISSP

Levels of significance: * = p < .05; ** = p <. 01; *** = p < .001

United States but also Sweden score clearly higher than Norway (the reference category in Model 1). The outcome for Ireland points in the same direction but is not statistically significant (albeit almost). In contrast to these outcomes, Denmark turns out to have an exceptionally low score. Finally, the Anglo-Saxon cluster has a distinctly higher coefficient than the Nordic (Model 2) regarding willingness to work more and earn more.

The results for 2015 are quite similar in certain respects. The four Anglo-Saxon countries all have significantly higher odds ratios than Norway (Model 1), while no important differences can be discovered across the four Nordic nations. As a consequence, we must expect a noticeably higher odds ratio for the Anglo-Saxon cluster than for the Nordic, and this is corroborated in Model 2.

As to control variables, a few results can be brought up. Males tend to be more willing than females to increase their work effort in order to earn more. Age is a significant factor as well. Compared to the oldest category, all other respondents—and in particular the youngest—are more inclined to choose the work more-earn more option. This option is distinctly less often selected by managers, professionals and semi-professionals in comparison with manual workers (the reference category).

Continuing with the analysis of preference to work more and earn more, we can now examine how it correlates with work mobilization rates (Figure 5.3). As can be seen, the correlations are quite strong: $R^2 = .64$ and $.62$ for the respective years. In 2005, the Anglo-Saxon nations are mainly placed in the upper right-hand part of the diagram, but Ireland is somewhat of an exception. Three of the Nordic countries appear in the lower left-hand quarter of the figure, whereas Sweden is more in the middle. The gap between the Nordic and the Anglo-Saxon clusters is even more marked in 2015. All the four Nordic countries are in the lower left-hand corner of the diagram and all the then four Anglo-Saxon countries are higher up and further to the right, without being very close to one another. The United States is rather remote from the fit line, both in 2005 and in 2015, because the proportion of American respondents answering that they want to work more and earn more is particularly high, while the work mobilization rates are not the highest.

In other words, in countries with high work mobilization rates respondents are more likely to answer that they want to work more in order to earn more. This variable, which explicitly includes financial motives, is positively correlated—and quite strongly so—to the measure of work mobilization, while non-financial employment commitment is negatively linked to that measure.

2005

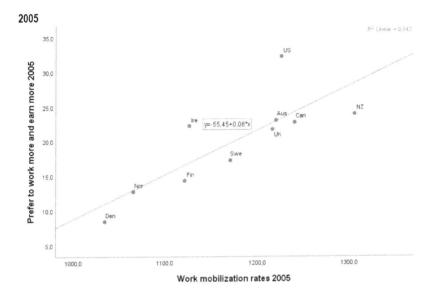

2015

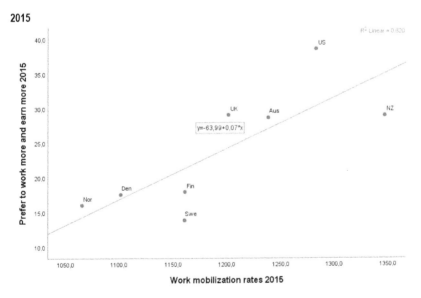

Figure 5.3 Relationship between preference to work more and earn more and work mobilization rates in Anglo-Saxon and Nordic countries, 2005 and 2015

Sources: OECD and ISSP

Concluding Discussion

A main conclusion from the above analysis is that, from 2005 to 2015, there has not been much change in the patterns under scrutiny. Overall, the results from my previous study (Furåker 2012) remain. The level of non-financial employment commitment tends to be higher in Nordic countries than in the Anglo-Saxon cluster. The least one can say is that willingness to take a paid job is definitely not lower in the former nations with their relatively generous welfare state arrangements than in the latter nations with their more limited welfare systems. This outcome holds for both 2005 and 2015 and it is in agreement with previous studies (Esser 2005, 2009; Hult and Svallfors 2002). Moreover, the association between non-financial employment commitment and employment rates is positive, although rather weak, in both of the surveys. People in the Nordic region do not only express a non-financial employment commitment, they are to a relatively great degree involved in work as well. We should observe that women tend to score higher on non-financial employment commitment and that female employment rates are higher in Denmark, Norway and Sweden, which is the reason why those countries have higher total employment rates than most of the Anglo-Saxon countries.

However, as emphasized several times in this chapter, we should not confuse employment rates with the amount of work that people actually carry out. People may have a job but still work relatively little. The explanation can be that they have part-time contracts or high levels of absence due to sickness, parental leave or other circumstances. Working hours can also be more or less strictly regulated through collective agreements or by law, for example, when it comes to statutory paid holidays. In terms of work mobilization rates, the Anglo-Saxon countries as a rule surpass the Nordic—and non-financial employment commitment is negatively linked to this indicator. For some forms of non-attendance in the workplace, welfare state provisions can be assumed to be highly important as much as they allow people to keep away from their job without very significant impact on their purchasing power. For example, a generous parental insurance gives parents, or at least one of them, the opportunity to stay home from work with their small children, while retaining some income.

Because non-financial employment commitment turned out to be negatively related to work mobilization rates, I directed my attention to other subjective items in the ISSP data set. The most interesting item is then a question aimed at capturing people's willingness to increase or decrease their work effort and accordingly their income. It is found to be rather strongly correlated with work mobilization rates. The proportion choosing the option work more and earn more is not very big, since most respondents want to keep their working hours and income as they are. Largely, however, compared to the Nordic quartet, the Anglo-Saxon cluster has higher proportions that prefer to work and earn more. This outcome goes hand in hand with the higher work mobilization rates in the latter.

Why are employees in the Anglo-Saxon countries to a larger extent willing to work and earn more? A possible explanation is that people in the market-oriented Anglo-Saxon world are more heavily dependent on a paid job. There is relatively little that they can get from other sources, unless they receive dividends from private property or the like. Among other things, their consumption of services relies to a greater degree on what is available in the market. To have a private nanny is a more common solution in the Anglo-Saxon countries. The public support systems in case of sickness, disabilities, unemployment, etc., are also generally weaker. Poverty rates tend to be rather high, and large segments of the population with low income need to work a great deal to have some minimum standard of living. It is difficult to avoid the costs for food, clothes, housing, transportation and other weighty needs. There are vivid stories describing how low-income earners sometimes must even have two jobs to keep their nose above the water surface (Ehrenreich 2002).

There is another possible interpretation of people's answer that they want to work longer hours and increase their income, fully compatible with the above. It emphasizes that individuals wish to improve their standard of living. Realizing that this can be done by an increased work effort, they may develop a positive attitude to supplying more of their time for the labour market. There are indeed many, probably often tempting, ways of using some extra money. The market constantly provides new things to buy, not only in the more fashion-oriented segments, but throughout. Some may just want to work more so that they can buy more or better goods and services. Such an attitude is perhaps sometimes a corollary of necessity, but we should not exclude that it is based on voluntariness.

Asking whether and to what extent people are motivated to engage in paid work, we should not merely focus on the notion of non-financial employment commitment. We need to have a broader approach to people's willingness to work and it requires that financial motives are taken into account. This is not to say that the work more and earn more question in the ISSP surveys is the final solution for that purpose. It is undoubtedly desirable if we could also develop other questions—or batteries of questions—to remedy the relative neglect of a financial dimension in many social science accounts.

Notes

1. In my previous analyses (Furåker 2003, 2012), I assumed that each individual could contribute 40 hours per week during 50 weeks; in view of that a full annual effort would be 2,000 hours. These assumptions were of course somewhat arbitrary; instead, we might, for example, suppose that people work 45 hours per week during 52 weeks (no vacation). This time, I do not worry about what a full annual work effort could be but choose a simpler measure. The idea is, after all, just to take into account the degree to which

the population is gainfully employed and how much work (in hours) each employed individual does.
2. A Finnish-speaking colleague pointed out that the word *enjoy* has been given a translation that makes it difficult for Finns to agree with the statement.

References

Berglund, T. (2012) 'Work Orientations in Western Europe and the United States', 47–66, in B. Furåker, K. Håkansson and J. C. Karlsson (eds) *Commitment to Work and Job Satisfaction*. London: Routledge.

Castles, F. G. (ed.) (1993) *Families of Nations: Patterns of Public Policy in Western Democracies*. Aldershot: Dartmouth.

Castles, F. G. (2004) *The Future of the Welfare State: Crisis Myths and Crisis Realities*. Oxford: Oxford University Press.

Dobbin, F. and T. Boychuk (1999) 'National Employment Systems and Job Autonomy: Why Job Autonomy Is High in the Nordic Countries and Low in the United States, Canada and Australia.' *Organizations Studies* 20(2): 257–291.

Ehrenreich, B. (2002) *Nickel and Dimed: On (Not) Getting By in America*. New York: Henry Holt and Company.

Esping-Andersen, G. (1990) *The Three Worlds of Welfare Capitalism*. Princeton, NJ: Princeton University Press.

Esser, I. (2005) *Why Work? Comparative Studies on Welfare Regimes and Individuals' Work Orientations*. Stockholm: Stockholm University, Swedish Institute for Social Research.

Esser, I. (2009) 'Has Welfare Made us Lazy? Employment Commitment in Different Welfare States', 79–105, in A. Park, J. Curtice, K. Thomson, M. Philips and E. Clery (eds) *British Social Attitudes: The 25th Report*. London: Sage.

Esser, I. and K. M. Olsen (2012) 'Perceived Job Quality: Autonomy and Job Security Within a Multi-Level Framework.' *European Sociological Review* 28(4): 443–454.

Furåker, B. (2003) 'Post-Industrial Profiles: North American, Scandinavian and Other Western Labour Markets', 241–261, in T. P. Boje and B. Furåker (eds) *Post-Industrial Labour Markets. Profiles of North America and Scandinavia*. London: Routledge.

Furåker, B. (2012) 'Work Attitudes, Employment and Work Mobilization: A Comparison Between Anglo-Saxon and Nordic Countries', 67–85, in B. Furåker, K. Håkansson and J. C. Karlsson (eds) *Commitment to Work and Job Satisfaction*. New York, London Routledge.

Gallie, D. (ed.) (2007a) *Employment Regimes and the Quality of Work*. Oxford: Oxford University Press.

Gallie, D. (2007b) 'Production Regimes, Employment Regimes, and the Quality of Work', 1–33, in Gallie (2007a), op. cit.

Gallie, D. and S. Alm (2000) 'Unemployment, Gender and Attitudes to Work', 109–133, in Gallie and Paugam, op.cit.

Gallie, D. and C. Vogler (1994) 'Unemployment and Attitudes to Work', 115–153, in D. Gallie, C. Marsh and C. Vogler (eds) *Social Change and the Experience of Unemployment*. Oxford: Oxford University Press.

Gallie, D. and S. Paugam (eds) (2000) *Welfare Regimes and the Experience of Unemployment in Europe*. Oxford: Oxford University Press.

Gallie, D., M. White, Y. Cheng and M. Tomlinson (1998) *Restructuring the Employment Relationship*. Oxford: Oxford University Press.

Hall, P. A. and D. Soskice (2001) 'An Introduction to Varieties of Capitalism', 1–68, in P. A. Hall and D. Soskice (eds) *Varieties of Capitalism. The Institutional Foundations of Comparative Advantage*. Oxford: Oxford University Press.

Hamermesh, D. S. (1979) 'Entitlement Effects, Unemployment Insurance and Unemployment Spells.' *Economic Inquiry* 17(3): 317–332.

Hamermesh, D. S. (1980) 'Unemployment Insurance and Labor Supply.' *International Economic Review* 21: 517–527.

Hammer, T. and H. Russell (2004) 'Gender Differences in Employment Commitment Among Unemployed Youth', 81–104, in D. Gallie (ed.) *Resisting Marginalization. Unemployment Experience and Social Policy in the European Union*. Oxford: Oxford University Press.

Hult, C. and S. Svallfors (2002) 'Production Regimes and Work Orientations: A Comparison of Six Western Countries.' *European Sociological Review* 18(3): 315–331.

ISSP (International Social Survey Programme) (2005, 2015) Work Orientations III and IV. Köln: GESIS—Leibniz-Institut für Sozialwissenschaften.

Korpi, W. (2000) 'Faces of Inequality: Gender, Class, and Patterns of Inequalities in Different Types of Welfare States.' *Social Politics* 7(2): 127–191.

Korpi, W. and J. Palme (1998) 'The Paradox of Redistribution and the Strategy of Equality: Welfare State Institutions, Inequality and Poverty in the Western Countries.' *American Sociological Review* 63(5): 661–687.

Lindbeck, A. (1995) 'Welfare State Disincentives with Endogeneous Habits and Norms.' *Scandinavian Journal of Economics* 97(4): 477–494.

Lindbeck, A. (2003) *An Essay on Welfare State Dynamics*. Stockholm University: Institute for International Economic Studies. Published in CESifo Working Paper Series. No. 976.

Nordenmark, M. (1999) *Unemployment, Employment Commitment and Well-Being. The Psychosocial Meaning of (Un)employment Among Women and Men*. Umeå: Umeå University, Department of Sociology.

OECD Database. https://data.oecd.org/.

Veblen, T. (1953/1899) *The Theory of the Leisure Class. An Economic Study of Institutions*. New York: Mentor Books.

6 Organizational Commitment
Cross-National Differences and Work-Related Factors

Bengt Furåker and Kristina Håkansson

Introduction

Organizational commitment is a matter of the bonds between employees and their workplace and employer. It implies that people are supportive of and loyal to their employing organization. Accordingly, employers may have a kind of immaterial asset at their disposal. It is likely that good employment and working conditions help to increase the degree of employees' organizational commitment, but we must be aware that there is often a trade-off in this respect. Employers, for their part, may have good reasons to make improvements for their employees, but improvements are frequently associated with costs, although sometimes win-win solutions can be found. Employees can no doubt benefit from being loyal to their work organization, if such a stance leads to better treatment by the employer. However, loyalty may also breed silence, preventing employees from putting forward demands that might be important for them.

Most studies of employees' organizational commitment have been conducted in North America, but some research involves other countries, showing similarities and differences across nations (e.g., Hattrup, Mueller and Aguirre 2008; Kirkman and Shapiro 2001; Lincoln and Kalleberg 1985, 1990; Luthans, McCaul and Dodd1985; Randall 1993; Sommer, Bae and Luthans 1996; Turunen 2011). Part of the research examines the role of work-related attributes, but often very different indicators are used. Another limitation is that many studies just involve one or a few countries. Our cross-national comparison covers 17 economically developed countries, which were included in the same survey waves in 2005 and in 2015. A crucial question is whether national differences disappear, or are at least clearly reduced, when data on the same work-related characteristics are controlled for. In addition, we wish further to explore and specify the impact of various work-related factors, also including some which have previously been considered very little or not at all. Besides this, the inclusion of two surveys—with 10 years in between—provides an opportunity to examine whether patterns are stable or not across time.

The Concept of Organizational Commitment

Organizational commitment is an established concept in the sociological and psychological literature (e.g., Allen and Meyer 1990; Gallie et al. 1998: Chapter 9; Meyer and Allen 1997; Mowday 1998; Mowday, Porter and Steers 1982; Mowday, Steers and Porter 1979; Porter et al. 1974). It may refer to different spheres of life, but in working life it is about the ties between employees and their work organizations. Some authors have used different terms for approximately the same phenomena. In a well-known book, Albert Hirschman (1970) discusses the relationship between exit, voice and loyalty. The main idea is that people can act in two different ways if they are dissatisfied with an organization (to which the individual has a relation as an employee, as a consumer or otherwise): they can exit or they can raise their voice—complain or protest. Their reactions are to some extent affected by their feelings of loyalty. If people are sufficiently dedicated to the organization they are likely to resort to voice rather than to exit, and this option is facilitated if they believe that improvements are possible and worth the effort. Hirschman (1970:75) even uses the term 'organizational loyalty' which more or less sounds like organizational commitment. A similar concept is organizational identification. It has been treated in different ways (for an overview see Riketta 2005). One of the definitions is that it refers to solidarity with and support for an organization as well as to feelings of fellowship with other members of it (Patchen 1970: 155). This is indeed close to how the concept of organizational commitment is usually understood.

An early interpretation of the concept of organizational commitment is that it involves three dimensions. The first of these means that people have 'a strong belief in and acceptance of the organization's goals and values'; the second that they are willing 'to exert considerable effort on behalf of the organization'; and the third that they have 'a definite desire to maintain organizational membership' (Porter et al. 1974: 604). This definition is a starting point for a great deal of the discussion in the literature on organizational commitment. It is also the point of departure for the Organizational Commitment Questionnaire (OCQ) (Mowday, Steers and Porter 1979).

Natalie Allen and John Meyer (1990) provide an elaborated definition of organizational commitment (cf. also Meyer and Allen 1991, 1997; Meyer et al. 2002). They point out that the nature of the link between employees and their employing organization can be of different kinds: 'Employees with strong affective commitment remain in the organization because they *want* to, those with strong continuance commitment because they *need* to, and those with strong normative commitment because they feel they *ought* to do so' (Allen and Meyer 1990: 3). Accordingly, the first subcategory is *affective commitment*, based on the assumption that emotional ties are important. People are committed to the organization because they like it and identify with it. The second subcategory, *continuance commitment*, focuses on the instrumental motives which may be involved. The idea is that people remain with an organization as long as they have something to gain from it. Exiting is associated with costs and existing alternatives may not be sufficiently attractive to be worth leaving for. For example, if employees have acquired company-specific skills and are rewarded for this, they have an incentive to stay in the workplace, as long as these skills are not transferable to other workplaces. The third category is *normative commitment*. It covers feelings of obligation to the organization, which may have to do with tradition as well as with personal ties with workmates and management. This classification into three categories has gained much attention among researchers in the field.

Yet another classification is found in the work that Duncan Gallie and his collaborators (1998: 237–239) have done on data from the Employment in Britain Survey. Using six questions from the OCQ, they identify *effort, flexibility* and *value commitment*. One of the OCQ items refers to people's readiness to work harder than necessary to help the organization succeed and this is the basis for singling out effort commitment. The second category is relevant when employees 'express a willingness to be flexible to the point of some personal sacrifice' (Gallie et al. 1998: 238). It is labelled *flexibility commitment* and is empirically built on employees' declarations that they would take almost any job to keep working for the organization and that they would consequently turn down an offer of a better-paid job. Finally, value commitment implies identification with the organization and its values.

Another distinction comes from a Swedish survey study of how job insecurity influences organizational commitment (Furåker and Berglund 2014). The dataset includes six items—in practice the same as those used by Gallie et al. (1998: 237–238). A principal component analysis generated two factors that were labelled *value commitment* and *willingness to stay* respectively. The first of these embraces both the value and the effort items in Gallie and his co-authors' analysis, as they turned out to be quite strongly correlated with one another. The second factor is about readiness to remain with the employing organization, thus coinciding with the Gallie teams' category of 'flexibility commitment'. In order to emphasize people's willingness to keep working for the organization the above label was preferred.

As pointed out in Chapter 2, commitment at work does not have to be about the employing organization as such but can be related to actors or phenomena connected with it (e.g., Fukami and Larson 1984; Meyer and Allen 1997; Reichers 1985; Wallace 1993). One example is provided in a British study of workplaces in the 'new economy', showing that employees' commitment to colleagues and to customers exceeded their commitment to the employer (Baldry et al. 2007: 99–103). In the case of temporary agency work, there is the question whether employees feel stronger commitment to the user firm than to the agency or vice versa (Håkansson and Isidorsson 2012; see also Chapter 7 in this book). We should thus be aware that there can be multiple and even competing loyalties in a workplace.

Theoretical and Empirical Starting Points

The exchange between an employer and employees can be described as an issue of quid pro quo (Parsons and Smelser 1956: 105). Employees are supposed to do something for the employer and they are paid for it. This exchange needs to be specified in several ways—for example, in terms of working hours or the quality of the performance or the produce. Employees receive payment and the level of compensation is not given; in a 'free' labour market, it is negotiable no matter whether trade unions are involved or not. In addition, there is a whole range of other employment and working conditions that are part of the exchange. Generally, we can suppose that all circumstances characterizing the exchange with the employer affect employees' commitment to their work organization. Hence, if there is little for employees to complain about—because pay is satisfactory, management is fair, job security is adequate, working conditions are decent, etc.—we can expect them to have a positive attitude and loyalty to their organization. This is particularly likely to be the case if comparisons with other workplaces fall out well and/or the possibilities to move to other workplaces are small, say due to limited demand for labour.

There are many studies of the relationship between job quality, or job properties, and organizational commitment (e.g., Allen and Meyer 1990; Lincoln and Kalleberg 1985, 1990; Pentareddy and Suganthi 2015; Randall 1993; Riketta 2005; Steers 1977; Welsch and LaVan 1981). Typically, they include rather different work-related variables. In the following, we provide some examples from the literature. Besides a personal characteristics scale, Richard Steers (1977: 49–50) utilized two different scales measuring work features (inspired by Hackman and Lawler 1971 and Buchanan 1974 respectively) as independent variables in his analysis of organizational commitment among hospital employees and scientists and engineers. The first is called job characteristics, measuring autonomy, variety, feedback, task identity and the opportunity for employees to develop close friendships at work. The second scale refers to work experiences and contains four dimensions: group attitudes to the organization; the degree to which the job meets respondents' expectations; views on one's personal importance to the organization; and the degree to which the organization is considered reliable in fulfilling its commitments to employees. Both these measures were strongly associated with organizational commitment and the association was especially strong for the work experience dimension.

In a survey of more than 8,000 employees in nearly 100 plants in Japan and the United States, James Lincoln and Arne Kalleberg (1985, 1990) identified several work-related variables. The main purpose of the study was to examine differences in organizational commitment (gauged by six QOC items) between workers in the two countries. It turned out to be less clear than might be expected that organizational commitment was greater in Japan. Some careful sifting of the data was required before this could be concluded.

Certain factors linked to the job came out as important for organizational commitment in Lincoln and Kalleberg's comparison. Having a position such as manager or supervisor had a clear impact. This is altogether in line with expectations. Managers and people in supervising positions are likely to be more inclined than others to be supportive and loyal to their organization, not least because they often have various kinds of privilege—for example, in terms of pay. In an analysis of the role of managers and supervisors in class relations, Erik Olin Wright (1997: 20–22) has given these privileged earnings a name: 'loyalty rent'. It is supposed to be a reward for being loyal to the employing organization.

In contrast to the outcomes for managers and supervisors, Lincoln and Kalleberg (1985) found little influence of employee tenure, which was perhaps more surprising as we might believe that remaining longer in an organization would be associated with a higher degree of commitment to it. However, age had significant effects and it turned out to be more important in Japan. A meta-analysis of a large number of previous studies, including data from 155 independent samples and more than 50,000 employees, showed that tenure and age correlated positively, but only weakly, with all three dimensions of organizational commitment identified above: affective, continuance and normative (Meyer et al. 2002). A noteworthy result in the latter investigation is the strong positive association between occupational commitment and affective commitment. Other researchers have pointed to a potential conflict between the two (e.g., Wallace 1993), but although the possibility of such conflicts should not be excluded, this result suggests that they are not so common (Meyer et al. 2002: 38).

Coming back to Lincoln and Kalleberg's (1985, 1990) study, we can highlight its conclusions that decentralized, participatory decision-making enhanced organizational commitment in both countries and that Japanese plants had a higher degree of participatory decision-making. It is also worth noting the impact of welfare services sponsored by the employer. Such arrangements were more common in Japan and they were positively associated with organizational commitment.

Some studies have examined the links between sectors of employment and organizational commitment. Despite somewhat disparate results, it appears that public sector employees often show lower levels of organizational commitment than private sector employees (Buelens and Van den

Broek 2007; Goulet and Frank 2002; Zeffane 1994). This holds also in comparison with nonprofit organizations.

A relatively recent study of knowledge workers in Australia, India, Singapore and the United States investigated the relationship between job characteristics and affective organizational commitment and how it is mediated through leadership complexity (or, more simply, leaders' abilities to handle competing demands) and psychological empowerment (Pentareddy and Suganthi 2015). The analysis included a scale based on four job traits: skill variety, task identity, task significance and feedback (as identified by Hackman and Oldham 1975 and 1976, but a fifth dimension, autonomy, was excluded because it was part of the other mediating measure). Psychological empowerment was assessed through a loan from the literature covering four aspects: meaning, competence, self-determination and impact (Spreitzer 1995). A major conclusion from the analysis is that both the mediating factors, leadership complexity and psychological empowerment of employees, contribute to making the influence of good job properties on affective commitment stronger (Pentareddy and Suganthi 2015: 316).

Job satisfaction is another relevant element in relation to organizational commitment. Past research has demonstrated rather strong correlations between the two. The meta-analysis by John Meyer and his colleagues (2002) revealed that overall job satisfaction is strongly correlated with affective organizational commitment. Similarly, Furåker and Berglund's (2014) survey mentioned above also shows clears links between overall job satisfaction and the two dimensions value commitment and willingness to stay. It is possible that the causal connection goes in both directions. Higher job satisfaction may lead to stronger organizational commitment, but strong commitment may also boost satisfaction. There has been some debate around the issue of causality (cf. Meyer 1997).

Conflicts regarding work roles may be coupled with the relationship between management and employees. Good relations of that kind are likely to make employees more inclined to be positive and loyal to their work organization. It is consequently an aspect that can enhance organizational commitment. In this context, the influence of trade unions should be considered. Lincoln and Kalleberg (1985) suggested that unionization could lead to an aggregation of grievances, thus creating a more adversarial workplace climate. Unions may present conflict-laden requirements to management, thereby maintaining or even sharpening a tense work environment. It was assumed that there might be a difference between the United States and Japan in this respect. The reason would be that unionism in Japan can be seen as a corporatist control structure, contributing positively to the performance of the company. Data indicated that the relationship between unionism and organizational commitment was negative in both countries, but more strongly so in the United States. A comparison between six countries—New Zealand, the

United States, Great Britain, West Germany, Norway and Sweden—by means of data from the 1997 International Social Survey Programme (ISSP) showed that the United States followed by New Zealand got the highest score on organizational commitment and Sweden the lowest just before West Germany (Hult and Svallfors 2002). Data were controlled for sex, age, education, social class and working time. It was suggested that the cross-national differences could have something to do with the strength of trade unions, as organizational commitment is about accepting employers' goals and approaches.

Worry about losing one's job is another subjective element to be taken into account. One interesting outcome in Gallie and his co-workers' study (1998: 244–245) is that fearing (unreasonable) dismissal was associated with higher flexibility and effort commitment among social sector employees. These findings fit in with Swedish results, disclosing that worry about losing one's job was strongly correlated with value commitment and willingness to stay (Furåker and Berglund 2014). Gallie and his team (1998: 244–245) proposed that being anxious about a job loss makes employees value their current job more, and hence they become more closely attached to their work organization (cf. also Bjarnason 2012). This seems logical, but it is also possible that strong commitment makes people worry more about losing their job because it implies that the organizational relationship is of particularly high value to them. We could add that individuals with strong attachments to their employing organization are likely to feel especially uncomfortable when there are threats of staff reductions if they imagine difficulties in finding an alternative that they would regard as equivalent to their current position.

Research Questions

There are several analytical purposes in this chapter: One is to examine whether or rather to what extent cross-national differences in organizational commitment are modified, when we control for work-related factors. It is unlikely that they completely disappear, but they may be more or less reduced. Our datasets have the advantage of covering random samples of employees in a large number of countries; many earlier studies are limited to a few industries in one or a few countries. We deal with 17 economically advanced capitalist nations; most of them are European but we also include Australia, New Zealand, Japan and the United States.

Moreover, we want to contribute further analysis of how various job properties are associated with organizational commitment by applying a comprehensive approach for these issues. We focus on employees' job characteristics in terms of working hours, sector of employment, position as supervisors of others, possibilities of deciding working time and the daily organization of work, job security, income, opportunities for advancement, and whether they see their job as interesting and as allowing work to be carried out independently. These can be seen as objective working conditions, although the information we have consists of answers to survey questions that is, requiring personal assessments.

Other significant dimensions include assessments of workplace relationships—between management and employees as well as between workmates. These elements are essential for the workplace climate. We can suppose that judging management–employees relations as positive indicates greater organizational commitment, whereas it is less clear what to expect in regard to relations between workmates. In this context, it is also of interest to take into consideration whether people are unionized or not. As pointed out above, unionization may imply an adversarial relationship to the employing organization and, hence, a lower degree of organizational commitment. Furthermore, we make use of information on whether respondents think that workers need unions. This could be another indicator of an oppositional attitude to the employer; a demand for a union counterforce might be equivalent to being distrustful and lacking loyalty. In other words, expressing that workers need unions is possibly associated with lower levels of commitment.

It is similarly appropriate to examine the role of job satisfaction. Good employment and working conditions can be expected to increase the chances that employees are satisfied with their job and their workplace, and we assume that high job satisfaction increases the likelihood for greater organizational commitment. Employment and working conditions are generally less favourable among those in the lower levels of the workplace hierarchies, but of course even employees higher up may be dissatisfied in one way or another; one aspect is if people feel that they have been maltreated.

Job satisfaction is dependent on a worker's employment and working conditions, but the impact of these is relative to those in other possible workplaces, too. It is probably also affected by employment chances in a wider sense. If unemployment is high in society or at least within the individual's own industry or occupation, he or she may be happy just to have a job. An indicator of this might be worry about losing one's job, which in turn may be linked to organizational commitment. In accordance with earlier research, we expect to see a positive correlation between the two factors. There are two possible, slightly different explanations to this. On the one hand, individuals may worry because they feel loyal to and want to stay with their organization, but on the other hand they may above all be worried about becoming unemployed and therefore cling to their workplace.

A related feature is perceived chances of finding another job. There are good reasons to study this aspect in connection with organizational commitment, as the possibility of getting another job represents the exit option, to use Hirschman's (1970) terminology. One problem here is that it is rather difficult for people to make proper judgments. We have access to answers to a question on how easy or difficult it would be for the respondent to get another equally good job. It is likely that some overestimate their chances in this respect, while others do the opposite. Still, the conclusion is not that it would generally be easier for an outside expert to make a reliable assessment. Instead, the concerned individuals themselves may be the best judges, not least because they know what they consider an equivalent job and because they have the relevant information about their personal situation (family situation, etc.). We therefore believe that this indicator can be useful. Being optimistic about chances to find another equally good job may make people less dependent on their employing organization and also less committed to it.

Finally, our investigation also aims at scrutinizing whether or to what extent the antecedents for organizational commitment are stable across time. By including data from two surveys from 2005 and 2015, we get an opportunity to see whether the results from the first wave remain the same—or approximately the same—10 years later. We also want to see how they stand compared to prior studies. Consequently, our analysis can help to confirm whether previously identified explanatory factors are robust or not.

Data and Variables

This analysis is based on data from two waves of ISSP carried out in 2005 and 2015. In the sense applied here, organizational commitment requires an employing organization and we therefore concentrate on employees. Self-employed with or without employees are not included because they have a different relationship to their organization. Likewise, we have excluded helping family members. Our focus is on employees living in 17 developed capitalist nations that participated in both surveys. The number of respondents in each of the two surveys is shown in Table 6.2, when all our variables are run simultaneously in the regression analyses. For more information on the collection of data, see the ISSP homepage.

The Dependent Variable

The dependent variable in our analysis is organizational commitment. It is based on three ISSP items which are phrased as follows in the two surveys: (a) 'I am willing to work harder than I have to in order to help the firm or organization I work for succeed'; (b) 'I am proud to be working for my firm or organization'; (c) 'I would turn down another job that offered quite a bit more pay in order to stay with this organization'. For each of the statements, respondents got five options for answering: 'Strongly agree', 'Agree', 'Neither agree nor disagree', 'Disagree' and 'Strongly disagree'. A principal component analysis shows that the three items make up one factor and we can thus use them as a measure of organizational commitment. The responses have been added to an index, ranging from 5 to 15. Cronbach's alpha for the index is .68 for 2005 and .66 for 2015. These figures are slightly below the desired criterion (.70), but if any of the three items are deleted Cronbach's alpha becomes lower.

Background Variables

We have access to a large range of independent variables, although some that would have been relevant, such as industry, size of the workplace, tenure and permanent/temporary employment contract, are not available. Four variables are background variables—that is, they are not directly related to the work situation: age, sex, education and country. Age is categorized, for the simple reason that this was done in one of the national surveys in 2015. The sex variable is dichotomous, distinguishing men and women. It is more complicated with education; the two surveys use different classifications of the variable highest educational achievement. We apply a classification from the lowest (basically mandatory education but including also a small number of respondents who had not even reached that level) to the highest (upper tertiary or university degree). The results regarding these control variables will not be presented in the table for the regressions, but we will mention a few words about them.

The final background variable is country. In this case, the results will be treated in a separate section, as a key research question is to what extent cross-national differences remain after controls for work-related indicators. To repeat, the analysis entails 17 countries that were included in both surveys. Four of them are Anglo-Saxon: Australia, New Zealand, the United Kingdom and the United States. From central and southern Europe we have Belgium, France, Germany, Spain and Switzerland. A comment is needed on the data from two of these countries in 2005, when the Belgian data refer only to Flanders and Germany is limited to West Germany. East Europe is represented by the Czech Republic, Latvia and Slovenia, and there is a Nordic cluster as well—with Denmark, Finland, Norway and Sweden. Lastly, Japan is included as the only Asian country. As mentioned, we are interested in how cross-national differences in organizational commitment are affected when various aspects of people's job situation are taken into account. The country variable is for that reason more than a control variable, but we have to insert a reservation here. A deeper analysis of how differences across countries can be explained would require a much more detailed nation-specific investigation than is possible within the scope of the current chapter.

Work-Related Independent Variables

The remaining variables are all work-related. There is a variable on whether respondents supervise others at work or not and it is likely to be a significant factor in relation to organizational commitment. As mentioned before, the two surveys have no industry variable, but there is a distinction between public and private sector employment, which we make use of. We also have information on working hours, presented in the form of five categories (1–19 hours, 20–34, 35–44, 45–54 and 55 and above).

The quality of jobs can be measured in different ways. To begin with, we have an additive index, summing up the answers on five items. People were asked to agree or disagree with a number of statements about their job: whether it is secure, whether their income is high, whether their opportunities for advancement are high, whether their job is interesting and whether they can work independently. The response options were the same as for the questions on organizational commitment. With five items, the maximum sum in the index can thus be 25 and the minimum is 5. Moreover, there are two variables measuring people's possibilities to decide their working hours and the organization of their daily work. The questionnaires provide other response options and these items are therefore treated separately. Another two variables deal with whether respondents' jobs include helping other people and whether they are useful for society. Once again, the response choices were the same as for organizational commitment. The two items have been added into a scale that we call 'job useful for others'. It has 10 as the highest score and 2 as the lowest.

Job satisfaction is a summary concept for people's feelings about their job. As a variable in the ISSP data sets, it is based on a question how satisfied respondents are in their current main job. Possible answers contained seven alternatives: 'Completely satisfied', 'Very satisfied, 'Fairly satisfied', 'Neither satisfied nor dissatisfied', 'Fairly dissatisfied', 'Very dissatisfied' and 'Completely dissatisfied'. This allows us to use it as a seven-point scale.

Respondents were also asked to answer a question on how they assess the relationship between management and employees and between workmates in their workplace. On both queries, they could choose to reply 'Very good', 'Quite good', 'Neither good nor bad', Quite bad' or 'Very bad'. We treat the two variables as five-point scales. Another piece of information concerns whether respondents are unionized or not. In addition, there is a variable on respondents' attitudes towards unions. It has slightly different wordings in the two surveys, but we do not believe that this difference is too big to make a comparison impossible. In 2005, respondents were asked to agree or disagree with a statement on whether working conditions would be much worse without trade unions. The response options were the same as for the other agree-disagree items mentioned above. In 2015, the wording of the statement is simpler, but the meaning is more or less same. Respondents could again choose between the same alternative answers.

Two variables touch upon people's labour market situation. One aspect is to what extent they worry about losing their current job. In this case, four responses were possible: 'I worry a great deal', 'I worry to some extent', 'I worry a little' and 'I do not worry at all'. The variable is included as a dummy variable. The other variable is about respondents' perceptions of labour market chances—that is, how easy or difficult it would be to get another equally good job. Answers could be 'Very easy', 'Fairly easy', 'Neither easy nor difficult', 'Fairly difficult' or 'Very difficult'. This variable is handled as a five-point scale.

We have also tried a measure of socioeconomic or occupational category, distinguishing managers, professionals, semi-professionals, service workers and manual workers. With some simplification, we can say that this categorization is a summary of job characteristics. It is accordingly left out in the regressions to be shown.

Results

We start by presenting some statistics on the dependent and the key independent variables used as scales. Table 6.1 summarizes this information for 2005 and 2015. The average on the organizational commitment 13-point scale for all the respondents in our analysis is 9.65 for 2005 and somewhat higher, 9.92, for 2015.

A principal independent variable is the job quality index. The average for all respondents on this 21-point scale is 16.63 for 2005 and 17.11 for 2015, an increase of .48 points. This might be interpreted as a general improvement of working conditions. Yet another essential independent variable is job satisfaction. Its corresponding averages are 5.17 in 2005 and 5.24 in 2015.

On the index called 'job useful for others' Table 6.1 shows an increase of the means from 7.61 in 2005 to 7.86 in 2015. In contrast, for the two indicators 'good relations management-employees' and 'good relations between workmates', the averages are fairly similar in both surveys. The same goes for the variable 'unions needed'. Finally, it does not seems to have become easier 'to find other equivalent job' in 2015.

Organizational commitment and the job quality index correlate quite strongly with each other. Pearson's R is .48 both years. The corresponding figures for organizational commitment and job satisfaction are slightly higher: .53 (2005) and .56 (2015). The association between the job quality index and job satisfaction is .50 in the first survey and .54 10 years later.

Next, we switch to regression analysis, in which we examine the role of the various independent variables. This examination starts with a presentation of the results for the work-related variables, but without displaying the outcomes for the background factors (including country), although they are controlled for (Table 6.2). A separate section below will be devoted to the cross-national differences.

Table 6.1 Key variables used as scales

	Min.	Max	2005		2015	
			Mean	Std. dev.	Mean	Std. dev.
Dependent variable						
Organizational commitment	3	15	9.67	2.52	9.92	2.48
Independent variables						
Job quality index	5	25	16.63	3.46	17.11	3.53
Job satisfaction	1	7	5.17	1.16	5.24	1.17
Job useful for others	2	10	7.61	1.82	7.86	1.78
Good relations management-employees	1	5	3.77	.97	3.80	.96
Good relations with workmates	1	5	4.18	.76	4.19	.78
Unions needed	1	5	3.66	1.05	3.71	1.07
Easy to find other equivalent job	1	5	2.69	1.13	2.56	1.11

Source: ISSP

Table 6.2 Factors associated with organizational commitment. OLS regressions, controlled for age, sex, education and country. Unstandardized b coefficients.

	2005	2015
Supervising others at work (ref. = No)		
Yes	.27***	.24***
Sector (ref. = Private)		
Public	–.10*	–.12*
Working hours (ref. 35–44 hours)		
1–19	–.01	.17
20–34	.01	.00
45–54	.15**	.15**
55+	.16*	.22**
Job quality index (21-point scale)	.17***	.16***
Can decide working hours (ref. = Cannot decide)		
Freely or within certain limits	.20***	.14**
Can decide organization of daily work (ref. = Cannot)		
Freely or within certain limits	.06	.12*
Job useful for others (9-point scale)	.10***	.12***
Job satisfaction (7-point scale)	.59***	.74***
Good relations management-employees (5-point scale)	.53***	.49***
Good relations between workmates (5-point scale)	.01	–.08**
Union member (ref. = No)		
Yes	–.07	–.03
Unions needed (5-point scale)	.01	-.07***
Worry about losing job (ref.= Not at all)		
A great deal	.48***	.42***
To some extent	.23***	.35***
A little	.16**	.17***
Easy to find other equally good job (5-point scale)	–.18***	–.09***
R²	.44	.44
N	8,863	8,873

Source: ISSP

*** = p < .001; ** = p < .01; * = p < .05

R^2 is rather high for both regressions: .44. The results for the background variables are not exposed in the table, but, as a beginning, some words can be said about three of them. We find no statistically significant age differences with respect to organizational commitment, either in 2005 or in 2015. The same applies to sex. On the third background variable, education, there is one outcome worth being observed: people with the highest education had lower levels of organizational commitment both years.

Work-Related Variables

As to the various job features appearing in Table 6.2, we first encounter what it means to be a supervisor of others at work. Not surprisingly, people in such roles score distinctly higher on organizational commitment than people in non-supervisory positions. Another significant variable is sector of employment. Public sector employees are distinguished by showing markedly lower levels of organizational commitment than private sector employees. Those working 35–44 hours per week are the reference category with regard to the next variable in the table. We find that respondents with longer hours get higher scores on organizational commitment. Respondents with shorter hours cannot be shown statistically to differ from the reference category.

The job quality index is strongly significant both years, implying that higher totals on the index are associated with stronger organizational commitment. One thing to pay attention to is that the job quality scale has 21 points, which means that although the coefficients are not the highest in the table, the effect is considerable. The two variables measuring the possibilities of deciding working hours and the organization of daily work are dichotomized. Respondents who answered that they could decide freely or within certain limits are compared with those who responded that they could not decide at all. The general pattern is that having some freedom in these respects is linked to greater organizational commitment, but this cannot be confirmed for deciding the organization of daily work in 2005.

It is noteworthy that perceiving the job as useful for others (a nine-point scale) goes hand in hand with higher levels of commitment to one's employing organization. The results on job satisfaction are indisputable. The more satisfied respondents are with their job, the more likely they are to score high on the commitment variable.

A very important factor promoting support and loyalty to people's work organization is whether relationship between management and employees is recognized as good. This is clearly verified in the table. The corresponding variable focusing on workmates is insignificant in the regression for 2005 and the outcome for 2015 suggests that it can even be negative in relation to organizational commitment. There is no indication that union membership matters, but the view that there is a need for unions is negatively associated with the dependent variable in 2015.

The variable measuring the degree of worry about losing one's job shows clear-cut results. More worry means a greater degree of organizational commitment. Finally, the outcome on perceived possibilities of finding another equally good job turns out to be as assumed. Those respondents who believe that it would be easy to get a job just as good as the one they currently have appear to be less attached to their employing organization.

Another conclusion from Table 6.2 is that the general patterns of how various factors impact on organizational commitment are quite similar in 2005 and 2015. Despite some differences in the outcomes in the two surveys, it is obvious that many of the results are very much alike. Just to mention some of the clearest findings, both years indicators on supervising others at work, sector of employment, working hours, job quality, having a job considered useful for others, job satisfaction, good management-employees relations, worry about losing one's job and assessments of one's chances to get another equivalent job are clearly associated, positively or—in a few cases—negatively, with organizational commitment. The analysis signals that these fallouts are robust and reliable.

Cross-National Differences

The most remarkable result with respect to the country variable is the high level of organizational commitment in Japan. With all our controls, it turns out to be higher than in any of the other countries. In the following presentation, we use Australia as the reference category because this country is close to the average in terms of organizational commitment. The first question to be dealt with is whether cross-national patterns are similar in the two survey waves. Controlling for all variables included in Table 6.2, we can examine the cross-national differences in the two surveys (Figure 6.1). For several countries, bars are closer to the zero-line—representing Australia—in 2015. The negative differences in relation to the reference category can then no longer be statistically verified for the Czech Republic, Denmark and Finland. At the same time, some results clearly go in the opposite direction. For example, Norway, New Zealand and the United Kingdom did not differ substantially from Australia in 2005, but the 2015 levels of organizational commitment in these countries are significantly higher. It is only Japan and the United States that score radically higher in 2005 as well as in 2015. Those with lower coefficients both years are France, Latvia, Sweden, Spain and Germany. In sum, it appears that, given our controls, cross-national differences were to some extent lower in 2015 compared to 2005, but we also come across both the opposite and very little change at all.

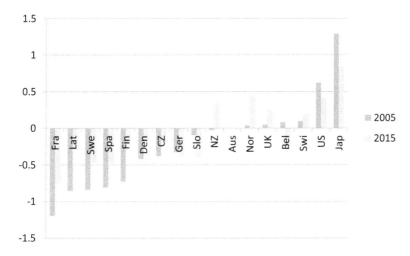

Figure 6.1 Relative levels of organizational commitment with control for all variables included in Table 6.2 and with Australia as reference category,
2005 and 2015, unstandardized b-coefficients

Source: ISSP

Note: In 2005, Belgium refers to Flanders and Germany refers to West Germany

In terms of country clusters, patterns are somewhat divided. Japan is a
specific case with its high levels of organizational commitment and the
four Anglo-Saxon countries are also found on the right-hand side of the
diagram. Among the Nordic countries, Norway stands out with a high
score in 2015, whereas the other three are lower—although not always
significantly lower—than the reference category. The European countries France, Spain and Germany are also characterized by less commitment, but Switzerland is approximately on par with Australia. The Czech
Republic and Latvia were clearly below the reference category in 2005,
and in 2015 we find Latvia together with Slovenia in the same position.

Then we want to see what our controls for work-related variables mean
for cross-national differences in terms of organizational commitment—
that is, compared to analyses with control only for background variables.
For that purpose we look at the data from the two survey waves separately (Figure 6.2). Two regression models are run for each of the data
sets: one comprising age, sex, education and country (A) and the other
embracing these four variables plus all work-related variables (B). The
latter model is the same as in the regressions shown in Table 6.2.

A remarkable outcome is that in 2005 the difference between Japan and
the reference category Australia is greater in Model B than in Model A.
In other words, controlling for work-related variables increases the gap

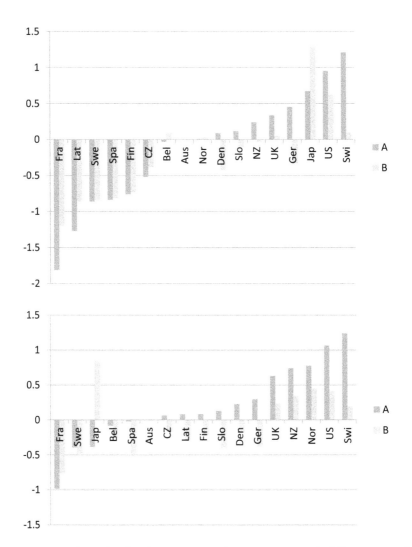

Figure 6.2 Relative levels of organizational commitment with different sets of control variables and with Australia as reference category, 2005 and 2015, unstandardized b-coefficients

Source: ISSP

between the two. The same holds for 2015, but then Japan is even below the reference category in Model A and this is statistically confirmed.

At first sight, it may seem that the controls for work-related variables imply lower cross-national differences. The most blatant example is Switzerland as both years gets clearly higher scores than Australia in Model

A, but in Model B this is statistically no longer the case. However, the picture is more complicated. None of Denmark and West Germany in 2005 or Spain, Slovenia, Germany, Latvia and Belgium in 2015 differs negatively from the reference category in Model A, but they are all significantly lower in Model B. It is obvious that controlling for work-related indicators does not eliminate cross-border dissimilarities, although these may be reduced. Accordingly, there must be other factors, not measured here, that influence the outcomes. It could be aspects of people's work situations not covered in the data sets. The impact of a cultural dimension should neither be ruled out, but that is a topic that must be left outside the present chapter.

Summarizing the results on the cross-national comparisons, with control for all our independent variables, we find that Japan shows higher levels of organizational commitment than all other countries, in 2005 as well as in 2015. Another country with relatively high commitment levels is the United States and, in 2015, this also goes for Norway, New Zealand and the United Kingdom. Cross-border differences partly come out as similar between the two years, but the patterns entail some variation. There are deviations in relation to the reference category with both higher and lower scores. The controls of work-related indicators show that although cross-border dissimilarities may become lesser they do not disappear. Japan is extreme; when work-related variables are included in the regressions its bars reach their highest both years.

Conclusions

What conclusions can be drawn from our analysis? To begin with, it should be repeated that the results are quite similar in both surveys used in our analysis. Of course, there are certain differences in the regression coefficients and the levels of statistical reliability, but the overall patterns are strikingly similar to each other. This suggests that the outcomes are quite robust; the most decisive explanations behind organizational commitment appear to be stable.

An important conclusion is also that even if national dissimilarities in terms of organizational commitment are sometimes lessened when we control for work-related characteristics, they do not vanish. Some countries typically have low and others typically have high levels of organizational commitment. On the whole, this configuration remains after we have included a large number of work-related factors in the analyses, even if the differences partly become smaller. Japan represents an exception because the controls make it have the highest level of organizational commitment among all the countries. Hence, work-related aspects do not have the same explanatory power in Japan. Not surprisingly, the Japanese ratings of working conditions are on average relatively low. It is plausible that cultural traits—not contained within our surveys—influence the outcome. The same goes for certain work-related factors such as tenure, type of employment contract and size of the workplace. Concerning country clusters, it seems that, besides Japan, the Anglo-Saxon countries, and in particular the United States, score relatively high on organizational commitment, whereas the patterns for the Nordic and the other European countries are split.

As expected, job features are strongly linked to organizational commitment. This is in accordance with much previous research (e.g., Lincoln and Kalleberg 1985, 1990; Pentareddy and Suganthi 2015; Randall 1993; Riketta 2005; Steers 1977; Welsch and LaVan 1981), but it should be kept in mind that the measurements applied in earlier studies differ a great deal. In the current inquiry, we have tried to specify a number of especially important variables for 17 countries. Among the many job traits that emerge as significant, we want to emphasize a few dimensions. First, there are some objective indicators clearly associated with higher levels of organizational commitment: having a position as a supervisor of others at work, being employed in the private sector and having longer working hours. Supervising others to some extent means being the representative of the employing organization and it is evident that this may produce feelings of loyalty. On the sector variable, it turns out that private sector employees are more inclined to convey organizational commitment (cf. Buelens and Van den Broek 2007; Goulet and Frank 2002; Zeffane 1994). The explanation for this is unclear, but we may speculate about the role of competition in markets for goods and services. It is essential for companies in the competitive sector to establish a brand and to get employees to stand behind it. This might be a driving force for creating organizational commitment in private sector workplaces. To work longer hours—often probably overtime—implies that the individual makes certain sacrifices for the employing organization. It can be seen as an expression of devotion or as a loyalty-generating mechanism or both.

Second, there is a job quality dimension (cf. Lincoln and Kalleberg 1985, 1990; Pentareddy and Suganthi 2015; Randall 1993; Riketta 2005; Steers 1977; Welsch and LaVan 1981). We have computed job quality as a summary index based on five different items. It comprises respondents' answers on to what extent they regard their job to be secure, their income to be high, their opportunities for advancement to be high, their job to be interesting and their job to allow independence in working. Each of these aspects constitutes a puzzle piece for people's assessment of the quality of their jobs. The index is significantly and positively associated with organizational commitment: the higher respondents score on this index, the stronger is their commitment. Some other factors that could not be entailed in the index—due to the construction of the questionnaires—point in the same direction, but not always so clearly. However, we must mention the possibilities of having some degree of freedom to decide working hours. It can be added that people's subjective relationship to their work is fundamental; those who have a higher degree of job sat-isfaction are distinctly more likely to be committed to their employing organization.

A third component in the picture is that respondents who consider their work useful for others show a higher level of organizational com-mitment. It suggests that occupational commitment—which is likely to be associated with thinking that one's work is useful for others—frequently goes hand in hand with support for and loyalty to employing organization. We should not therefore rule out that there may sometimes be conflicts between the two (cf. Meyer et al. 2002: 38; Wallace 1993).

Fourth, an important job-related dimension is the climate in the work-place between management and employees. As expected, if respondents judge the relationship between the two parties to be good, the more likely they are to have a high degree of organizational commitment. A positive workplace climate thus encourages employees' backing of the employ-ing organization. The downside is that it may be difficult to bring up discontent, although a positive atmosphere should allow this to hap-pen. Notably, trade union membership does not prove to be important. By comparing the results for various countries with very different lev-els of union density (not shown), we can find rather similar outcomes on organizational commitment. Nevertheless, if respondents agree that workers need unions in the workplace, it may be taken as an indication of a tense climate. In the 2015 survey wave, we discover that individuals in agreement with such a need also have lower commitment levels.

A fifth dimension has to do with people's labour market situation. Higher degrees of worry about losing one's job are associated with higher levels of organizational commitment. As we have noted previously, the direction of causality can be discussed (cf. Bjarnason 2012; Furåker and Berglund 2014; Gallie et al. 1998: 244–245). On the one hand, individu-als who feel that their job is threatened may become more inclined to appreciate what they have, including the organization they work for. On the other hand, the mechanism can also operate the other way around. High organizational commitment may lead to greater worry when people experience the risk of job loss. Furthermore, the easier respondents think it would be for them to find another equally good job, the less inclined they are to be committed to their current employer.

References

Allen, N. and J. P. Meyer (1990) 'The Measurement and Antecedents of Affec-tive, Continuance and Normative Commitment to the Organization.' *Journal of Occupational Psychology* 63: 1–18.

Baldry, C., P. Bain, P. Taylor, J. Hyman, D. Scholarios, A. Mars, A. Watson, K. Gilbert, G. Gall and D. Bunzel (2007) *The Meaning of Work in the New Economy.* Houndmills, Basingstoke: Palgrave Macmillan.

Bjarnason, T. (2012) 'Work Attitudes in a Crisis', 162–180, in B. Furåker, K. Håkansson and J.Ch. Karlsson (eds) *Commitment to Work and Job Satisfaction*. New York, London: Routledge

Buchanan, B. (1974) 'Building Organizational Commitment: he Socialization of Managers in Work Organizations.' *Administrative Science Quarterly* 19: 533–546.

Buelens, M. and H. Van den Broek (2007) 'An Analysis of Differences in Work Motivation between Public and Private Sector Organizations.' *Public Administration Review* 67: 65–74.

Fukami, C. V. and E. W. Larson (1984) 'Commitment to Company and Union: Parallel Models.' *Journal of Applied Psychology* 69(3): 367–371.

Furåker, B. and T. Berglund (2014) 'Job Insecurity and Organizational Commitment.' *Revista Internacional de Organizaciones* 13: 163–186.

Gallie D., M. White, Y. Cheng and M. Tomlinson (1998) *Restructuring the Employment Relationship*. Oxford: Clarendon Press.

Goulet, L. R. and M. L. Frank (2002) 'Organizational Commitment Across Three Sectors: Public, Non-Profit, and For-Profit.' *Public Personnel Management* 31(2): 201–210.

Hackman, J. R. and E. E. Lawler III (1971) 'Employee Reactions to Job Characteristics.' *Journal of Applied Psychology* 55: 259–286.

Hackman, J. R. and G. R. Oldham (1975) 'Development of the Job Diagnostic Survey.' *Journal of Applied Psychology* 60: 159–170.

Håkansson, K. and T. Isidorsson (2012) 'Temporary Agency Workers and Organizational Commitment', 181–198, in B. Furåker, K. Håkansson and J.Ch. Karlsson (eds) *Commitment to Work and Job Satisfaction*. New York and London: Routledge.

Hattrup, K., K. Mueller and P. Aguirre (2008) 'An Evaluation of the Cross-National Generalizability of Organizational Commitment.' *Journal of Occupational and Organizational Psychology* 81(2): 219–240.

Hirschman, A. E. (1970) *Exit, Voice and Loyalty. Responses to Decline in Firms, Organizations, and States*. Cambridge, MA: Harvard University Press.

Hult, C. and S. Svallfors (2002) 'Production Regimes and Work Orientations: A Comparison of Six Western Countries.' *European Sociological Review* 18 (3): 315–331.

ISSP (International Social Survey Programme) (2005, 2015) *Work Orientations III and IV*. Köln: GESIS—Leibniz-Institut für Sozialwissenschaften.

Kirkman, B. L. and D. L. Shapiro (2001) 'The Impact of Cultural Values on Job Satisfaction and Organizational Commitment in Self-Managing Work Teams: The Mediating Role of Employee Resistance.' *The Academy of Management Journal* 44 (3): 557–569.

Lincoln, J. R. and A. L. Kalleberg (1985) 'Work Organization and Workforce Commitment: A Study of Plants and Employees in the U.S. and Japan.' *American Sociological Review* 50(6): 738–760.

Lincoln, J. R. and A. L. Kalleberg (1990) *Culture, Control, and Commitment. A Study of Work Organization and Work Attitudes in the United States and Japan*. Cambridge: Cambridge University Press.

Luthans, F., H. S. McCaul and N. G. Dodd (1985) 'Organizational Commitment: A Comparison of American, Japanese, and Korean Employees.' *The Academy of Management Journal* 28(1): 213–219.

Meyer, J. P. (1997) 'Organizational Commitment', 175–228, in C. L. Cooper and I. T. Robertson (eds) *International Review of Industrial and Organizational Psychology*. Chichester: Wiley.

Meyer, J. P. and N. J. Allen (1991) 'A Three-Component Conceptualization of Organizational Commitment.' *Human Resource Management Review* 1(1): 61–89.

Meyer, J. P. and N. J. Allen (1997) *Commitment in the Workplace: Theory, Research, and Applications*. Thousand Oaks, CA: Sage.

Meyer, J. P., D. J. Stanley, L. Herscovitch and L. Topolnytsky (2002) 'Affective, Continuance, and Normative Commitment to the Organization: A Meta-analysis of Antecedents, Correlates, and Consequences.' *Journal of Vocational Behavior* 61: 20–52.

Mowday, R. T. (1998) 'Reflections on the Study and Relevance of Organizational Commitment.' *Human Resource Management Review* 8(4): 387–401.

Mowday, R. T., L. W. Porter and R. M. Steers (1982) *Employee-Organization Linkages: The Psychology of Commitment, Absenteeism and Turnover*. New York: Academic Press.

Mowday, R. T., R. M. Steers and L. M. Porter (1979) 'The Measurement of Organizational Commitment.' *Journal of Vocational Behavior* 14: 224–247.

Parsons, T. and N. J. Smelser (1956) *Economy and Society: A Study in the Integration of Economic and Social Theory*. London: Routledge & Kegan Paul.

Patchen, M. (1970) *Participation, Achievement, and Involvement on the Job*. Englewood Cliffs, NJ: Prenctice Hall.

Pentareddy, S. and L. Suganthi (2015) 'Building Affective of Commitment Through Job Characteristics, Leadership and Empowerment.' *Journal of Management & Organization* 21(3): 307–320.

Porter, L. W., R. M. Steers, R. T. Mowday and P. V. Boulian (1974) 'Organizational Commitment, Job Satisfaction and Turnover Among Psychiatric Technicians.' *Journal of Applied Psychology* 59(5): 603–609.

Randall, D. M. (1993) 'Cross-Cultural Research on Organizational Commitment: A Review and Application of Hofstede's Value Survey Module.' *Journal of Business Research* 26: 91–110.

Reichers, A. E. (1985) 'A Review and Reconceptualization of Organizational Commitment.' *Academy of Management Review* 10(3): 465–476.

Riketta, M. (2005) 'Organizational Identification: A Meta-Analysis.' *Journal of Vocational Behavior* 66: 358–384.

Sommer, S. M., S.-H. Bae and F. Luthans (1996) 'Organizational Commitment Across Cultures: The Impact of Antecedents on Korean Employees.' *Human Relations* 49(7): 977–993.

Spreitzer, G. M. (1995) 'Psychological Empowerment in the Workplace: Construct Definition, Measurement, and Validations.' *Academy of Management Journal* 38(5): 1442–1465.

Steers, R. M. (1977) 'Antecedents and Outcomes of Organizational Commitment.' *Administrative Science Quarterly* 22(1): 46–56.

Turunen, T. (2011) 'Commitment to Employment and Organisation: Finland in a European Comparison.' *Research on Finnish Society* 4: 55–66.

Wallace, J. E. (1993) 'Professional and Organizational Commitment: Compatible or incompatible?' *Journal of Vocational Behavior* 42(3): 333–349.

Welsch, H. P. and H. LaVan (1981) 'Inter-Relationships Between Organizational Commitment and Job Characteristics, Job Satisfaction, Professional Behavior, and Organizational Climate.' *Human Relations* 34(12): 1079–1089.

Wright, E. O. (1997) *Class Counts. Comparative Studies in Class Analysis.* Cambridge: Cambridge University Press.

Zeffane, R. (1994) 'Patterns of Organizational Commitment and Perceived Management Style: A Comparison of Public and Private Sector Employees.' *Human Relations* 47(8): 977–1010.

7 Commitment in Organisations Using Temporary Agency Workers

Kristina Håkansson and Tommy Isidorsson

The labour market has changed dramatically in recent decades. Technological innovations have changed the organisation of production of goods and services in decisive ways. Demand for accessibility and just-in-time production have raised employers' demands for flexibility in staffing. One way to obtain this flexibility is to use staff temporarily, which is often called numerical flexibility (Atkinson 1984; Kalleberg 2001). Temporary staff can be employed directly by an employer on a temporary contract or hired from a temporary work agency. In the latter case, the agency worker is employed by the agency but performs work in client organisations. Hence, agency workers and client organisation employees perform work in the same organisation but with different employing organisations. These different employment relations for the two groups could potentially have consequences for the employees' loyalty to the workplace—that is, organisational commitment. In general, conceptualisations of commitment include a bond to the organisation, a disposition to stay with it (Allen and Meyer 1990, Meyer and Herscovitch 2001). The aim of this chapter is to describe and explain the degree of commitment of client organisation employees and temporary agency workers in workplaces where the two groups work together.

Agency workers could be assigned to client organisations for varying durations and could be integrated in the organisation and work together with the client organisation's employees or be assigned to separate tasks. These various forms of using agency workers affect the work organisation in different ways. The presence of agency workers in a workplace affects both agency workers and client organisation employees (Håkansson and Isidorsson 2012a). However, knowledge about how the use of agency workers affects commitment is scarce.

Research on organisational commitment has developed over several decades (cf. Chapter 6 in this volume). Most of it is based on traditional staff—that is, workers employed by the employer of the workplace. Thus, theories are built on employees' identification and engagement with one organisation—an employment relationship where the employer and the workplace coincide. However, with the introduction of temporary work agencies, this traditional employment relationship has become more complicated. Temporary agency work is affected by the triangular relationship within the agency work industry, consisting of the 'employment' relationship between the agency worker and the agency, the 'management' relationship between the agency worker and the client organisation, and the 'business' relationship between the client organisation and the temporary work agency (Bergström and Storrie, 2003: 9; Håkansson Isidorsson and Kantelius 2012; Storrie, 2007: 106) (Figure 7.1)

From a temporary agency worker perspective, there is a split between the employer and the workplace. In the workplace the agency worker is not under the supervision of the employer but under the management of another organisation. There is thus a split employer-management relationship. The employment relationship concerns employment conditions such as employment contracts and payment, while the management relationship is about job characteristics in the day-to-day activities. The 'business' relationship between the temporary work agency and the client organisation dictates that the client organisation buys work from the temporary work agency temporarily or until further notice.

The scarce amount of research on temporary agency workers' commitment suggests that commitment is primarily linked to the work situation and not the employer (Håkansson and Isidorsson 2012b). Less is known about how the use of temporary agency workers shapes organisational commitment to the client organisation for both traditional workers and temporary agency workers. This chapter is based on a study of a workplace in which traditional permanent employees and temporary agency workers work side by side performing the same work tasks. Hence, this case could be characterized as a 'critical case' (Yin 2014), given that the job content and organisational context are almost equal, but the employers differ. This design, where we can separate the employer relationship

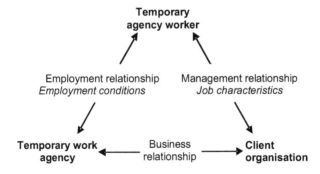

Figure 7.1 The triangular relationship in the temporary agency work industry between the agency worker, the temporary work agency and the client organisation

with its employment conditions from the management relationship with its job characteristics, gives us the opportunity to understand what constitutes commitment. In addition, given the same employment status—both client organisation employees and agency workers have permanent contracts—our study makes it possible to modulate the commitment concept.

The Swedish Context

Prior to 1993, it was illegal in Sweden to run private work agencies for profit-making purposes (Berg 2008: 106). New legislation in that year made this allowed (Swedish Code of Statutes 1993, No 440). In Sweden, as in many OECD countries, the number of agency workers has increased rapidly during the last two decades. Although it has been subject to extensive debate, temporary agency work remains a marginal phenomenon in the labour market. Agency workers account for approximately 1.6 percent of all employees in Sweden, and approximately 1.9 percent in Europe according to World Employment Confederation (2017: 12). According to the statistics from the same organisation, long contract periods dominate in Sweden: 70 percent of all assignments last longer than three months (CIETT 2013, 2014).

Even though the industry accounts for a small fraction of employment, its effects on the labour market must not be underestimated; more than 50 percent of all Swedish workplaces with at least 100 employees use agency workers (Håkansson and Isidorsson 2016). The work organisation in client organisations must be adjusted in response to the use of agency workers, meaning that the use of a small number of agency workers affects many more employees. Agency workers' commitment to the client organisation might also influence the commitment of the employees of the client organisation.

The operations of temporary work agencies in Sweden are regulated by the Private Employment Agencies and Temporary Labour Act (Swedish Code of Statutes 1993, No 440; 2012, No 854). There are no restrictions, either in the length of time or the cumulative duration of assignments, on using temporary agency workers. The regulation of the agency work industry is weak in Sweden (OECD 2013). However, the legislation also protects the employees in the agency industry by explicitly emphasising that employees may not be prevented from being employed by the client organisation to which they are assigned. Working conditions in the Swedish agency industry are regulated via collective agreements in the same way as in other industries. The collective agreement for blue-collar temporary agency workers states that they must have an hourly wage that corresponds to the average hourly wage for comparable groups at the client organisation (Staffing Agreement, 2017, Section 3, Subsection 2). The collective agreement also maintains the right to pay between assignments for temporary agency workers. This compensation payment is approximately 80–90 percent of the regular salary. Equivalent compensation is possible in a few other countries, although sometimes at a low level (OECD 2013). Moreover, the Swedish Employment Protection Act (Swedish Code of Statutes 1982, No 80), which prescribes that the normal form is an open ended employment contract, usually called a permanent position, applies also to employees of the agency industry. Hence, a temporary agency worker can have a permanent employment contract with a temporary work agency. This is also possible in some other European countries but not all of them (OECD 2013). The widespread use of agency workers and the regulation via collective agreements indicates that temporary work agencies could be seen as institutionalized in Sweden (Bergström et al. 2007; Håkansson and Isidorsson 2016).

Research Overview and Theoretical Framework

Organisational commitment has received a lot of interest since it was first conceptualized by Howard Becker in 1960 and, since then, has developed into a multidimensional concept (Cohen 2007; WeiBo, Kaur and Jun 2009) According to Becker's (1960) 'side-bet' theory, the main explanation for remaining in an organisation was that the individual had made some investments in that organisation. The individual's loyalty was then explained by the high cost of leaving the organisation. Later theories include the psychological attachment to an organisation, or affective dependence (Porter et al. 1974; Mowday and Steers 1979). Meyer and Allen (1991) formulated a theory including three dimensions of commitment. They distinguished between affective, continuance and normative commitment. Affective commitment refers to the emotional bond to the organisation; the employee *wants* to stay and is loyal to the organisation. The second dimension, continuance commitment, is used when the employee must stay with the organisation; the cost of changing organisations is believed to exceed the cost of staying, so the employee *needs* to stay. This dimension is close to Becker's (1960) first attempts to define commitment. In contrast to affective commitment, a good job offer from another organisation would break the employee's loyalty to the present organisation. Finally, normative commitment is shown when the employee has a feeling of obligation to the organisation. The employee perceives that he or she *ought* to stay. Even though the three dimensions are theoretically differentiated, empirical studies show difficulties in distinguishing between affective and normative commitment (Allen and Meyer 1990). Therefore, some researchers only use affective and continuance commitment (Coleman, Irving and Cooper 1999: 996). This chapter focuses on temporary agency workers' and client organisation employees' emotional attachment to, identification with, and involvement in organisations they are related to—that is, affective commitment (Allen and Meyer 1990: 2).

Employment Conditions and Job Characteristics as Explanations of Commitment

Previous research into organisational commitment has mainly dealt with people working in traditional employment relations. This research suggests that age has some importance, but not gender and education. The most important antecedents for commitment refer to job characteristics such as job challenges, goal clarity and participation in decisions (Allen and Meyer 1990; cf. Chapter 6 in this volume). Research about agency work has also paid attention to employment conditions (Håkansson and Isidorsson 2012b).

In the context of temporary agency workers, job security relates to the employment relationship (Figure 7.1), while employability could be related to both organisations (Håkansson and Isidorsson 2019). The agency is responsible for finding new client organisations and is thus interested in keeping their employees employable. Even though the responsibility for competence development lies with the employer—that is, the work agency—client organisations can also offer the job training required for performing the daily work. The agency workers might thus gain experiences that could also be useful for other client organisations. It has been shown that an agency worker who perceives training as something facilitating the possibility to remain within the organisation will respond with commitment (Chambel et al. 2015).

Job characteristics relate to possibilities and conditions in the organisation, such as participation, feedback and equity (Allen and Meyer 1990; Mowday, Porter and Steers 1982). Previous research is based on traditional employees, but several studies have confirmed that job characteristics also explain agency workers' commitment to the client organisation (Slattery et al. 2010; Håkansson and Isidorsson 2012b). There is also empirical evidence of a positive association between agency workers' organisational support and commitment (Connelly, Gallagher and Gilley 2007; Giunchi, Chambel and Ghislieri 2015). Similarly, skill investments such as competence development and training foster agency workers' commitment (Woldman et al. 2018). Although competence development is formally the employer's responsibility, temporary workers mostly expect it from the organisation where they perform the daily work—that is, the client organisation.

Integration as Explanation of Commitment

Agency workers could be used in different ways that possibly affect their commitment as well as the commitment of client organisation employees.

There is a widespread view that the use of temporary agency workers is a means to achieve flexibility. This flexibility refers to the employer's wish to vary the number of staff, as illustrated in the model of the flexible firm by John Atkinson (1984). The same notion of temporary agency workers appears in several later studies (Houseman 2001; Kalleberg 2001; Kalleberg, Reynolds and Marsden 2003: 532; Kauhanen 2001; Mitlacher 2007). According to this view, agency workers are assigned to work tasks with a short induction time (in practice, these are often routine work tasks that can be carried out by unqualified and easily replaceable staff), while client organisation employees perform the more qualified and firm-specific work tasks. Hence, the use of agency workers results in a division into core and periphery. This kind of use entails frequent changes of workplaces for the agency workers, resulting in lower commitment to the client organisation (Håkansson and Isidorsson 2012b). However, organisations can use temporary agency workers for other reasons. There can be an employment strategy where the agency workers are used long term in case of a downturn in the future (Holst, Nachtwey and Dörre 2010). In this case, the agency workers are more intertwined with the client organisation employees and the division into core and periphery is blurred.

Agency workers who are integrated into the client organisation and who participate in training and development work show stronger commitment to the client organisation (Giunchi, Chambel and Ghislieri 2015; Håkansson and Isidorsson 2012b; Toms and Biggs 2014). Some studies have revealed a spillover effect between the organisations (Fontinha, Chambel and De Cuyper 2012; Slattery et al. 2010). Håkansson and Isidorsson (2012b) found that agency workers' integration in the client organisation leads to a dual effect—that is, commitment to both the client organisation and the agency. This integration even outweighs job security as an explanation for commitment. A qualitative study revealed that agency workers on long-term assignments felt more integrated in the client organisation, resulting in stronger commitment (Toms and Biggs 2014). Other researchers have found similar results (Kuvaas and Dysvik 2009). However, the way in which client organisation employees' commitment is affected by the integration of agency workers is not known. In case of a downturn, the agency workers are the first to leave, thus strengthening the job security for client organisation employees (Håkansson and Isidorsson 2015).

Social Exchange and Psychological Contract as Explanation to Commitment

Previous research comparing agency workers' and permanent workers' commitment has shown mixed results. In a literature review, it was noted that one explanation for the contradictory results might be the heterogeneity in the group of contingent workers (Connelly and Gallagher 2004: 962). This is also one of the conclusions in a theoretical chapter on the psychological contract (De Cuyper and De Witte 2008). Moreover, one study emphasized that agency workers have different ways of gaining access to the internal labour market of the client organisation (Broschak, Davies-Blake and Block 2008: 30). It found high commitment to the client organisation in cases where the agency worker perceived career opportunities in the client organisation. Several authors have used theories of social exchange and psychological contracts to explain agency workers' commitment (Chambel, Castanheira and Sobral 2016; Chambel et al. 2015; Coyle-Shapiro and Morrow 2006; Woldman et al. 2018). According to social exchange theory, there is a reciprocal relation—agency workers who perceive good job quality and skill investments will respond with commitment to the client organisation. In a comparative study of agency workers and client organisation employees in Portugal, it was found that agency workers showed even higher commitment in cases where their expectations were exceeded (Chambel, Castanheira and Sobral 2016). In these cases, the client organisation had HR practices that agency workers perceived as investments.

In sum, recent research suggests that temporary agency workers' commitment to the client organisation could be explained as a response to the job quality offered by the client organisation and the social exchange of commitment as a response to this. However, most studies are based on data solely from temporary agency workers. There is a lack of studies comparing agency workers and client organisation employees in the same work context, including client organisation employees' commitment.

This chapter compares commitment of client organisation employees and temporary agency workers. The aim is to describe and explain the level of commitment among client organisation employees and temporary agency workers in workplaces where the two groups work together. More specifically, we try to answer the following research questions:

- What are the differences and similarities between agency workers' and client organisation employees' commitment to the client organisation?
- How is client organisation employees' commitment affected by the use of agency workers?
- How can agency workers' and client organisation employees' degree of commitment be explained?

Data and Methods

Our analysis is based on a case study of a medium-sized manufacturing plant in Sweden. The plant has been using temporary agency workers for blue-collar work since 2004. Prior to that date, the client organisation experienced a decline in demand and reduced its employees accordingly, laying off a large number of employees in 2003. When demand increased in 2004 due to a large order, the client organisation decided to use temporary agency workers since the increased need for staff was thought to be temporary. Although the use of temporary agency workers began as a temporary solution for a large order, with no intention on the part of the client organisation to continue the hiring of personnel after this peak, the plant has been using temporary agency workers on a fairly regular basis ever since. Most assignments have been staffed by the same agency workers for a considerable period of time, exceeding two years in some cases. In the wake of the financial crisis in 2008, the corporate executive board required local plants to provide for 30 percent flexibility. Thus, this new use of temporary agency workers is not directly linked to an increase in orders, but rather to a strategic management decision (cf. Holst, Nachtwey and Dörre 2010). With the new staffing strategy, the management of the client organisation considered how temporary agency workers could be integrated into the work organisation more efficiently than before, a reorganisation that was an important part of the shift towards long-term strategic use. According to the managers, all staff, temporary agency workers and client organisation employees are treated equally. The temporary agency workers are used in the same way as client organisation employees: they receive on-the-job training and participate in job rotation. The induction time in the production unit is about two to three months.

Since the workplace we investigate uses temporary agency workers who are fully integrated into production, and who perform the same work tasks as regular employees and participate in the same work rotation, this case gives us a unique opportunity to compare affective organisational commitment among client organisation employees and temporary agency workers. Furthermore, it is also possible to control for type of employment contract, as both groups mainly have open-ended contracts. Because our selection of workplace and individuals is not random, it is impossible to generalize our results to the labour market. Hence, it is not appropriate to use tests of significance. Rather, this study can be seen as a critical case (Yin 2014) to test the importance of the employment relationship. As temporary agency workers and client organisation employees work together and perform the same work tasks, differences in organisational commitment could be assigned to the employment relationship.

We make use of survey data from client organisation employees in the production unit and temporary agency workers assigned to this unit. A questionnaire was distributed at the workplace during a monthly production stop and staff meeting. The production stop lasted for 60 minutes and gave us a total time of 30 minutes to inform the workers about the survey and to have the workers fill in the questionnaire. Everyone at the workplace that day had the opportunity to participate in the survey.

Hence, this is a total investigation of a critical case and not a sample representing the situation on the Swedish labour market. This arrangement required our access to the company's ordinary meeting time, so the questionnaire had to be distributed and collected in one day. The response rate among the staff was extremely high; it was more than 90 percent. However, the single-day distribution meant that absent employees could not participate. If the staff on sick leave and on business trips were taken into account, the response rate would be around 80 percent.

In total, 139 blue-collar employees at the client organisation and 30 temporary agency workers returned the questionnaire. The questionnaires given to client organisation employees and temporary agency workers were almost identical, although some wordings were adapted in order to apply to the two different groups of respondents.

The dependent variable in this study is affective organisational commitment, measured by four questions developed and used by Allen and Meyer (1990: 6). We used the same questions but asked for organisational commitment to the employer *and* to the client organisation. Thus, the following items were included:

(1) I would be very happy to spend the rest of my career with my temporary work agency/client organisation.
(2) I enjoy discussing my temporary work agency/client organisation with people outside it.
(3) I really feel as if this agency's/client organisation's problems are my own.
(4) I think that I could easily become as attached to another organisation as I am to this agency/client organisation (reversed).

The fourth question was excluded because a factor analysis showed that this question distinguished itself from the other three questions. This could be due to the special character of agency work, where the employees are expected to change workplaces on demand. Thus, the index that we use for commitment are made up of three questions or statements and respondents were asked to take a stand on them. Five response alternatives were given on each statement: 'strongly agree', 'slightly agree', 'neither agree nor disagree', 'slightly disagree' and 'strongly disagree'. The index thus ranges from 3 to 15.

The independent variables included in the questionnaire were personal characteristics (age), employment conditions and job characteristics. Employment conditions are measured as satisfaction with salary and job security on five-point scales, ranging from very dissatisfied to very satisfied. Employability is an index consisting of two inquiries: whether the respondent has acquired knowledge that is useful for other companies, and an estimation of the possibilities of getting a similar or better job. This index ranges from 2 to 8. Job characteristics include satisfaction with competence development offered by the client organisation, and satisfaction with the manager, both measured on five-point scales ranging from very dissatisfied to very satisfied. Feedback is measured by the question whether or not the respondent has had a development discussion with the employer during the last 12 months. Autonomy is a scale that includes one item about influence how to perform the job and one item about influence in working time. This scale ranges from 2 to 10.

Analyses

In our first analysis we investigated whether the agency workers and the client organisation employees differ in terms of commitment. We added factors relating to the management relationship and the employment relationship stepwise in OLS regressions. Due to the small number of agency workers, we were not able to perform separate analyses for the two groups of workers, but carried out some bivariate analyses. The second analysis focused on client organisation employees. Our interest was to highlight the effect of the use of temporary agency workers. Attitudes to agency workers were measured by two statements: 'I think it is good to have agency workers at my company' and 'The company should give ordinary employees (client organisation employees) better opportunities for development compared to agency workers'. Response alternatives ranged from strongly disagree to strongly agree.

Findings

Client organisation employees and agency workers differ in several respects. Most agency workers have an upper secondary school education, while one third of the client organisation employees have a nine-year compulsory school education. There are also some similarities; all respondents have open-ended contracts, albeit with different employers—agency workers have open-ended contracts with the temporary work agency. Both groups of employees have clearly higher proportions of males, resembling the gender distribution in the manufacturing industry. Table 7.1 provides some further information. Agency workers are younger and, accordingly, also have shorter tenure. The two groups differ regarding perceptions of employment conditions and job characteristics: agency workers are less satisfied with job security but more satisfied in all other aspects.

Salary, job security and feedback (development discussion) relate to the employer relationship (see Figure 7.1). Temporary agency workers' salaries are set as the average salaries paid to client organisation employees in the same positions. This is in accordance with the national blue-collar collective agreement within the temporary work industry. The salary level in this client organisation is high compared to other client

Table 7.1 Descriptives: respondents' backgrounds, employment conditions and job characteristics. Means and SD (in parenthesis).

	Client organisation employees	Temporary agency workers
Age	48 (9.2)	29 (6.6)
Tenure in years	21 (8.8)	2.7
Satisfaction with salary (range 1–5)	3.36	4.47
Satisfaction with job security (range 1–5)	3.74	2.97
Autonomy (range 2–10)	6.74	7.53
Satisfaction with manager (range 1–5)	3.51	4.13
Satisfaction with competence development at client organization (range 1–5)	3.08	3.41
Feedback (have had development discussion, share in percent per group)	60%	33%

organisations in the area, which means that agency workers' high satisfaction is not surprising. Temporary agency workers are less satisfied with their employer in terms of job security compared to client organisation employees. They have also received less feedback from their employer. The job characteristics, which relate to the management relationship, are perceived more positively among agency workers. Agency workers and client organisation employees work side by side and perform the same tasks. However, agency workers *perceive* more autonomy and are more satisfied.

Previous research suggests that commitment increases by age, indicating that client organisation employees in our case would report higher commitment. Also, the long tenure in a Swedish context entails good chances of remaining employed in case of redundancies, as the Swedish labour law applies the principle of 'last in—first out'. In this specific case there are very few newly employed people in the client organisation, indicating that even those with long tenure could be affected in case of a downturn. However, it must be stressed that the main buffer is constituted by the temporary agency workers, thus giving the client organisation employees high stability at the expense of the agency worker's long-term instability. All in all, we could assume that the differences in background characteristics imply higher organisational commitment among client organisation employees.

In the next analysis, we sought different explanations for commitment (Table 7.2). In Model 1, we investigated the impact of the employment

Table 7.2 Factors influencing organisational commitment. OLS regression, beta-values

	Model 1	Model 2	Model 3
Employer (ref. = client organisation)			
Temporary work agency	.18	.04	.05
Age	.23	.19	.19
Factors in respect of the management relation			
Autonomy		.16	.15
Satisfaction with management		.23	.20
Satisfaction with competence development at the client org.		.35	.30
Factors in respect of the employment relation			
Satisfaction with salary			.08
Satisfaction with job security			.10
Employability			.00
Have had feedback discussion (ref. = no)			.01
R^2	.03	.40	.41

relationship and personal characteristics (age). In Model 2, we added factors relating to the management relationship—that is, job characteristics. Previous research based on employees with a traditional employment relationship has shown that job characteristics are the most important antecedents (cf. Chapter 6 in this volume); the question here is whether this also holds true for temporary agency workers. In Model 3, we add factors relating to the employment relationship, such as satisfaction with salary and job security.

Model 1 shows that temporary agency workers are more committed compared to client organisation employees, but these differences largely disappear in Model 2 when we control for management relationship factors. The results from Model 2 also seem to be quite robust when we add factors linked to the employment relationship in Model 3. The latter factors do not really contribute to the explanation of commitment; R^2 increases only with one percentage point. So far, the results confirm the importance of job characteristics and age, regardless of whether the individual is an agency worker or client organisation employee.

The small sample of agency workers in our data does not allow separate regression analyses. However, separate bivariate analyses reveal that the impact of job characteristics on commitment differs between the two groups. For client organisation employees, job characteristics are an important explanation for commitment, but this impact is weaker for agency workers. The job characteristic of job autonomy has a very weak influence on agency workers' commitment, even though they perceive more autonomy compared to client organisation employees. Hence, for client organisation employees, job characteristics seem to be the main antecedents to affective commitment in accordance with previous research, while this explanation is much weaker for agency workers.

In the next analysis, we turn to the client organisation employees. The question is whether their commitment is affected by the use of agency workers (Table 7.3). To be able to discern the effect of agency workers, Model 1 shows only the factors that have already been tried in Table 7.2. In Model 2, we added factors that relate to the use of agency workers, whether agency workers are included in the team, and the attitudes towards agency workers.

Adding factors relating to the use of temporary agency workers increases R^2 significantly, from .49 to .62. The results from Model 1 in Table 7.3 seem to be quite robust, and satisfaction with competence development even increased in importance. The presence of agency workers has no effect, but attitudes regarding the use of such workers does seem to matter. Client organisation employees who are positive about agency workers show a stronger commitment. The same holds true for client organisation employees who are of the opinion that they should have better opportunities for competence development compared to agency workers. Both attitudes are in line with the idea of using temporary agency workers as a buffer in case of a downturn, benefitting the position as a client organisation employee.

Table 7.3 Factors influencing commitment among client organisation employees. OLS regressions, beta-values.

	Model 1	*Model 2*
Age	.16	.17
Factors in respect of the management relation		
Autonomy	.26	.24
Satisfaction with management	.19	.23
Satisfaction with competence development at the client organization	.32	.42
Factors in respect of the employment relation		
Satisfaction with salary	–.01	–.05
Satisfaction with job security	.11	.14
Employability	–.10	–.08
Have had feedback discussion (ref = no)	–.03	–.12
Factors in respect of the use of agency workers		
Agency workers are included in the team (ref. = no)		–.03
Good to use agency workers		.13
Client organization employees should have better opportunities		.13
R^2	.49	.62

Conclusion

The aim of this study has been to describe and explain the degree of commitment of client organisation employees and temporary agency workers in a workplace where the two groups work together. We have formulated three main research questions. The first of these was to examine similarities and differences in commitment between agency workers and client organisation employees. Our analysis revealed no clear differences between the two groups. According to our study, both groups of workers are committed to the client organisation to about the same extent.

Our second research question concerned the people employed by the client organisation, asking whether their commitment is affected by the use of temporary agency workers. There is no previous research on this issue. When agency workers are doing the same work tasks, including those that require competence development, the client organisation employees may perceive themselves as replaceable. That would theoretically challenge their psychological contracts and affect their commitment negatively (De Cuyper and De Witte 2008). In the workplace we investigated, there is an explicit strategy to use agency workers as a long-term buffer (cf. Holst, Nachtwey and Dörre 2010). This solution implies stronger job security for client organisation employees. However, their commitment is not affected by the use of agency workers in the work group; the presence of these workers does not seem to make any difference.

An interesting result is that those client organisation employees who have a positive attitude towards the use of agency workers at the plant show stronger organisational commitment. At the same time, the client organisation employees who express that they should have better opportunities for development compared to agency workers also show stronger commitment. The pattern of attitudes is obviously double-edged. On the one hand, using temporary agency workers can create protection in case of a downturn. In a situation with redundancy, the agency workers are the first who have to leave, thus strengthening the job security for client organisation employees (Håkansson and Isidorsson 2015). We think that this can contribute positively to commitment. On the other hand, the use of agency workers could also imply that client organisation employees perceive themselves as replaceable, which might decrease their organisational commitment. It could be possible to counteract such a scenario by giving client organisation employees better opportunities for development. Our analysis is in line with the idea of having temporary agency workers as a buffer in case of a downturn, offering job stability for the client organisation's employees.

The third and final research question was how to explain agency workers' and client organisation employees' level of commitment. Factors associated with the management relation appear to outweigh the explanations linked to the employment relation. Previous research has shown that job characteristics are very important antecedents to commitment (Allen and Meyer 1990; Mowday, Porter and Steers 1982). In our study, this is confirmed for client organisation employees, but the explanation looks weaker for agency workers. Another aspect to consider is that temporary agency workers' commitment has to do with their expectations and hopes of becoming employed by the client organisation. Hence, our results could be interpreted in line with some other previous research on social exchange and psychological contract in which expectations have been considered an antecedent for agency workers' commitment (Chambel et al. 2015; Chambel, Castanheira and Sobral 2016; Coyle-Shapiro and Morrow 2006; Woldman et al. 2018). Job characteristics that might be temporary, because they are not connected to the employer, do not seem to produce much commitment. Instead, temporary agency workers may show commitment in exchange for any future employment at the client organisation, thereby leaving the buffer position to another agency worker.

References

Allen, N. J. and J. P. Meyer (1990) 'The Measurement and Antecedents of Affective, Continuance and Normative Commitment to the Organization.' *Journal of Occupational Psychology* 63(1): 1–18.

Atkinson, J. (1984) 'Manpower Strategies for Flexible Organization.' *Personnel Management*, August.

Becker, H. (1960) 'Notes on the Concept of Commitment.' *American Journal of Sociology* 66(1): 32–40.

Berg, A. (2008) *Bemanningsarbete, flexibilitet och lokabehandling. En studie av svensk rätt och kollektivavtalsreglering med komparativa inslag.* Lund: Juristförlaget.

Bergström, O. and D. Storrie (eds) (2003) *Contingent Employment in Europe and the United States.* Cheltenham, Northampton: Edward Elgar.

Bergström, O., K. Håkansson, T. Isidorsson and L. Walter (2007) *Den nya arbetsmarknaden. Bemanningsbranschens etablering i Sverige.* Lund: Academica Adacta.

Broschak, J. P., A. Davies-Blake and E. S. Block (2008) 'Nonstandard, Not Substandard. The Relationship Among Work Arrangements, Work Attitudes, and Job Performance.' *Work and Occupations* 35(1): 3–43.

Chambel, M. J., F. Castanheira and F. Sobral (2016) 'Temporary Agency Versus Permanent Workers: A Multigroup Analysis of Human Resource Management, Work Engagement and Organizational Commitment.' *Economic and Industrial Democracy* 37(4): 665–689.

Chambel, M. J., F. Sobral, M. Espada and L. Curral (2015) 'Training, Exhaustion, and Commitment of Temporary Agency Workers: A Test of Employability Perceptions.' *European Journal of Work and Organizational Psychology* 24(1): 15–30.

CIETT (2013) *The Agency Work Industry Around the World. 2013 Edition. Based on Figures Available in 2011.* Brussels: International Confederation of Private Employment Agencies.

CIETT (2014) *Economic Report. 2014 Edition. Based on Data of 2012/2013*. Brussels: International Confederation of Private Employment Agencies.

Cohen, A. (2007) 'Commitment Before and After: An Evaluation and Reconceptualization of Organizational Commitment.' *Human Resource Management Review* 17: 336–354.

Coleman, D. F., G. P. Irving and C. L. Cooper (1999) 'Another Look at the Locus of Control—Organizational Commitment Relationship: It Depends on the Form of Commitment.' *Journal of Organizational Behavior* 20(6): 995–1001.

Connelly, C. and D. G. Gallagher (2004) 'Emerging Trends in Contingent Work Research.' *Journal of Management* 30(6): 959–983.

Connelly, C., D. G. Gallagher and K. M. Gilley (2007) 'Organizational and Client Commitment Among Contracted Employees: A Replication and Extension with Temporary Workers.' *Journal of Vocational Behaviour* 70: 326–335.

Coyle-Shapiro, J. A. M and P. C. Morrow (2006) 'Organizational and Client Commitment Among Contracted Wmployees.' *Journal of Vocational Behaviour* 68: 416–431.

De Cuyper, N. and H. De Witte (2008) 'Job Insecurity and Employability Among Temporary Workers: A Theoretical Approach Based on the Psychological Contract', 88–107, in K. Näswall, J. Hellgren and M. Sverke (eds) *The Individual in the Changing Working Life*. Cambridge: Cambridge University Press.

Fontinha, R., M. J. Chambel and N. De Cuyper (2012) 'HR Attributions and the Dual Commitment of Outsourced IT Workers.' *Personnel Review* 41(6): 832–848.

Giunchi, M., M. J. Chambel and C. Ghislieri (2015) 'Contract Moderation Effects on Temporary Agency Workers' Affective Organizational Commitment and Perceptions of Support.' *Personnel Review* 44(1): 22–38.

Håkansson, K. and T. Isidorsson (2012a) 'Work Organizational Outcomes of the Use of Temporary Agency Workers.' *Organization Studies* 33(4): 487–505.

Håkansson, K and T. Isidorsson (2012b) 'Temporary Agency Workers and Organizational Commitment', 181–198, in B. Furåker, K. Håkansson and J. C. Karlsson (eds) *Commitment to Work and Job Satisfaction: Studies of Work Orientations*. New York, London: Routledge.

Håkansson, K. and T. Isidorsson (2015) 'Temporary Agency Workers—Precarious Workers? Perceived Job Security and Employability for Temporary Agency Workers and Client Organization Employees at a Swedish Manufacturing Plant.' *Nordic Journal of Working Life Studies* 5(4): 3–22.

Håkansson, K. and T. Isidorsson (2016) 'Användningen av inhyrd arbetskraft i Sverige.' *Arbetsmarknad & Arbetsliv* 22(3/4): 47–67.

Håkansson, K. and T. Isidorsson (2019) 'Job Quality for Temporary Agency Workers and Client Organization Employees at a Swedish Manufacturing Plant', 177–199, in T. Isidorsson and J. Kubisa (eds) *Job Quality in an Era of Flexibility. Experiences in a European Context*. London, New York: Routledge.

Håkansson, K., T. Isidorsson and H. Kantelius (2012) 'Temporary Agency Work as Means of Achieving Flexicurity.' *Nordic Journal for Working Life Studies* 2(4): 153–169.

Holst, H., O. Nachtwey and K. Dörre (2010) 'Temporary Agency Work. Functional Change of a Non-Standard Form of Employment.' *International Journal of Action Research* 6(1): 108–138.

Houseman, S. N. (2001) 'Why Employers Use Flexible Staffing Arrangements: Evidence from an Establishment Survey.' *Industrial and Labor Relations Review* 55(1): 149–170.

Kalleberg, A. L. (2001) 'Organizing Flexibility: The Flexible Firm in a New Century.' *British Journal of Industrial Relations* 39(4): 479–504.

Kalleberg, A. L., J. Reynolds and P. V. Marsden (2003) 'Externalizing Employment: Flexible Staffing Arrangements in US Organizations.' *Social Science Research* 32(4): 525–552.

Kauhanen, M. (2001) *Temporary Agency Work in Finland. Background Document on Temporary Agency Work in Europe.* Helsinki: Labour Institute for Economic Research.

Kuvaas, B. and A. Dysvik (2009) 'Perceived Investment in Permanent Employee Development and Social and Economic Exchange Perceptions Among Temporary Employees.' *Journal of Applied Social Psychology* 39(10): 2499–2524.

Meyer, J. P. and N. J. Allen (1991) 'A Three-Component Conceptualization of Organizational Commitment.' *Human Resource Management Review* 1(1): 61–89.

Meyer, J. P. and L. Herscovitch (2001) 'Commitment in the Workplace: Toward a General Model.' *Human Resource Management Review* 11(3): 299–236.

Mitlacher, L. W. (2007) 'The Role of Temporary Agency Work in Different Industrial Relations Systems—A Comparison Between Germany and the USA.' *British Journal of Industrial Relations* 45(3): 581–606.

Mowday, R. T., L. W. Porter and R. M. Steers (1982) *Employee-Organizational Linkages. The Psychology of Commitment, Absenteeism, and Turnover.* New York: Academic Press.

Mowday, R. T. and R. Steers (1979) 'The Measurement of Organizational Commitment.' *Journal of Vocational Behaviour* 14: 224–247.

OECD (2013) 'Protecting Jobs, Enhancing Flexibility: A New Look at Employment Protection Legislation,' 65–126, in *OECD Employment Outlook 2013.* París: OECD Publishing.

Porter, L. W., R. M. Steers, R. T. Mowday and P. V. Boulian (1974) 'Organizational Commitment, Job Satisfaction, and Turnover Among Psychiatric Technicians.' *Journal of Applied Psychology* 59(5): 603–609.

Slattery, J. P., T. T. Selvarajan, J. E. Anderson and R. Sardessai (2010) 'Relationship Between Job Characteristics and Attitudes: A Study of Temporary Employees.' *Journal of Applied Social Psychology* 40(6): 1539–1565.

Staffing Agreement (2017) Staffing Agreement 2017-05-01-2020-04-30 between the Swedish Trade Union Confederation and the Staffing Industries.

Storrie, D. (2007) 'Temporary Agency Work in the European Union—Economic Rationale and Equal Treatment', 103–122, in B. Furåker, K. Håkansson and J. C. Karlsson (eds) *Flexibility and Stability in Working Life.* Houndmills, Basingstoke: Palgrave Macmillan.

Swedish Code of Statutes (1982) No 80. Lag om anställningsskydd [The Employment Protection Act].

Swedish Code of Statutes (1993) No 440. Lag om privat arbetsförmedling [Act on Private Employment Agencies].

Swedish Code of Statutes (2012) No 854. Lag om uthyrning av arbetstagare [Act on the Hire of Workers].

Toms, S. and D. Biggs, (2014) 'The Psychological Impact of Agency Worker Utilisation.' *Employee Relations* 36(6): 622–641.

WeiBo, Z, S. Kaur and W. Jun (2010) 'New Development of Organizational Commitment: A Critical Review (1960–2009).' *African Journal of Business Management* 4(1): 12–20.

Woldman, N., R. Wesselink, P. Runhaar and M. Mulder (2018) 'Supporting Temporary Agency Workers' Affective Commitments: Exploring the Role of Opportunities for Competence Development.' *Human Resource Development International* 21(3): 254–275.

World Employment Confederation (2017) *Economic Report. Enabling Work, Adaptation, Security & Prosperity.* Brussels: World Employment Confederation.

Yin, R. (2014) *Case Study Research. Design and Methods*, 5th ed. London: Sage.

8 'There Is No Future for Us Oldies'

Sensing Dignity and Alienation in the Cabin

Ann Bergman and Jan Ch. Karlsson

Introduction

Organizational commitment can be treated as 'a matter of the bonds between employees and their workplace and employer. It implies that people are supportive of and loyal to their employing organization' (Furåker and Håkansson, Ch. 6: 124 in this book). Further, organizational commitment is strongly correlated to job characteristics, or working conditions, and to job satisfaction (e.g., Furåker and Berglund 2014; Lincoln and Kalleberg 1990; Meyer et al. 2002). We approach this causal cluster by using a theoretical framework based on the concepts of subjective *dignity* and *alienation*. The empirical material consists of a homogenous group of respondents: Swedish middle-class, middle-aged women who have been working long-term as cabin attendants at a full-service carrier airline. The purpose is to show how and explain why commitment to work and job satisfaction can shift rather quickly as the working conditions and the work change from being dignified to alienating. The main body of the chapter is focused on the conceptual pair dignity and alienation.

Some years ago, it was said that cabin attendants probably were 'under-studied, in spite of Arlie Russell Hochschild's *The Managed Heart*' (Hodson 2008: 756), but the situation has changed. Still, most research is concentrated on further theorizing and mapping of empirical trends in emotional labour (Bolton and Boyd 2003; Spiess and Waring 2005; Taylor and Tyler 2000; Williams 2003). However, some recent studies focus on other aspects, such as ageing, vulnerability and working conditions (Bergman and Gillberg 2015; Curley and Royle 2013), and collective mobilization and resistance (Taylor and Moore 2015). Hence, recent research indicates that studies of cabin attendants benefit from analyses that do not only focus on the emotional labour carried out in their encounters with passengers.

'There is something special about flight attendants', Per Gustafson writes (2003: 69; our translation), pointing out that the job of cabin attendant is one of few occupations in which women engage in an activity that has historically been linked to men—in this case, travel. Female-dominated occupations have rarely been associated with mobility or high status. Against this backdrop, the job of cabin attendant is special since it has been characterized by a rather unusual mix of femininity, service, high status, glamour, urbanity and mobility. In a study comparing perceptions of the statuses of various occupations, it was found that the cabin attendant is one of the few female-dominated occupations with a relatively high status (Ulfsdotter Eriksson 2006). Today, the occupation's status is not what it used to be and the decline has been rapid. As far as status is concerned, cabin attendants had their glory days during the postwar period, and status was associated with the exclusivity of flying, as air travel was restricted to a privileged few and associated with a feeling of luxury. It is no coincidence that the term *jet set*, denoting a class of wealthy, international people, is directly connected to air travel. The aura surrounding the exclusiveness of flying had a spillover effect on cabin crew, as did the high status of pilots. The occupation became desirable and was a ticket to the world, primarily for middle-class women. The occupation's popularity persisted even after scheduled flights became more accessible to the general public. Throughout this period, and until the present, the cabin attendant has embodied the airlines' image and been seen as a symbol of them (Barry 2007). Another aspect making the occupation somewhat exclusive is that it is quite small in numbers. In 2016, there were 2,310 cabin attendants in Sweden of which 80% were women and 20% men (SCB 2016). The total number of passengers at Swedish airports was in the same year 36.3 million (Transportstyrelsen 2016).

The industry has been subject to continuous reshaping since the postwar period—for instance, via the technical developments that have made flights possible that are faster, longer, higher and carry more passengers. Between the years 2007 and 2017, the total number of people globally traveling by commercial aviation rose from 2.4 billion to 4.1 billion (IATA 2018). In 1995, fewer than 10,000 unique city pairs were globally connected by commercial aviation, while in 2017 there were more than 20,000 such pairs. While air travel has become more accessible, airfares have simultaneously gone down. Between 1995 and 2017, the cost of air travel for consumers decreased by more than half in real (inflation-adjusted) terms (IATA 2018).

In Sweden, overseas flights were deregulated in 1991 and domestic flights in 1992; since then, the number of actors has constantly been increasing with more (smallish) airports coming into service. In 1997, European Union deregulations opened up the market so that any commercial company could service any destination at any price (Boyd and Bain 1998; Unionen 2014). In 2016, low-cost carriers had 35–40% of the market in the Nordic countries (Transportstyrelsen 2016). Thus, the deregulations together with economic recessions in the Eurozone contributed to full-service carriers adapting to a number of the cost efficiency practices used by low-cost carriers in order to be competitive (Dobruszkes 2006). Therefore, the earlier division between full-service carriers and low-cost carriers is increasingly blurred, resulting in hybrid models.

Cheap airfare and accessibility have created passenger groups showing a greater variation in terms of, for example, class and lifestyle, thus generating a broader range of expectations regarding service. The airlines' goal is to safely transport passengers from point A to point B as fast and cost-efficiently as possible, while those passengers simultaneously are being induced to consume. Consequently, the occupational role, working conditions and status of cabin attendants have transformed from 'a touch of class' to 'fast and good enough'. The cabin attendants at low-cost carriers are recruited into an already modified occupational role, while long-serving cabin attendants at full-service carriers have experienced the transformation in their work practices. Therefore, at full-service carriers the cabin attendants, according to Phil Taylor and Sian Moore (2015), work under a 'double burden' through the airlines' strategy of cutting costs while requiring a relatively high service quality. The once so attractive job was created by an industry that no longer can afford to keep up its original standards (Barry 2007; Bergman and Gillberg 2015).

Method

The data are based on in-depth interviews and follow up email conversations with eight female cabin attendants of which seven were conducted during the autumn and winter of 2013 and one in the fall of 2015. At the time, the women were aged between 50 and 55 and they all had middle-class backgrounds. They had been in the occupation for between 24 and 30 years, and had worked for their then employer, a full-service carrier airline, between 16 and 23 years. Despite the fact that there were individual variations and that each respondent had her own story, living conditions and experience, much was similar. They described what a closely knit group they had become during a long period of savings and rationalizations undertaken by the company since the end of the 1990s. In this connection, it is noticeable that the respondents spoke of 'us' and 'we' much more often than of 'I' when telling us about their work. 'We' did not stand for the interviewed as a group, but for all long-serving, middle-aged, middle-class women working as flight attendants for the company.

The interviews were open, unstructured conversations about the respondents' experiences of their work situation. Their own concerns and interests guided the conversations. Of course, there were follow-up questions, but each interview started with a request to talk about the job and what they thought of it. One part of the conversation was recorded and the other was not; instead notes were taken. After turning off the recorder, the respondents kept on talking—we would not say more freely or critically, but more personally. After the interviews, there were some follow-up discussions by email, and one of the respondents wrote a short 24-hour diary.

In the first coding of the empirical material, we soon came to think of the concepts of alienation and dignity, including relations between them. We then went to the literature on these concepts, eventually forming a precoding list with codes from the model in Table 8.2. We were searching for expressions of the category *Dignity* (using the codes Autonomy, Meaningful work, Respect and Flourishing) and the category *Alienation* (using the codes Powerlessness, Meaningless work, Disrespect and Self-estrangement). Eventually, we added other codes—namely, those of High and Low work–life quality—in order to capture the relationship between work and nonwork, as this turned out to be an extremely important part of the cabin attendants' narratives of their experiences of changes in work. (This dimension was then added to the model.) The subsequent analysis was guided by these analytical categories and codes. We used them as a filter through which we scrutinized the cabin attendants' descriptions of their present situation, which they constantly related to their experiences in the past. This analytical filter, or grid, forms the framework in which we present the results. The voices of the respondents set the narrative in motion and hence the number of interview quotes is high. Our methodological approach, then, has not been a straightforwardly inductive or deductive one. Instead, we have constantly moved between and combined these analytical strategies (cf. Karlsson and Bergman 2017: 10–11). However, the study can also be regarded as one concerning a critical case (Yin 2003: 40) in that we are testing the Dignity–Alienation Model that we developed during the analysis on an occupational group of a certain age that seems suitable for such a test. The cabin attendants we interviewed had been working in their occupation for such a long time that they had experienced dramatic changes in their working conditions. The critical case concerns whether their experiences can be interpreted and explained through seeing them in the light of the model.

We are aware that there is always the risk of nostalgia when talking about an occupation in retrospect. Since all respondents were long serving and were recruited into the occupation by the present airline company or other airline companies during the 1980s, there is a need to be cautious about the comparisons between the past and the present made by the respondents when it comes to working conditions. On the other hand, their prior experiences in the occupation make them an interesting group to study—a critical case. Younger, newly recruited cabin crew would probably tell a different story, partly due to their lack of earlier experiences in the occupation and to the fact that they were recruited on other types of contracts.

However, evidence from other sources, such as the trade union, indicates that the working conditions have in fact deteriorated and the occupation and the industry have undergone big changes due to deregulation and increased competitiveness (Unionen 2014). Further, there are some objective facts concerning, for example, working hours, rotas and retiring age that support their subjective comparisons between the past and the present. Nevertheless, it is the experience of the cabin attendants themselves that is of importance in this chapter. Their experiences reveal the causes of their shift from being satisfied and committed to work to the opposite—or in other words, from subjective feelings of dignity to feelings of alienation.

Dignity and Alienation

The concept of *alienation* has a long history in philosophy and the social sciences (Israel 1971), and for a couple of decades from the 1950s on it had a central position in the sociology of work. Part of this involved a turn to a subjective interpretation of the concept rather than the objective one found in Marx. There is a common saying expressing this—namely, that work creates 'blue-collar blues, white-collar woes and managerial discontent'. The most common social science reference is to Melvin Seeman (1959), although other sociologists took this turn before he did (e.g., Goffman 1957). Seeman's fame is largely due to Robert Blauner (1973) taking his dimensions of alienation as a point of departure for his analysis of alienation and freedom in industrial settings.

The dimensions of alienation presented by Seeman came, he says (1959: 783), from the 'basic ways in which the concept of alienation has been used' in sociology. Further, he emphasizes that his perspective on alienation involves 'a consistent focus on the individual's expectations or values' (1959: 788), leaving social conditioning and the behavioural consequences of these subjective dimensions to others to study. One reason for choosing this perspective is that he wants to avoid the critical element of the concept in favour of adapting it for empirical research. Seeman's dimensions are: (1) powerlessness, or the feeling that you cannot determine the outcomes you seek in life; (2) meaninglessness, or thinking that you do not understand the workings of the social organization to which you belong, leading to the impossibility to predict the outcomes of your behaviour; (3) normlessness, or the expectation that you have to use socially unacceptable means to reach your goals; (4) isolation, or the implication that you do not value those things that are highly regarded in your society; and finally, (5) self-estrangement, or performing activities only instrumentally and not in an engaged way.

Blauner later used four of Seeman's dimensions of alienation in an investigation of the variations of the intensity of alienation in different types of industry: powerlessness, meaninglessness, social alienation or isolation and self-estrangement. He describes (1973: 182–183) the main results as an inverted U-curve. In craft industries, there is a low level of alienation in all four dimensions, giving workers maximum freedom in their work. The level of alienation rises steeply in machine industries, such as textiles, especially when it comes to powerlessness. Alienation reaches its peak in industries using assembly-line production, such as car manufacturing. Here all dimensions of alienation are intensified. However, this development is reversed in continuous-process, automated industries, with chemical plants as Blauner's main example, where there is a decline of the experience of powerlessness, meaninglessness, isolation and self-estrangement, leading to high degrees of feelings of freedom for workers. In Blauner's analysis, there is also a time element, implying a development from craft, to machine and conveyor belt industries to automation. He therefore predicts that the future holds less alienation and a growing degree of freedom for industrial workers. Like most social science forecasts, this has turned out to be empirically false (Hodson 1996).

For a period during the late 20th and the beginning of the 21st century, the concept of alienation was less popular in the social sciences. One of the reasons was probably the intense criticism launched at Blauner's analysis, mainly for its methodological deficiencies and for being an expression of technological determinism (e.g., Eldridge 1971; Gallie 1978). A beginning of a renaissance of the concept can, however, be discerned through the analysis in Marek Korczynski's (2014) *Songs of the Factory*, a book that has attracted much attention. This ethnographic study was carried out in a Taylorized blinds factory with work tasks of deadening monotony. In his analysis, Korczynski (2014: 68–69) reintroduces the concept of alienation:

> I want to reclaim the usefulness of the concept of alienation for sociologists of work, as a way of understanding the lived experience of labor as a social process. In particular, I argue for the importance of understanding how workers *sense* alienation. . . . Workers sensing alienation was also a social process in that they constantly fought back against their senses being dominated by alienation.

The sense of alienation was triggered by the immediate working conditions, such as the monotonous work and abuse from supervisors, but was put out of play whenever work was not performed, such as during breaks.

Although cabin attendants are not working on an assembly line and produce services, not goods, the notion of subjective alienation plays a crucial role in our understanding of how they experience their working conditions and how they are affected by them. This is in line with Hochschild (2003: 7), who states that one can become alienated in a service producing as well as in a goods producing society. In comparison to Hochschild, who sees alienation as an outcome of the emotional labour enacted by the cabin attendants in the service encounter, we understand it as an outcome of the working conditions in general.

So, what is the opposite of alienation? In Blauner's analysis, the antonym of alienation is freedom, leading to a scale of the dimensions: powerlessness vs. control, meaninglessness vs. purposefulness, isolation vs. belonging and self-estrangement vs. self-expression. However, in her seminal analysis of emotional labour, Hochschild (2003: 184) indicates that the opposite of alienation is dignity, although she does not elaborate on the point. Blauner too sometimes mentions *dignity* as a term for *non-alienation* (1964: 164–165). Further, Korczynski specifies both implicitly (e.g., 2014: 123) and explicitly (2014: 128) that dignity is the opposite concept of alienation. A minimal definition in the social sciences of dignity at work is that it should at least entail 'the ability to establish a sense of self-worth and self-respect, and to appreciate the respect of others' (Hodson 2001: 3). There is, however, a more elaborate characterization (Sayer 2007: 567): working conditions that provide employees with 'integrity, respect, pride, recognition, worth and standing or status, are positively related to dignity', while conditions that result in 'shame, stigma, humiliation, lack of recognition, or being mistrusted or taken for granted are negatively related to dignity'.

Finally, Sharon C. Bolton (2007, 2010) has suggested a Dimensions of Dignity at Work Model, underlining the importance of its construction (2010: 166):

> Thinking in terms of dimensions allows for a detailed analysis of dignity at work that covers many important issues in the world of work and how experiences may differ. For example, many people enjoy dignity in work as they have some autonomy and/or meaning in the type of work they do, but not dignity at work in the sense that they do not enjoy good terms and conditions of employment. Yet others may carry out mundane and monotonous work but benefit from dignity at work in that they gain from a physically healthy working environment and secure terms and conditions. Combined, a dimension of dignity model represents a useful opportunity for a holistic analysis of work in its blend of the inherent dignity of the human person with people management policies and practices that may either support or deny this human condition.

The dimensions are classified as the subjective factors of dignity in work and the objective factors of dignity at work. The former are, of course, the most interesting in this book. Bolton's dimensions of the factors in work are autonomy, job satisfaction, meaningful work, respect, and learning and development, which we call flourishing. Bolton does not discuss antonyms of the dimensions, but it is clear that they are autonomy vs. powerlessness, job satisfaction vs. job dissatisfaction, meaningful work vs. meaningless work, respect vs. disrespect, and flourishing vs.

self-estrangement. The way the two models relate to each other can be seen in Table 8.1.

Some of these dimensions are theoretically problematic for our purposes. First, there is the dimension of job satisfaction. The concept job satisfaction 'designates the degree to which people are content with their job' (Furåker, 2012: 11). Thereby it comprises most of the Bolton–Blauner model, without differentiating in the way we need. Second, 'respect' is one of Bolton's dimensions, but it lacks an antonym in those of Blauner. This seems, however, easy enough to solve by simply adding 'disrespect' on the Blauner side (cf. Sayer's definition of dignity above). Finally, the concept of 'isolation' in the right-hand column does not have an opposite in the left-hand column. It is also quite a vague concept (cf. Israel 1971: 212) and we leave it out of the present argument. Another theme is so strong in the interviews that we have to add a further dimension to the above. The interviewees talked a lot and with great emphasis about the relation between their jobs and family life when discussing their experiences of work; the relation between work and the total life situation was an important aspect. We therefore add the dimension 'high work–life quality' and 'low work–life quality' to our model. By *work* we mean paid work and by *life* we mean life outside of working hours, such as family and leisure.

Obviously, in our interpretation, the first term in each conceptual pair is a dimension of dignity while the second is a dimension of alienation. The result, the Dignity–Alienation Model, can be found in Table 8.2.

Table 8.1 Relationship between Bolton's and Blauner's models

Bolton: Dignity in work	Blauner: Alienation
Autonomy	Powerlessness
Job satisfaction	
Meaningful work	Meaningless work
Respect	
Flourishing	Self-estrangement
	Isolation

Table 8.2 Subjective dimensions of dignity and alienation in work

Dignity	↔	Alienation
Autonomy	↔	Powerlessness
Meaningful work	↔	Meaningless work
Flourishing	↔	Self-estrangement
Respect	↔	Disrespect
Work–life balance	↔	Work–life conflict

Bolton seems to regard the dimensions of dignity as absolute classifications as she does not discuss opposite concepts, while Blauner treats the dimensions as endpoints on a scale. In Table 8.2 we do the same as Blauner: a phenomenon can in principle be categorized at any point between dignity and alienation as it is a continuum. The more dignity there is, the less alienation there is, and vice versa.

As the concepts are abstractions and the cabin attendants and their subjective experiences are not, the results presented below are not as neat and tidy as the model. The dimensions are interrelated and overlap and therefore they need to be understood in relation to each other. Subjective alienation emerges due to the interactions of the dimensions.

Working in the Sky

As mentioned, our emphasis in the presentation of the results is on the shift from subjective dignity to subjective alienation in order to show how these two aspects are interrelated in several dimensions and causally connected to objective working conditions. The experiences presented are unevenly spread along the continuum of each dimension and there is a variation in the empirical starting and ending points of the different continua. The results are not exact measurements of changes on these continua, but a result of our analysis of the cabin attendants' stories about their working lives, which all show a drift from dignity towards alienation. The presentation below is both a description of each dimension, with the dignity endpoint described first, and an attempt to create a coherent narrative.

Autonomy and Powerlessness

Autonomy entails the sense of being in control of your work, being able to lay down—individually or collectively—the rules followed in performing work tasks and determining other circumstances. The opposite concept, powerlessness, refers to the sense of not being able to control or modify your work environment and conditions. An autonomous worker experience being an active agent, but a powerless worker is deprived of agency. A lack of autonomy is related to the unpredictability of working hours and whether the cabin attendants will have their recovery time. Their lack of experienced autonomy is thus related to high demands of unpredictable availability for and flexibility at work, which develop into feelings of not being in control of their lives.

The cabin attendants said that the first significant deterioration in their work situation came in 2004. Before that, cabin attendants were scheduled on a fixed, regular and cyclical rota, in which a full-time position involved five days of work followed by four days off. Since this rota continued yearly, it made their work predictable. It was possible for them to plan their leisure time and family life accordingly. The possibilities of long-term planning made it easy to swap days with colleagues, or apply for vacation if needed. They also knew that one work period of five days often, but not always, started with an overnight stop between day one and day two and that they came home on day two. On day three, they also came home after working during the day/evening and between days four and five they again had an overnight stop somewhere. Altogether, these factors enabled the cabin attendants to plan their lives in a way that helped them to develop feelings of being in control. As a result of the company's increased demand for flexible staff due to a more competitive and uncertain market, the cabin attendants' working conditions took a turn for the worse. Moira said:

> Even if it started earlier in 2002 after 9/11 and a decrease in passengers, with Ryan Air becoming a serious competitor, it was in 2004 we got catastrophic rotas with more working hours and variable schedules.

They all stress it was a major downturn when they had to let go of the earlier system and instead went on a variable rota, which to them presented a more inflexible and unpredictable schedule. It became almost impossible to swap days with colleagues as well.

The next big deterioration in their autonomy was the agreement entered into at the end of 2012 that increased the maximum number of working hours from 45 to 47.5 hours per week and from 10.5 to 13 hours per day. Daily working hours could be increased to 15 hours per day and to 60 hours per week in the event of certain unforeseen circumstances, such as delays and the replanning of rotas. The Swedish Working Hours Act only regulates parts of the working time for cabin attendants, since it makes an exception for certain groups of flight personnel. Instead, their working hours are regulated by the European Aviation Security Agency, which allows up to 60 hours per week and 190 hours per month. Replanning and changes became more common along a whole rota, but also over a single shift. Rebecca stated:

> You often begin early on the first day of a rota and finish late on the last day, and in between, you can do just about anything. They keep redoing the rotas all the time. Either they call you or you find out when you check in. They can postpone a flight by two hours whenever necessary. So, imagine that I'm supposed to finish at 7 pm, but it can be at 9 pm instead, and I find this out on the very same day. We have small time margins and, on the days when we work, the company can in principle utilize every hour of the day and does what it wants with us.

The company's extended demand for flexibility resulted in instability for the cabin personnel. It made the working day less porous and reduced breaks on the ground between flights. Suzy said: 'We no longer have the right to meal breaks on the ground between flights; instead lunch and other breaks are often being taken on board during flights'. The cabin attendants experienced these changes as further decreasing their autonomy, since they earlier could use such breaks to make phone calls, read a newspaper or just rest. In addition, time for recovery was affected negatively. Suzy continued: 'You are entitled to 12 hours [of] rest between the shifts and then you' are expected to be fit for work again. The thing is that our 12-hour rest period can occur whenever—for example, during the day'. Not being able to predict or influence when free time is scheduled results in a feeling of powerlessness and of being entirely in the hands of the company and technology. Hannah said:

> They put everything into the computer [crew, flights] and the system then spits out the most efficient result. There is no will or intent [from management] to schedule us in another way. The result of the scheduling works on paper and it is according to the collective agreement—but not for us.

The cabin attendants received their rotas for the coming month on the 15th of each month. Hence, they did not know their rotas until two weeks prior to them being implemented. This is yet another aspect that increased their lack of autonomy, since it reduced their possibilities to plan ahead.

The experience of not being listened to by the management or the union increased the feelings of powerlessness. Lorna said: 'I have no possibilities to influence my work situation. . . . They want to have a human being that works whenever they want it to, on their conditions, and that doesn't make any demands'. In the same way, Moira stated, 'Our managers are angry with us since we do not appreciate the situation. They want us to keep on working, look happy and think it is totally fine to work 14 hours a day'. Rebecca spoke of how she went up to her manager after the agreement was signed between the union and the company in 2012:

> I told her that this change will have enormous consequences. She answered that there was no danger and that it would turn out exactly as in 2004. That it would blow over. Now one year has passed and we are still upset. It has not blown over. It is different now.

Rebecca said that there used to be very good communication between them, but now she 'feel[s] an enormous contempt for those people who just look at us and say: Things will turn out fine'. Hence, the cabin attendants experienced that there was no dialogue between staff and management and that the only way management communicated was through directives or printed messages. Esther exclaimed: 'I wish they would listen more to us, but they don't. We don't have their ear, they don't hear us at all'. Further, the cabin attendants did not think that they received any support from either the worker safety representatives or the labour union in this matter. Moira continued: 'We have just had an email from the union where it says that they are disappointed with us because we are disrupting and destroying things now when we need to stick together'. The union representatives claimed, on the other hand, that they had to accept drastically worsened working conditions in order to keep the jobs in Sweden, which was their first priority.

The work in the cabin of each member of the crew has always been strictly regulated by safety routines and standards during a flight. However, even more standardization has been introduced in their work of serving the passengers in order to increase efficiency, which has led to an experienced decrease in autonomy. Carol said:

> Our company management used to say that you do whatever you yourself think you need to do in a specific situation in order to give good service. Today we are more directed by standards. How to serve, all the elements and the service encounters with the passenger.

In summary, although the flight attendants only had some amount of autonomy in the early years, there was a sharp turn towards their sensing powerlessness from the middle of the 2000s. Several factors contributed to this. They felt that the management, but also the union, did not listen to them anymore. Their original responsibility for the service encounter was changed by new managerial standards. Further, without them being able to influence the decisions, their regular rotas could be changed at short notice, the workday was extended and they lost their meal breaks on the ground. In all, there was a considerable movement on the continuum from some degree of autonomy, related to predictability, to a high degree of powerlessness. This sense of powerlessness is closely related to the feelings of meaninglessness that are presented next.

Meaningful and Meaningless Work

Work is meaningful if workers sense that what they do is part of a larger whole, but it can also be meaningful in relation to an individual's preferences. Workers feel that they contribute to something that they see in a positive light, but also that the work itself is seen in a positive light. Meaninglessness results when workers cannot sense such connections to, for example, the final product or good service to customers, or when the work itself is experienced negatively. What is regarded as a meaningful job is influenced by work tasks, working conditions and colleagues, but also by a worker's life situation as a whole. Although the work–non-work relationship is discussed at length in a later section, it also plays an important role in this dimension. The result shows that a sense of resignation is related to meaninglessness. This resignation grew from a conviction that the ongoing deregulation and competition in the industry would not stop. Further, the cabin attendants were certain that they belonged to an unwanted group due to their age and their resistance to the ongoing changes.

The cabin attendants said that the job had always involved irregular working hours, being away from home and a rather heavy physical workload. However, this was not regarded as a problem since they experienced that they always had the possibility to recuperate and enjoy a good balance between work and rest, and that the pros of the work far outweighed the cons. Their irregular working hours were often described as a positive part of the job, forming the basis of an appreciated lifestyle. Rebecca stated:

> For many years of my life, I've had the privilege of having a good job which I've truly loved. It hasn't been the best job in the world as regards career, working conditions, wages or things like that. Instead, it used to be the best shitty job in the world! It's lively, with people on the go, and constantly new encounters.

The 'best shitty job in the world' captures the paradox of having a job which was not regarded as the most meaningful and best job on the whole, but at the same time was fun and made it possible to live a life that they felt had meaning. Common traits among these cabin attendants recruited in the mid-1980s include their middle-class backgrounds, not being too highly educated and viewing their jobs as offering better opportunities than many other possible jobs. Suzy noted, 'Most of us have some form of upper secondary education, which means that the job of cabin attendant was, for all that, a good one, given our education'. The work presented opportunities such as good wages and possibilities to travel. Esther remembered: 'I started in 1986 and was before that working as a nurse and had SEK 4,800 a month. Then when I became a cabin attendant I got SEK 7,900 a month and felt so wealthy!'

The cabin attendants all highlighted and appreciated their encounters with a great variety of people, such as other crew members, multitudes of passengers and the diversity of persons and occupational groups within aviation at large. Hannah stated: 'I always liked working with people; before I started here I was at a childcare centre. I still enjoy meeting people. That is what I really like about being a cabin attendant.' They all stressed the social dimension of their work in the cabin, and mentioned aspects such as being able to handle different people, create a good atmosphere and give good service as making the work meaningful. Rebecca said: 'I don't need a manager that pats me on the head and tells me that I'm good. I get that from my passengers'. However short and intense the meetings on board during flights were, they all high-lighted the importance of being able to provide good service, along with their responsibility for health and safety, as important for their sense of meaning. At the time of the interviews, the cabin attendants experienced that there was less time to provide good service, which made them feel unsatisfied and frustrated with themselves and their jobs. Lorna declared:

> Today, service is something totally different from five to ten years ago. Then we had something to serve with. Today we are a walking kiosk and a sales person and in the midst of this selling, you are trying to create a nice environment.

Their frustration over their work situation led to a distancing, whereby the cabin attendants ceased to engage emotionally and cognitively in their work. They also described how they had lowered their work standards by not delivering the same level of service and by not being there for their employer in the same way as before. They expressed that they felt that there was no meaning to being loyal and committed to work and that this was a result of not being able to do a good job. Rita commented: 'I want to feel that I'm doing a good job, that's very satisfying. The way it is now, I feel that I don't live up to what I want'.

The reshaping of the industry has had consequences for the occupation, which has been degraded in terms of both working conditions and status; however, at the same time, the women included in this study carry with them experiences of earlier times and they were socialized into a different occupational role. Lorna expressed it in this way:

> The older ones among us find the low level of service difficult. For the younger ones, who don't know anything other than quickly, quickly, hurry, hurry, it's a lot easier not to care. They're different. They're tougher than us and don't care as much about the passengers and others [as we do].

There existed a strong collective memory in the group of older cabin attendants about what it was like when they felt their work was meaningful to them as well as their company. Carol mentioned, 'There is a picture of how we want it to be, but we'll never be able to get back to that again. Therefore—resignation'. Suzy said, 'I don't think the company has any choices since this is all regulated by the EU. There is no return'. Hannah stated, 'We're a dying species. When we quit there will be young people on hourly contracts who work here for a couple of years while they study. This occupation has changed'. The cabin attendants stressed that what was happening to the company was a consequence of an ongoing and irreversible trend. They described the company's continuous financial rescue packages, their frozen wages and heavy cutbacks in their allowances for expenses in the previous couple of years. Along with impaired working conditions, the lack of possibility to change the situation and a conviction that what was happening in the industry was impossible to change, the situation was experienced as devoid of meaning.

In summary, the preconditions for providing good service, something the cabin attendants thought was important and which made them feel proud, were not there anymore. Further, they did not sense any hope of those conditions ever returning. This led to resignation in the face of less meaningful work. Also in this dimension, there was a clear movement on the continuum from dignity towards alienation. The cabin attendants' experiences of an increase in their feelings of meaninglessness are interrelated with the next dimension—respect and disrespect.

Respect and Disrespect

Respect can be defined as the 'imputed worth accorded to one person by one or more others' (Spears et al. 2006: 179). However, for our purposes two additions are needed (Rogers and Ashforth 2017). First, it concerns how employees subjectively sense this worth as directed towards them from others, and second, respect can be directed towards an individual as well as a whole group—in our case the occupational group of cabin attendants. The cabin attendants experienced that their work and they as employees had gone from being respected to becoming disrespected. These experiences were mainly related to a fall in occupational status, declines in working conditions and benefits at large and the feeling that the company wanted to get rid of them.

Rebecca declared:

> All the deteriorations in our situation have made us worn out and feel like junk that has no value. In the 1980s, when I started, and into the 1990s, we were the airline's frontline staff. We were respected and treated accordingly. We had a value, in simple terms, and things like that are important for your self-esteem and well-being.

As mentioned above, the cabin attendants were all socialized into their occupational role during a period when passenger service was important and the frontline staff was deemed important as well as professional. Carol stated: 'Then as well as today we are a combination of nurse, fireman and waitress, but back then we were more into fine-dining than fast-food'. Their status and being respected were tightly bound up with safety and service and highlighted by the company in its marketing. The safety dimension is still of importance, but onboard service has changed due to the company's conversion to cheap mass transportation. Along with the shift in service provided by the company and expectations from the passengers, the occupation's status has declined. Moira reflected upon the past and said:

> We could run ourselves into the ground, almost, to please the passengers; nothing was impossible. However, there was no way we were being pushed around. We received enormous support from the company. We were their public face and we always heard that we'd been chosen and how important and skilful we were. Imagine the 80s! Imagine the moment of truth! That was us! [laughter]

They all felt that they once had been involved in shaping the airline and its image and that they at that time were significant and valuable as persons—and as Moira added: 'Isn't that what all people want in their work—to be able to feel dignity and respect?' There was a common understanding that the company had let them down by the deteriorating working conditions and that they did not receive the same recognition as before. They felt that their well-being and even their basic needs no longer were of any interest to the company. Lorna said:

> The company seems to have forgotten that its staff are people who need to sleep, rest, eat and visit the toilet. The company is entirely addressing its own needs and sucking the maximum out of its employees, and we won't be able to take an unlimited amount of that.

Rebecca said, 'In the past I felt privileged, but now I feel contempt and just want to leave the company. The working conditions are inhuman and—surprise—I am still human!' Some of the biggest problems for the cabin attendants were related to what they saw as their basic needs such as sleeping and eating regularly. Since there were flights around the clock, the loops worked by cabin attendants did not run either clockwise or anticlockwise, but could be completely varied. Rita exemplified some of the difficulties with switching between clockwise and anticlockwise rotations for sleep, work and mealtimes. She said:

> We are getting insomnia, stomach problems and increased ill health. Before flying New York I can have two full days of 10 hours each day and then get up at 3:30 [in the morning] and fly to New York. After these shifts, you can be sure of nosebleeds and your stomach being in a mess.

The women also described that they felt as if they were seen as too old and too sick, but also too burdensome for the company due to their salaries and their outspoken resistance to the ongoing changes. Although the company claimed that their age was not a problem, they were all convinced that it was their age, in combination with their attitudes and wages, that was troublesome and Hannah claimed, 'They have a hidden agenda; they want to get rid of us'. Lorna declared:

> There is no one from the company who says, 'What good work you are doing!' Our managers don't care at all about us and we just have to like it or leave it. From being the face outward we are now easily replaceable.

Their own understanding was that they had been very loyal to the company and shown a high degree of work morale as a way of returning their appreciation for being recognized and their good working conditions. There was a tendency among the cabin attendants to talk about their employer almost as a person to which they had a personal relationship, or as Rebecca said:

> I've been in harmony with my company, been there through thick and thin, and now it's over. They ended it with me first, and then I ended it with them. It gets so personal when such a long-term relationship ends.

It was not only the way the cabin attendants were treated by the company in terms of status decline that affected them; they felt a lack of respect in the cabin while interacting with the passengers, but also beyond that. Rita expressed the following:

> Even though this wasn't the most qualified of jobs, I was still proud of being a cabin attendant. I stood tall in my uniform and was able to walk with my head held high. All the time, we were reminded that we'd been chosen. Today, I curl up and am almost ashamed to show myself in my uniform, on the metro or on the bus.

Esther reflected upon how she felt regarding the company's respect for them and said: 'If we'd started to treat our passengers in the same way as our company treats us we'd go bankrupt'.

In summary, the fall in job status meant that the cabin attendants sensed much less recognition and respect from the company both as individuals and as an occupational group. They even felt disrespected to such an extent that they suspected that the company planned to terminate their employment. From sensing that they were the face of the company, representing it outwards, they felt that they were a burden to it. Working under conditions that they thought did not even meet the most basic needs strengthened their feelings of being disrespected and betrayed. The movement on the respect–disrespect dimension has strongly been in the direction of alienation. The next dimension, flourishing and self-estrangement, is closely related to all three dimensions described above.

Flourishing and Self-Estrangement

In the Aristotelian tradition to which we adhere, 'flourishing consists in cultivating a *range* of different virtues, relationships, activities and "excellences"' (Sayer 2007: 30–31; cf. Gorski 2013). Flourishing in work would have been a contradiction in terms for Aristotle, but here it means the sense of 'self-actualization' through being engaged in work for intrinsic reasons. Its antonym is therefore 'self-estrangement' through not being engaged in your work or only doing it for money (for which another term is 'instrumental orientation', cf. Furåker, Ch. 2 in this book). Among the cabin attendants, self-estrangement was expressed by a sense of having reached a dead-end, with no hope of changing the direction of development for the company or for themselves. Their ageing and their limited chances to obtain desirable jobs outside of aviation were related to feelings of being trapped in an undesirable situation.

A crucial part of the cabin attendants' feelings of what is here understood as manifestations of self-estrangement was caused by the agreement between the employer and the union in 2012, which came into force in 2013. Rebecca said, 'You can't believe it's true that this is an agreement between a union and an employer in Sweden of today. There seems to be no way to change what is happening'. As mentioned above, their conviction that their future in the company and occupation would not get better, but even worse, gave rise to feelings of despair. This experience was strongly related to their age and to their impaired intention of staying in the company until retirement. As mentioned, the respondents were aged between 50 and 55 when interviewed. They were aiming, up until the 2012 agreement, to retire at 60, which was the previous retirement age. Along with other deteriorations, the retirement age was raised from 60 to 65, at the same time as other pension conditions were degraded. The change in the retirement age was seen as a considerable setback, since they all had planned to retire at 60. Esther expressed it like this: 'Working the way you do in your 60s and beyond is not really that good for you. Long hours, irregular hours, high altitude, starts and landings wear you down. It's simply harder for us older ones to recover'.

Hence, ageing was a central concern among the cabin attendants, not only because of worries about their health but also because of their sense of the difficulties of getting another job. Hannah commented: 'Many are in their fifties and have done this for a very long time and do not really have anything to fall back onto. This is a big problem for many'. There was a strong feeling of being locked in based on their sense of being unwanted by both the company and the labour market at large. Lorna said: 'I've realized, after having applied for as many jobs as I have done, that I'm no longer of interest as I don't have any certificates and I'm old'. The cabin attendants said that a common discussion among them in the cabin and on breaks was about what they could do to be able to quit and what jobs they had a chance of getting. They were all looking for another job and said that they would never recommend their present job to anyone they knew and that they felt sorry for colleagues who were in their 60s. Suzy said: 'The ones close to retirement, they just bite the bullet and are trying to last, but the ones my age are almost all thinking of alternative jobs and ways out'.

As the company claimed that continued efforts to increase revenues and reduce costs were required for survival, while simultaneously emphasizing safety, punctuality and also a high quality of service—the cabin attendants were of the opinion that staying in the company and occupation was devastating health-wise and socially. They were convinced that these degraded working conditions were normalized and had set the standard as regards the kind of cabin crew the company preferred. The ideal employee was depicted as a malleable (young and/or contracted) person who works for a couple of years under flexible forms of employment, an insight that shattered the cabin attendants' future prospects in the occupation. As a way of coping with the present situation, physically and psychologically, all the respondents were working part time. Some also attended different kinds of education to increase their employability, but also as a way to earn the right to work part time.

Previously, the cabin attendants argued, they all shared a belief that if they were there for the company in hard times, then the company would be there for them. Now they experienced that this had not been the case, and the feelings of being respected and being in it together were replaced with disappointment. Rebecca said: 'They have let us down so many times. There's no work ethic left. It's crumbled away because of how we've been treated. I'm so damned angry, but also really sad about what's happened'. Lorna expressed the same letdown while at the same time referring to her own well-being and said:

> We've been so loyal, so terribly loyal. We've gone along with 'We are fixing this'. Then we were dropped. You get sadder and sadder and more and more resigned. There doesn't seem to be an end to it. You're always selling a part of yourself, but there are limits to everything. For my part, it isn't worth what it costs me to stay there in terms of body and soul. There is no future for us oldies.

There was a certainty that the younger cabin attendants did not share the same experiences, since they belonged to a new type of employee just passing through the job. Hence, this sense of self-estrangement in and of the work was related to this older group of cabin attendants' perception of their present situation due to their collective experiences in the past.

In summary, the possibilities for flourishing have diminished continuously and the cabin attendants have replaced commitment, loyalty and a will to work for the company until retirement with a desperation to find a way to quit—an exit. Having to continue working five more years after the age of 60 was contributing to an instrumental attitude to work and to a sense of self-estrangement. Their awareness of being locked into an unwanted and demanding situation with an ageing body further increased these feelings along with a strong sense of being betrayed by the company. Being worried about health and well-being as well as the chances to find ways out of a detrimental situation is not a driver for flourishing. Also when it comes to the dimension of flourishing and self-estrangement, there is a movement from dignity towards the alienation point of the continuum.

High Work–Life Quality and Low Work–Life Quality

Related to the conceptual pair of high and low work–life quality is the concept of work–life balance. We do not intend to participate in the vibrant debate about the concept's relevance. Instead, we make use of it in a rather pragmatic way in order to illustrate the shift along the work–life quality dimension. A balanced life results, according to Catherine Kirchmeyer (2000: 81), when 'achieving satisfying experiences in all life domains'. In a similar way, Sue Campbell Clark (2000: 751) defines work–life balance as the 'satisfaction and good functioning at work and at home, with a minimum of role conflict'. High work–life quality is experienced when the input of a person's resources, such as energy, time, involvement and commitment, are distributed and used in the different domains of life in a way that the person understands as balanced and fair, and thus satisfactory (cf. Greenhaus, Collins and Shaw 2003). The subjective notion of having enough time and energy for the different domains of life is important for well-being and a sense of dignity.

The interviews highlighted a decreasing work–life quality, caused by an increased workload, less time for recovery, less time for family and friends, and diminished possibilities to use earlier tactics to balance work and life. Overall, the interviewees shared the opinion that the lack of balance between work and nonwork was ruining their work–life satisfaction at large and thus their entire life quality.

The cabin attendants all mentioned that they originally did not plan to stay in the occupation for long, but they stayed because the job facilitated a highly valued lifestyle and a high degree of work–life quality. Hannah explained: 'Many of us who started in the 1980s imagined that we'd work for a maximum of five years and then do something else. It didn't turn out that way. Many of us have stayed, and we wonder how that happened'. When asked why, they explained that before the drawbacks, the shifts and rotas were arranged in such a way that there was enough time to rest and recover and a lot of free time for themselves. As Carol said, 'The women created spaces for themselves. Flying gave me time for myself—my own time'.

The work was something that became even more appreciated when they had children since it made possible a mix of work, family and own time. The fixed rotas enabled them to plan the division of labour at home and their social lives more broadly. They described how the whole family got used to their work. As stated by Rita:

> Sure, we worked a lot and we were away a lot. On the other hand, however, I was at home a lot, too. My children never complained that I was away, and they also have a dad. It was more that they wondered from time to time if it would soon be time for me to go away on long haul. Then, I'd been at home too long!

The women's absence from their homes contributed towards their partners' assuming greater family responsibilities, which had a positive effect on their sense of work–life quality. Their being away from home tilted the traditional gendered division of labour into a more egalitarian shape. Esther noted, 'My husband is the one on top of things. He is cooking, cleaning, and taking care of the kids. I am away and he is home—simple as that!' The possibility to reduce working hours due to small children was something that they further experienced as a driver for a high degree of work–life quality. Suzy recalled, 'When we had our children I worked 75% and it was fantastic since I was working five days and then free for seven days. I had time to do the musts but also time to recover'. As a single parent, Carol called to mind:

> When I began in 1987, I met so many strong female role models who went through divorces but could live by themselves thanks to working conditions and finances that made ends meet. They all seemed so independent to me, and then I became one of them as well.

By the time of the interviews, and as described in the previous sections, the increased workload and unpredictable demands of temporal and spatial availability for work had negative consequences on the cabin attendants' work–life quality. The opportunities to recover and to be available in other spheres of life, such as family and friends, diminished drastically. Rebecca claimed:

> Since the new agreement, I have no time to recuperate. Think about those who have children. How does that work? On the other hand, there are very few parents of young children working here now. This is not a family-friendly workplace anymore.

Beside the longer and more flexible working hours the cabin attendants were, after the agreement, no longer entitled to five but only to a maximum of three weeks' holiday between mid-May and mid-September. Not being able to have summer vacation together with the family to the same extent as earlier lowered their satisfaction with their work and their overall work–life quality. In addition, there was a decrease in the number of free weekends each month, from two to one. This meant that the cabin attendants could be working six weekends in a row. They felt that the situation both at work and at home became more and more strained, which affected quality of life both for themselves and for their families. Hannah told us:

> Many are on sick leave and they are in a psychologically bad shape because they can't make ends meet at home. The ones with children living at home don't have an easy time. Sometimes they're crying. My children have moved out so it's my husband who doesn't see me much.

The restriction of free weekends and the number of weeks during the summer holiday reduced their possibilities of social contact and activities with, not only their families, but also friends. Rita said: 'You are losing many friends now, since you are never available for them. You are at home at odd hours and when you are home, you want to do the musts and then rest'. They were all dedicating a large part of their free time to rest and recovery at the expense of other things. Rebecca said: 'A lot of the time when I'm not at work is spent on ensuring that I have the energy to be at work'. Accordingly, they were all concerned about their health and physical fitness and tried to live as healthy a life as possible.

The cabin attendants described how the new work situation triggered questions about them staying in the occupation by partners, family and friends. They were also aware of their feelings of being too tired to do something else when they did not work—and apart from that never being able to plan anything in advance. Their feeling was shared with their families. Suzy recalls how the lack of planning affected her marriage: '"Aren't you too old to be playing around like this?" my ex-husband asked me when I was away too much and we weren't able to plan ahead'. She said that they managed perfectly well before the variable, short-notice rotas and both thought they had found a good balance. Feelings of turning into an absent or tired mother gave rise to dissatisfaction, especially if or when the children noticed the state of affairs. Moira told us about when she struggled with burnout symptoms: 'My little daughter wanted to come with me to my work and help me so I didn't have to work so hard and become so tired'.

The cabin attendants felt their work–life quality fading away at the same time as they were certain that their situation was impossible to change. While waiting for an exit option, they were all trying to cope with the situation in order to sustain a decent work–life quality. One strategy was to work part time, while another one was to call in sick. Moira said that as loyalty to the company grew fainter, their bad conscience at calling in sick when they felt they were tired disappeared too.

This strategy was also used in order to cope with the company's strict policy regarding days off. Moira continued: 'We never get days off either if we ask to be free for a day or so. Now, people have stopped asking for a day off or vacation—they call in sick instead. We'd never entertain the thought of seeing that as treachery'.

In summary, the cabin attendants all describe how their former possibility to maintain a good work–life quality, but also independence, was one of the main reasons that they stayed in the occupation for so long. Although they always had been away from home and worked irregular hours, the situation and workload were not only manageable but also highly valued. However, due to the changes in their working conditions their present situation no longer allowed a decent work–life situation, but rather a situation in which recovery of body and soul was one of the main concerns and where their time and energy was used up by the company, leaving little for the family. The shift from a high degree of work–life quality to a low degree in the continuum is unmistakable, thus moving from dignity to alienation.

Summary and Conclusion

In this chapter, we have shown how and explained why job satisfaction and commitment to work among the cabin attendants shifted rather quickly as the working conditions and the work changed from dignified to undignified. We constructed a five-dimensional Dignity–Alienation Model, in which four dimensions were based on Bolton's model of dignity in work and Blauner's model of alienation, while the fifth emerged when analysing the data. Four of the dimensions are related to the workplace and the working conditions and the fifth dimension depicts the relationship between work and life outside work. The latter is an important indication that the spheres of work and nonwork are interconnected in such a way that one cannot exclude nonwork factors, such as family, when understanding subjective notions of dignity and alienation. This dimension is therefore important when analysing job satisfaction and commitment to work, especially when taking into account the gender dimension. Although Sweden has been a forerunner as one of the most gender equal countries since the 1960s, women have done and still do more of the unpaid household and care work (Grönlund and Öun 2018; Hagqvist, Gillander Gådin and Nordenmark 2017).

The Dignity–Alienation Model was used to capture how long-serving cabin attendants were subjected to and experienced a change in their working conditions. We have shown that the working conditions are causal factors bringing about feelings that we have analysed as autonomy/powerlessness, meaning/meaninglessness, flourishing/self-estrangement, respect/disrespect, and high/low work–life quality. Changes in working conditions from good to bad have been shown to cause a movement from a sense of dignity to a sense of alienation. Although the cabin attendants struggled against alienation and strived for dignity, they were pushed in that direction by their working conditions. The situation was amplified by their own vulnerability as aging, low-educated women with small chances of employment elsewhere (cf. Bergman and Gillberg 2015).

To recapitulate, a certain lack of autonomy was also part of the cabin attendants' jobs in their early years of working for the company, but they felt they could plan ahead and thus manage their lives. From the beginning of the 2000s, they had felt more and more powerless as the rota system was changed in such a way that planning their lives was made increasingly difficult. Their feelings of powerlessness increased during the next decade with the lengthening of the workday and workweek. During this time, they had an increasing sense that their voices were not being heard. They felt that neither the company nor their union listened to them. Along the autonomy–powerlessness dimension, there is a clear movement from dignity towards alienation.

The cabin attendants found a certain amount of meaning in their work earlier on. The possibility of providing passengers with good service was important for that judgement, as were the general social relations at work. The job also provided them with the basis for living a meaningful life in relation to family and friends. All this was described as deteriorating in later years, creating a strong slide towards meaninglessness and alienation. Further, they mainly talked about respect and disrespect in collective terms—namely, as their occupation's loss of status. There was a common feeling that the company had deserted them. The movement in this dimension—from the dignity of being respected by the company to the alienation caused by a strong feeling of disrespect—is perhaps the most dramatic negative move in all the dimensions. When it comes to flourishing and self-estrangement, the dimension starts out closer to the alienation endpoint than the other dimensions. Factors that increased their feelings of self-estrangement included the prolonged retirement age, their increased problems with health and well-being, aging bodies and limited possibilities to find alternative employment. However, the insight that their loyalty was being exploited by the company fed into feelings of betrayal, which drove them into even more alienation.

The final dimension is high and low work–life quality and the change from being satisfied with the overall everyday situation in regards to work and life quality to arriving at a state close to despair can be understood as one of the faces of alienation. Not having the time and energy to invest in activities and social relationships in the private sphere undermines the foundations of dignity. The cabin attendants' feelings of not having the time and the energy to uphold their roles as mothers, spouses or friends strengthen a state of mind close to alienation.

Both dignity and alienation need to be understood as multidimensional, where the dimensions causally reinforce or weaken the sense of dignity or alienation. In some cases, they can also generate ambivalent and contradictory feelings. However, the shift is clear and thorough. Subjective experiences of dignity and alienation are related to factors that shape agency, such as gender, age and class. As shown, being a middle-aged woman without formal higher education results in a situation of being heavily circumscribed and locked in (cf. Furåker, Nergaard and Saloniemi 2014). Yet another aspect is that female-dominated occupations and sectors tend to score low on working conditions, Sweden not excluded (c.f. Sverke et al. 2016). The cabin attendants' stories shed light on both their lack of agency and the inferior working conditions in the female-dominated service sector. In contrast to Korczynski (2014), who reported that the sense of alienation was put out of play whenever work was not performed, we found that subjective alienation can be a rather enduring feeling. In our material, the sense of alienation is following the cabin attendants throughout their present life situation—such as their understanding of their labour market possibilities as well as work-life quality and well-being.

Turning back to organizational commitment, we started by referring to Bengt Furåker and Kristina Håkansson (Ch. 6: 124), who suggest that organizational commitment can be seen as 'the bonds between employees and their workplace and employer' with committed employees being supportive of and loyal to the organization. It was also pointed out that organizational commitment is dependent upon the quality of the job characteristics—that is, working conditions—and on the degree of job satisfaction (e.g., Furåker and Berglund 2014; Lincoln and Kalleberg 1990; Meyer et al. 2002). In this chapter, we have shown how these bonds, the relationships between employees and their employer, in a specific occupational and organizational context had changed from commitment to aversion. Korczynski (2014: 68) argues that subjective alienation is a fruitful tool to understand the 'lived experience of labour as a social process' as it is formed by the immediate working conditions. We have demonstrated how the lived experiences of worsening working conditions changed the cabin attendants' supportive and loyal attitude into the opposite. Our argument has been that good working conditions are a driver for dignity. Dignity—all dimensions considered—generates job satisfaction that feeds into organizational commitment. Bad working conditions drive alienation. Alienation—all dimensions considered—generates job dissatisfaction, which feeds into organizational aversion.

References

Barry, K. M. (2007) *Femininity in Flight: A History of Flight Attendants*. Durham, NC: Duke University Press.
Bergman, A. and G. Gillberg (2015) 'The "Cabin Crew Blues". Middle-aged Cabin Attendants and Their Working Conditions.' *Nordic Journal of Working Life Studies* 5(4): 23–39.

Blauner, R. (1964) *Alienation and Freedom: The Factory Worker and His Industry*. Chicago: University of Chicago Press.

Bolton, S. C. (2007) 'Dignity in and at Work: Why It Matters', 3–16, in S. C. Bolton (ed.) *Dimensions of Dignity at Work*. London: Butterworth-Heinemann.

Bolton, S. C. (2010) 'Being Human: Dignity of Labor as the Foundation for the Spirit—Work Connection.' *Journal of Management, Spirituality and Religion* 7(2): 157–172.

Bolton, S. C. and C. Boyd (2003) 'Trolley Dolly or Skilled Emotion Manager?' *Work, Employment and Society* 17(2): 289–308.

Boyd, C. and P. Bain (1998) ' "Once I Get You up There, Where the Air is Rarefied": Health, Safety and the Working Conditions of Airline Cabin Crews.' *New Technology, Work and Employment* 13(1): 16–28.

Clark, S. C. (2000) 'Work/Family Border Theory: A New Theory of Work/Family Balance.' *Human Relations* 53(6): 747–770.

Curley, C. and T. Royle (2013) 'The Degradation of Work and the End of the Skilled Emotion Worker at Aer Lingus.' *Work, Employment and Society* 27(1): 105–121.

Dobruszkes, F. (2006) 'An Analysis of European Low-cost Airlines and Their Networks.' *Journal of Transport Geography* 14(4): 249–264.

Eldridge, J. E. T. (1971) *Sociology and Industrial Life*. London: Michael Joseph.

Furåker, B. (2012) 'Theoretical and Conceptual Considerations on Work Orientations', 11–25, in B. Furåker, K Håkansson and J. C. Karlsson (eds) *Commitment to Work and Job Satisfaction. Studies of Work Orientations*. New York: Routledge.

Furåker, B. and T. Berglund (2014) 'Job Insecurity and Organizational Commitment.' *Revista Internacional de Organizaciones* 13: 163–186.

Furåker, B., K. Nergaard and A. Saloniemi (2014) 'Lock-in Patterns Among Employees: A Nordic Comparison.' *International Journal of Comparative Labour Law and Industrial Relations* 30(4): 435–458.

Gallie, D. (1978) *In Search of the New Working Class: Automation and Social Integration Within the Capitalist Enterprise*. Cambridge: Cambridge University Press.

Goffman, E. (1957) 'Alienation from Interaction.' *Human Relations* 10(1): 47–60.

Gorski, P. S. (2013) 'Beyond the Fact/Value Distinction: Ethical Naturalism and the Social Sciences.' *Society* 50(6): 543–553.

Greenhaus, J. H., K. M. Collins and J. D. Shaw (2003) 'The Relation Between Work—Family Balance and Quality of Life.' *Journal of Vocational Behavior* 63(3): 510–531.

Grönlund, A. and I. Öun (2018) 'In Search of Family-friendly Careers? Professional Strategies, Work Conditions and Gender Differences in Work–Family Conflict.' *Community, Work & Family* 21(1): 87–105.

Gustafson, P. (2003) 'Det märkliga med flygvärdinnor' ('The Remarkable Thing With Airline Hostesses'), 69–82, in M. Blomsterberg and T. Soidre (eds) *Reflektioner: Perspektiv i forskning om arbetsliv och arbetsmarknad (Reflections: Perspectives in Research on Working Life and the Labour Market)*. Gothenburg: Gothenburg University, Department of Sociology.

Hagqvist, E., K. Gillander Gådin and M. Nordenmark (2017) 'Work–Family Conflict and Well-Being across Europe: The Role of Gender Context.' *Social Indicators Research* 132(2): 785–797.

Hochschild, A. R. (2003) *The Managed Heart: Commercialization of Human Feeling*. Berkeley: University of California Press.

Hodson, R. (1996) 'Dignity in the Workplace Under Participative Management: Alienation and Freedom Revisited.' *American Sociological Review* 61(5): 719–738.

Hodson, R. (2001) *Dignity at Work*. Cambridge: Cambridge University Press.

Hodson, R. (2008) 'Review of Whitelegg: Working the Skies.' *Work, Employment and Society* 22(4): 756–757.

IATA (2018) *IATA Annual Review 2018*. www.iata.org/publications/Documents/iata-annual-review-2018.pdf.

Israel, J. (1971) *Alienation: From Marx to Modern Sociology: A Macrosociological Analysis*. Boston: Allyn and Bacon.

Karlsson, J. C. and A. Bergman (2017) *Methods for Social Theory: Analytical Tools for Theorizing and Writing*. London: Routledge.

Kirchmeyer, C. (2000) 'Work-Life Initiatives: Greed or Benevolence Regarding Workers Time', 79–93, in C. L. Cooper and D. M. Rousseau (eds) *Trends in Organizational Behavior*. West Sussex, UK: Wiley.

Korczynski, M. (2014) *Songs of the Factory: Pop Music, Culture and Resistance*. Ithaca: ILR Press.

Lincoln, J. R. and A. L. Kalleberg (1990) *Culture, Control, and Commitment. A Study of Work Organization and Work Attitudes in the United States and Japan*. Cambridge: Cambridge University Press.

Meyer, J. P., D. J. Stanley, L. Herscovitch and L. Topolnytsky (2002) 'Affective, Continuance, and Normative Commitment to the Organization: A Meta-analysis of Antecedents, Correlates, and Consequences.' *Journal of Vocational Behavior* 61(1): 20–52.

Rogers, K. M. and B. E. Ashforth (2017) 'Respect in Organizations: Feeling Values as "We" and "Me".' *Journal of Management* 43(5): 1578–1608.

Sayer, A. (2007) 'Moral Economy and Employment', 21–40, in S. Bolton and M. Houlihan (eds) *Searching For the Human in Human Resource Management. Theory, Practice and Workplace Contexts*. Basingstoke: Palgrave Macmillan.

SCB (2016) www.scb.se/hitta-statistik/statistik-efter-amne/arbetsmarknad/sysselsattning-forvarvsarbete-och-arbetstider/yrkesregistret-med-yrkesstatistik/pong/statistiknyhet/yrkesregistret-med-yrkesstatistik-2016/

Seeman, M. (1959) 'On the Meaning of Alienation.' *American Sociological Review* 24(6): 783–791.

Spears, R., N. Ellemers, B. Soosje and N. R. Branscome (2006) 'The Individual Within the Group: Respect!', 176–195, in T. Postmes and J. Jetten (eds) *Individuality and the Group: Advances in Social Identity*. London: SAGE.

Spiess, L. and P. Waring (2005) 'Aesthetic Labour, Cost Minimisation and the Labour Process in the Asia Pacific Airline Industry.' *Employee Relations* 27(2): 193–207.

Sverke, M., H. Falkenberg, G. Kecklund, L. Magnusson and P. Lindfors (2016) *Kvinnor och mäns arbetsvillkor: Betydelsen av organisatoriska faktorer och psykosocial arbetsmiljö för arbets- och hälsorelaterade utfall*. RAP 2016:2. Stockholm: Arbetsmiljöverket.

Taylor, P. and S. Moore (2015) 'Cabin Crew Collectivism: Labour Process and the Roots of Mobilization.' *Work, Employment and Society* 29(1): 79–98.

Taylor, S. and M. Tyler (2000) 'Emotional Labour and Sexual Difference in the Airline Industry.' *Work, Employment and Society* 14(1): 77–95.

Transportstyrelsen (2016) *Utveckling av luftfarten 2016*. www.transports tyrelsen.se/sv/publikationer-och-rapporter/rapporter/Rapporter-luftfart/ utveckling-av-luftfarten-2016/

Ulfsdotter Eriksson, Y. (2006) *Yrke, status och genus (Occupation, Status and Gender)*. Gothenburg: Gothenburg University, Department of Sociology.

Unionen (2014) *Flygets framtid: om villkoren för de anställda och möjligheterna för svenskt flyg (Future of Airlines: About Working Conditions for the Employed and the Possibilities for Swedish Aviation)*. Rapport: Unionen.

Williams, C. (2003) 'Sky Service: The Demands of Emotional Labour in the Airline Industry.' *Gender, Work & Organization* 10(5): 513–550.

Yin, R. K. (2003) *Case Study Research: Design and Methods*. Thousand Oaks, CA: Sage.

9 Young Workers' Job Satisfaction in Europe

Belgin Okay-Somerville, Dora Scholarios and Edward Sosu

Introduction

Provision of decent work for young people (aged between 15 and 24) is a global challenge and policy concern for developing and developed nations (O'Higgins 2017). Young people, particularly due to their lack of human and social capital, are vulnerable to labour market fluctuations, such as economic recessions (Verjans, De Broeck and Eeckelaert 2007). Although there is considerable national variance, the average youth unemployment rate in Europe has been reported to be twice that of the total unemployment rate (Eurostat 2018b). The majority of academic and policy attention on youth employment has therefore focused on extrinsic features of young people's work as reflected in adequacy of hours and pay (Edwards, Garonna and Ryan 2016). The decent work agenda, however, goes beyond earning a living wage to include intrinsic aspects of work, such as meaningful work that improves young workers' capabilities and allows sustainable, independent career development (Egdell and McQuaid 2016). Across Europe, we observe an unprecedented increase in the level of tertiary education (Eurostat 2018a): between 1995 and 2012, tertiary graduation rates have increased from 18% to 38% (OECD 2013). Although improving employability and employment opportunities is a priority in the Europe 2020 strategy (European Commission 2010), youth underemployment in jobs that do not match their skills and/or qualifications remains substantial (Bell and Blanchflower 2018; Holmes and Mayhew 2015), with negative implications for work-related attitudes, especially job satisfaction (Sánchez-Sánchez and McGuinness 2015).

High unemployment rates make it particularly difficult for young people to find jobs to match their qualifications (Peiró, Agut and Grau 2010). Therefore, the transitions from formal education to work typically involve young workers accepting jobs for which they are overqualified (Alba-Ramírez and Blázquez 2003; Kalleberg 2018). The aim of this chapter is to examine young workers' job satisfaction in relation to skill use and skill/career development opportunities offered at work. Job satisfaction is an important outcome of job quality (Van Aerden et al. 2016) and an indicator of work-related well-being (Judge and Klinger 2008), and is associated with key work outcomes, such as innovation and creativity, job performance, organisational commitment and turnover intentions (De Moura et al. 2009; Judge et al. 2001; Krumm, Grube and Hertel 2013). Young workers are argued to be more sensitive to the effects of conditions at work and labour market opportunities because they have little previous experience to build up resilience (De Witte, Verhofstadt and Omey 2007). Thus, understanding young workers' job satisfaction in relation to skill use and development at work has implications for improving working conditions and for sustainable labour market participation and career development for the individual (Semeijn et al. 2015). Although there is a plethora of research evidence on the skill underutilisation and job satisfaction of university leavers (e.g., Abel and Deitz 2017; Henseke and Green 2017), young workers without tertiary education are rarely included in these analyses.

Globally, the Great Recession of 2008–09 had a disproportionately hard impact on the quantity and quality of opportunities afforded to young people (Bell and Blanchflower 2011). Particularly in more liberal institutional regimes, where skills policies tend to overemphasize supply-side pressures for provision of skills yet neglect their deployment and development at work (Buchanan et al. 2010), young people are exposed to high risks in securing and maintaining work with implications for job satisfaction at work, and general well-being. The chapter contextualizes young people's job satisfaction by examining the importance of these predictors pre- and postrecession, and across two contrasting institutional regimes in Europe (i.e., Social Democratic and Liberal). For advancing our understanding of work attitudes, the chapter, therefore, aims to provide a more nuanced understanding of job satisfaction as it is experienced by Europe's young workers, pre- and postrecession and across institutional regimes.

Building on theoretical perspectives to work attitudes and well-being (Oldham and Hackman 2010; Hackman and Oldham 1976; Karasek and Theorell 1990; Karasek 1979) and using the European Working Conditions Surveys (2005–2015), this chapter provides a contextualized examination of job satisfaction as predicted by skill utilisation and skill/ career development. More specifically, the chapter contextualizes job satisfaction by examining the following:

- The importance of skill utilisation, skill development and career opportunities for young workers, through experienced meaningfulness of work, on job satisfaction, in comparison to the rest of the working population in Europe;
- The changing importance of skill utilisation, skill development and career opportunities on job satisfaction for Europe's young workers, pre- and postrecession;

- The impact of skill utilisation, skill development and career opportunities on job satisfaction for young workers in Social Democratic and Liberal regimes in postrecession Europe.

Skills, Meaningful Work and Job Satisfaction

Job satisfaction refers to an emotional state resulting from the evaluation or appraisal of one's job experiences in relation to one's work values (Locke 1969). As one of our concerns in this chapter is to understand how youth job satisfaction may be improved through employer practices or job design with implications for skill use and development, we draw from theories which have identified relevant objective job characteristics. These include, but are not limited to, Frederick Herzberg's (1966) two-factor theory differentiating between motivators and hygiene factors; Richard Hackman and Greg Oldham's (1976) job characteristics model, postulating five core job characteristics and three psychological states as determinants of job satisfaction; socio-technical systems theory (Trist 1981), which takes into account the social milieu within which work is done; Robert Karasek's (1979) job demand-control (-support) model; and the job demands-resources model of burnout (Demerouti et al. 2001). Common across these theories is the role of skill use and development on the job for improving job satisfaction. Perceived skill utilisation has consistently been found to be among the strongest predictors of job-related affective well-being (Morrison et al. 2005), especially of job satisfaction (O'Brien 1983; Okay-Somerville and Scholarios 2019). Moreover, underemployment, especially in the form of overskilling and overqualification, has been shown to be negatively associated with job satisfaction (Kifle, Kler and Shankar 2018; McKee-Ryan and Harvey 2011; Feldman, Leana and Bolino 2002) and job-related negative affective well-being in general (Karasek 1979; Karasek and Theorell 1990). Positive work attitudes, such as job satisfaction, are strongly related to management practices that are associated with use and development of skills, rather than maintenance of work performance (Kooij et al. 2010; Morrison et al. 2005).

According to Hackman and Oldham's (1976) job characteristics model, when a task requires staff to engage in activities that challenge or stretch their skills and abilities, that task almost invariably is experienced as meaningful by the individual. The person, therefore, reports higher work motivation and job satisfaction. One legacy of the job characteristics model is its emphasis on the role of intrinsic aspects of work for experienced meaningfulness of work (Wrzesniewski and Dutton 2001; Grant and Parker 2009; Grant 2008). Experienced meaningfulness refers to 'the degree to which the individual experiences the job as one which is generally meaningful, valuable, and worthwhile' (Hackman and Oldham 1976: 256).

Deriving meaning from events has been described as a 'fundamental human motive' (Britt, Adler and Bartone 2001: 54). Empirical research shows that people who experience meaningfulness of work also report better psychological adjustment, well-being and job satisfaction (Steger, Dik and Duffy 2012; Arnold et al. 2007; Lysova et al. 2019). One mechanism through which meaningful work improves work outcomes is through its effects on self-efficacy (Rosso, Dekas and Wrzesniewski 2010)—that is, on beliefs about one's capabilities (Bandura 1995). Individuals who experience higher self-efficacy through work perceive that they have the capacity and capability to exercize control over their environment and therefore experience work as more meaningful (Baumeister and Vohs 2002).

It can be argued that skill use and development through work—which encompasses a range of skill-related concepts, including perceived skill utilisation, development of skills (e.g., through on-the-job or external training) and the provision of career development opportunities— improves experienced meaningfulness at work and hence job satisfaction because the individual will feel more capable of accomplishing work tasks. In fact, skill use and development have been shown to be central to the enhancement of work-related self-esteem, self-realisation, fulfilment, identity-making at work and work engagement (Felstead et al. 2016; Boxall, Hutchison and Wassenaar 2015; Fujishiro and Heaney 2017). We, therefore, expect *skill use and development* at work (a term we use throughout as shorthand to represent job-related skill use, skill development and career opportunities) to be associated with job satisfaction and for this effect to be partially explained by employee experience of meaningfulness at work (see Figure 9.1). This is formulated in our first hypothesis as follows:

> *Hypothesis 1 (H1)*: Skill use and development at work will be (a) directly and (b) indirectly, via meaningfulness, associated with job satisfaction.

Age and Job Satisfaction

It is argued that goals and motivation related to work are age dependent (Kanfer, Beier and Ackerman 2013) and that job satisfaction increases linearly with age (Kalleberg and Loscocco 1983). There is also evidence that the relationship is U-shaped, declining from a moderate level in the early years of employment and then increasing steadily up to retirement (Clark, Oswald and Warr 1996; Gazioglu and Tansel 2006).

One explanation of the age dependency of job satisfaction is that it is linked to changes in employee needs, particularly those for personal growth and development, and security (Kooij et al. 2010). It has been argued that as we age our regulatory focus shifts: our need for self-actualisation/personal growth declines but the need for security increases

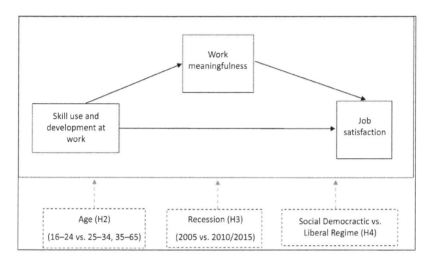

Figure 9.1 Conceptual framework for the effects of skill use/development on job
satisfaction for young people across Europe

Note: Solid boxes and arrows indicate baseline model (H1)

(Freund 2006; Kanfer and Ackerman 2004). Thus, the developmental
features of jobs, such as further skill development, become less important for well-being as we age (Kooij et al. 2013). Growth through work
experience is particularly important for young people in contemporary
labour markets (Helyer and Lee 2014), as experience is often a precursor
for employability. Many young people find themselves in an 'experience
trap' (Bell and Blanchflower 2011), where employers prefer experience
over credentials.

Having the opportunity to use and develop skills through work (e.g.,
through training or further career development opportunities) may
therefore be especially important for younger workers' sense of competence and employability in comparison to the rest of the working
population. Hackman and Oldham's (1976) job characteristics model
also predicts that the relationships between job features, experienced
meaningfulness and work attitudes will be moderated by the strength of
one's personal growth and development needs. Assuming that younger
workers have a higher need for growth, we therefore expect, compared
to the rest of the working population, young workers' job satisfaction
to benefit more from skill use and development and experienced meaningfulness at work.

Hypothesis 2 (H2): The (a) direct and (b) indirect effects of skill use
and development at work on job satisfaction will be stronger for
young workers compared to the rest of the working population.

The Increasing Importance of Skills Following Recession

The Great Recession of 2008–09 has been argued to have hit younger workers disproportionately hard (Bell and Blanchflower 2011). Although there is cross-national variation, across Europe the youth unemployment rate, on average, has risen by 35% between 2008 and 2011 (O'Higgins 2017, 2012). It can therefore be argued that the recession has had a significant impact on the employment opportunities of younger workers (Peters and Besley 2013). It has been shown, for instance, that graduating from university during the economic downturn is associated with lower starting salaries and a slower pace of pay progression within the first 10 years of one's career, in comparison to graduating during prosperity (Oreopoulos, von Wachter and Heisz 2012). Young workers who joined the labour market after the Great Recession may be exposed to higher risks and precarity in the labour market—including unemployment—the prevalence of temporary contracts and lower starting salaries (Chung, Bekker and Houwing 2012).

The opportunity for skill use and development at work, especially development which enhances job prospects, may improve well-being when workers are experiencing heightened labour market insecurity (Chung and Van Oorschot 2011), by improving—as noted above—work-related self-efficacy and self-esteem. In fact, recent research shows that in organisations that implemented some recessionary action, investing in employee skill development and deployment is associated with higher employee skill utilisation, job satisfaction and work-related affective well-being (Okay-Somerville and Scholarios 2019). Finding first-time employment and poor quality jobs that offer little development and progression opportunities are key challenges for young workers in Europe, particularly following the Great Recession (Chung, Bekker and Houwing 2012). Contemporary postrecessionary European labour markets are characterized by increasing flexibility among other factors, such as education-jobs mismatch. The implication for youth employment is a lack of stable employment and career opportunities (O'Reilly et al. 2015). Jobs that offer skill use, skill development and career advancement opportunities in postrecessionary climates may therefore help overcome the negative attitudinal consequences of labour market insecurity and may be associated with higher work meaningfulness and stronger attitudes towards the job than that in prerecessionary labour markets. Hence, it can be argued that skill use and development for young workers in postrecessionary labour markets may be more important for job satisfaction than for those in prerecessionary climates who may have experienced fewer labour market insecurities.

> *Hypothesis 3 (H3):* The (a) direct and (b) indirect effects of skill use and development at work on young workers' job satisfaction will

be stronger in a postrecessionary context compared to a prerecessionary context.

Institutional Regimes and Youth Job Satisfaction

Socioeconomic conditions and institutional structures may also influence the skill ecosystems within which skills are developed and deployed (Buchanan et al. 2010; Anderson 2010). Skill ecosystems refer to the range of contextual factors (such as the business setting, policy frameworks, modes of engaging labour, the structure of jobs, and level and type of skill formation) that shape approaches to skill development and use (Payne 2007). This recognizes the wider context of skills policies, including state intervention with respect to skill utilisation at both supply and demand ends of the labour market. Institutional regimes have been categorized in a number of ways, including criteria based on the degree of universal social protection (e.g., Esping-Andersen 1990); varieties of capitalism (Hall and Soskice 2003); and product, financial and educational markets more specifically (Amable 2003; Hall and Thelen 2009). In this chapter, we use an employment regimes theory approach (Gallie 2009b, 2009a), which takes into account the more specific aspects of institutional regimes. Employment regimes theory focuses on the relative power of employers and workers and provides a comprehensive account of the variation in institutional regimes with implications for cross-national job quality differences within Europe (Gallie 2007; Holman 2013; Holman and Rafferty 2017).

More specifically, we contrast two institutional regimes with regard to the implications of skill use and skill/career development opportunities on the job satisfaction of young workers in postrecessionary Europe: Social Democratic (Denmark, Sweden and Finland) and Liberal (UK and Ireland). The former provides employment rights throughout the working population, and participation of organized labour in decision-making is highly institutionalized. There is a strong strategy to promote employment growth and significant protection from unemployment. The value of employee skills is high, and a tight labour market operates, with low levels of unemployment. By comparison, Liberal institutional regimes are characterized by little state regulation of working conditions, and employment levels are assumed to be regulated by the market. Organized labour has little involvement in decision-making. There are low levels of employment protection and the labour market is rather fluid, with little employer interest in investment in training/skills beyond business needs (see Holman 2013 for a more comprehensive review of institutional regimes).

Previous research has shown that institutional regimes explain part of the cross-national variation in job quality. For instance, David Holman (2013) shows that high-quality jobs (i.e., jobs that are relatively high in job resources, skills and development, wages, security and flexibility) are more commonly observed in Social Democratic regimes in comparison to the rest of the EU. With respect to skill use and career development opportunities, graduates in Liberal regimes report higher skill underutilisation than those in Social Democratic regimes (Holmes and Mayhew 2015). Further evidence shows that a substantial proportion of Swedish young workers reported opportunities for development on the job in comparison to older workers (European Foundation for the Improvement of Living Working Conditions 2013), whereas in the UK, organisations that rely on young workers were found to be less likely to offer training and development opportunities (UKCES 2012). Recent evidence from postrecessionary Denmark and Sweden (two of the three EU27 countries categorized as Social Democratic) shows declining social investment in skill matching and upskilling, including the provision of job-related training in the workplace or classroom, and an increasing emphasis on incentive reinforcement and employee assistance towards labour market entry and progression (Bengtsson, de la Porte and Jacobsson 2017). Evidence from the UK shows that the impact of the recession on training expenditure and training participation was negligible (Felstead, Green and Jewson 2012), with most employers choosing 'training smarter'—for example, prioritizing courses likely to have most impact on business performance (Jewson, Felstead and Green 2015).

With regards to understanding job satisfaction resulting from jobs which provide high skill use and career development opportunities in postrecessionary Social Democratic and Liberal regimes, empirical evidence from the working population and theory offer alternative predictions. Youth job satisfaction trends across the EU27 countries is mixed. A positive trend in the job satisfaction of young people (defined 15–29 years) is observed in some countries—for example, Austria, Germany and Finland—and a reverse trend in others—for example, Sweden, Denmark and Ireland (Eurofound 2013); but how does this relate to job quality? Notwithstanding the postrecessionary shifts in social investment in skills noted above in Social Democratic regime countries (Bengtsson, de la Porte and Jacobsson 2017), empirical evidence regarding the quality of jobs in each regime (e.g., Holman 2013) still suggests higher skill use and development in Social Democratic compared to Liberal regimes. Assuming young workers have access to similar skill use and development opportunities as the overall working population, those in Social Democratic regimes may be more likely to show a strong association between high skill use/career development opportunities and job satisfaction through their effect on experienced meaningfulness. The rationale for this lies in the expected association between higher job quality (more enriched job characteristics in terms of the skill variety and challenge provided by the job) and work-related attitudes. This is consistent with Hackman and Oldham's (1976) depiction of experienced meaningfulness in work as almost invariably associated with greater skill variety and challenge.

An alternative possibility considers the contrasting labour market contexts for young people and how higher skill investment is interpreted. Given their generally higher levels of skills underutilisation at work (Holmes and Mayhew 2015), youth in Liberal regimes may demonstrate a stronger positive reaction to skills investment as a result of perception of relative deprivation (Hu et al. 2015) and associated social comparisons to others (Bashshur, Hernández and Peiró 2011). For young people in Liberal regimes, skill use and career development opportunities provided by an employer may be scarce, and so represent not only better internal employment opportunities but also better external employability given that these young people experience less employment protection at work. In Social Democratic regimes, young people are likely to have fewer such external worries regarding their employability. Given also the relatively compressed wage structure in Social Democratic regimes compared to the UK (Berglund and Esser 2014), investment in skill development may be less salient for these young workers, resulting in a weaker link between job quality and job satisfaction.

We formulate our final hypothesis to reflect the former position, with Social Democratic regimes expected to demonstrate stronger positive effects on job satisfaction than those in Liberal regimes. However, we recognize the possibility that individuals may interpret employer investment in skill differently according to the wider labour market and employment context. As such, we tentatively suggest the direction of this hypothesis but regard this as part of a theory building process regarding contrasts across employment regimes in how job quality relates to job satisfaction.

> *Hypothesis 4 (H4):* Within the postrecessionary context, the direct and indirect effects of skill use and development at work on young workers' job satisfaction will be stronger for those in Social Democratic, compared to Liberal, employment regimes.

Methodology

Data and Sample

The analyses presented in this chapter are informed by the European Working Conditions Surveys (EWCS). The EWCS provides data on working conditions in Europe. Topics covered in the survey include many aspects of working lives relevant for job quality and job satisfaction—for example, work intensification, working time, skills, discretion and other cognitive aspects of work—employment prospects, social environment, job and organisation context and working life perspectives (including job satisfaction and work fulfilment). The target population of the EWCS is residents aged 15 and above (16 in the UK, Bulgaria, Norway and Spain) and in employment at the time of the survey. Multistage, stratified, random sampling is used in each country. The data is collected in the form of face-to-face interviews conducted at the participant's home. The interviews took 45 minutes on average (see Technical Report for a detailed review of the sampling strategies and fieldwork (IPSOS 2016)).

For testing each hypothesis, the data set was reduced to match the target population as follows: H1 and H2 included data from the EU27 sample for cohorts from 2005, 2010 and 2015; H3 only included young workers (16–24) in the EU27; H4 only included postrecessionary data (2010 and 2015) from young workers in Social Democratic (Denmark, Sweden and Finland) and Liberal employment regimes (UK and Ireland). Only those with complete data on the key variables of interest were retained for analysis. Table 9.1 provides a description of the sample at each step of the analysis.

Measures

Measures included four broad categories: skill use and development, meaningfulness at work, job satisfaction and control variables. Following Holman (2013), *skill use and development* involved four separate items: (a) *perceived skill use* was measured using responses to the question 'Which of the following statements would best describe your skills in your own work?' Responses were recoded into a dummy variable with responses 'I need further training to cope well with my duties' and 'My present skills correspond well with my duties' representing 'Utilisation' (1), while the response 'I have the skills to cope with more demanding duties' represents 'Underutilisation' (0); (b) *career development opportunities* was based on responses to the statement 'My job offers good prospects for career advancement', measured on a five-point scale (1 = strongly disagree', 5 = strongly agree; (c) *employer-paid training* (0 = no, 1 = yes); and (d) *on-the-job training* (0 = no, 1 = yes).

Meaningfulness at work was measured with three items ('Your job gives you the feeling of work well done'; 'You are able to apply your own ideas in your work'; 'You have the feeling of doing useful work'). All items were measured on a five-point scale (1 = never, 5 = always). A confirmatory factor analysis suggests a good factor structure for this construct (CFI = 1.00; TLI = 1.00) with the standardized factor loadings for items (.49–.78) indicating good reliability. A composite *meaningfulness at work* score based on the average of the three items was subsequently computed and used for the analysis.

Job satisfaction was a single-item measure ('On the whole, are you very satisfied, satisfied, not very satisfied or not at all satisfied with working conditions in your main paid job?'; four-point scale, 1 = not at all satisfied, 4 = very satisfied).

Table 9.1 Description of the sample and measures at each step of the analysis

	H1: EU27	H2: EU27			H3: EU27 & youth			H4: EU27 & youth & postrecession	
		16–24	25–34	35–65	2005	2010	2015	Social Democratic	Liberal
N	77125	5836	17104	54185	2017	2049	1770	392	373
Job satisfaction	3.07	3.09	3.07	3.06	2.99	3.06	3.24	3.14	3.33
Meaningfulness	4.00	3.70	3.97	4.06	3.63	3.72	3.77	3.85	3.59
Perceived skill use[1]	.69	.68	.68	.69	.64	.69	.72	.71	.60
Career development opportunities	2.84	3.08	3.08	2.72	2.94	2.99	3.34	2.98	3.57
Employer paid training[1]	.35	.30	.37	.35	.21	.32	.38	.33	.46
On-the-job training[1]	.33	.41	.36	.30	.33	.40	.51	.53	.60
Female	.46	.45	.47	.46	.44	.45	.48	.51	.47
Education	3.44	3.09	3.68	3.40	3.04	3.09	3.16	2.95	3.13
Job security	3.92	3.75	3.81	3.98	3.78	3.58	3.88	3.69	4.04

[1] 0 = No; 1 = Yes.
The values indicate the proportion of participants who responded 'Yes'.

Control variables included: gender (1 = female, 0 = male), education (measured as a continuous variable on a seven-point scale from 0 = preprimary to 6 = second stage tertiary education) and perceived job security (single item: 'I might lose my job in the next six months'; 1 = strongly agree, 5 = strongly disagree).

Analyses

Hypotheses were tested using path analyses. Path analysis is a structural equation modelling technique that allows researchers to test prior hypotheses about causal relationships among variables. An advantage of this approach is the ability to simultaneously consider multiple independent and dependent variables in contrast to a conventional regression approach, which is restricted to a single dependent variable. Testing of H2, H3 and H4 involved multigroup path analyses, comparing three age groups (16–24, 25–34, 35–65), pre-/postrecession data (2005 vs. 2010 and 2015) and employment regimes (Social Democratic vs. Liberal) respectively. H3 and H4 were tested only using youth data (aged 16–24). Moreover, H4 was further restricted to postrecession data sets (2010 and 2015). Model fit indices and direct and indirect path coefficients are reported. All analyses were undertaken in Mplus 8 and taking into account cross-national weights for the EU27 group of countries. Models were evaluated using established goodness of fit indices with comparative fit index (CFI) and Tucker-Lewis index (TLI) values above .95 as well as the root mean square error of approximation (RMSEA) value below .05 indicating good model fit (Hu and Bentler 1999; Marsh, Hau and Wen 2004).

Limitations

The European Working Conditions Survey allowed us to examine the job satisfaction and working experience of a representative European sample of young workers against the general working population at different time periods (2005, 2010 and 2015), and provided wide coverage of a range of employment variables. Despite the advantages of such secondary data, there are inevitable limitations for the purposes of our hypothesis tests. First, the data set provides cross-sectional data from multiple cohorts rather than longitudinal data following individuals. This means that the contrasts between pre- and postrecessionary contexts rely on different cohorts. While we used control variables to account for some cohort differences (e.g., gender, education, perceived job security), the number of variables included and our reduction of the sample for some analyses to young people/postrecession precluded the inclusion of some significant variables (e.g., workplace variables, such as industry or size, or other dimensions of intrinsic job quality, such as task discretion and variety).

A second limitation is the definition of and comparisons between age cohorts across the different time periods. In the absence of longitudinal data for individuals, we make assumptions about the comparability of young people across time, even though these cohorts may vary in preferences and work orientations (Twenge et al. 2010). However, our interest in the relationship between skills and job satisfaction does not assume any generational cohort effects, which are controversial in the literature (Costanza et al. 2017), and the inclusion of control variables accounts for variations in perceived labour market differences (a primary concern with regard to the effects of skills) as well as for potential effects of gender and education.

Finally, the secondary data set restricts the ability to measure some variables. The EWCS uses a single item measure of job satisfaction, our dependent variable. Although single item measures are generally discouraged for psychological constructs, a meta-analysis by Wanous, Reichers and Hudy (1997) indicated convergent validity between single-item and scale measures of overall job satisfaction. Another concern is the measurement of skill use provided by the EWCS, which is based on categorical or dichotomous items, such as whether employer-based or on-the-job training was provided or not. We recognize that this provides a narrow operationalisation of perceived skill utilisation. Other work in this area has attempted to refine the operationalisation of skill utilisation to include, for example, whether training provided is actually perceived to enhance skills for one's job (Felstead et al. 2016). The secondary data set meant we could not replicate such complex measures of skill utilisation; however, in an effort to create a comprehensive measure, we relied on four different aspects of skills use, as suggested by Holman (2013), provided by the EWCS.

Findings

Table 9.2 summarizes model fit for each analysis and provides path coefficients for the models tested. It can be observed from fit indices (i.e., RMSEA, CFI and TLI) that all models were good-fit with the data. Tests of the baseline model (H1 column) showed that job satisfaction was directly and positively associated with all predictors, except for employer-paid training. Moreover, job satisfaction was positively and indirectly associated with career opportunities (β = .05, SE = .002, p < .001) and employer-paid training (β = .01, SE = .002, p < .001), and negatively associated with on-the-job training via meaningfulness at work (β = −.01, SE = .002, p < .001). Skill use, however, did not predict meaningfulness and was not indirectly associated with job satisfaction. These findings partially support Hypothesis 1.

Multigroup analyses examining the strength of the relationships predicting job satisfaction by age (Table 9.2, H2 columns) show that across

Table 9.2 Path analyses coefficients predicting job satisfaction

Direct effects	H1	H2 (EU27)		
	EU27	16–24	25–34	35–65
Skill use[1]→Meaningfulness	-.010 (.006)	.044 (.023)	.004 (.012)	-.028 (.007)***
Career opp→Meaningfulness	.212 (.006)***	.325 (.021)***	.261 (.013)***	.200 (.007)***
Training (paid for)[1]→Meaningfulness	.034 (.006)***	.016 (.022)	.021 (.013)	.028 (.008)***
Training (on-the-job)[1]→Meaningfulness	-.045 (.006)***	-.046 (.022)***	-.030 (.013)*	-.034 (.007)***
Meaningfulness→Job satisfaction	.243 (.006)***	.261 (.025)***	.229 (.013)***	.246 (.007)***
Skill use[1]→Job satisfaction	.016 (.006)***	.030 (.022)	.009 (.011)	.017 (.007)**
Career opp→Job satisfaction	.263 (.006)***	.249 (.023)***	.286 (.012)***	.250 (.007)***
Training (paid for)[1]→Job satisfaction	.007 (.006)	.005 (.021)	.022 (.012)	.004 (.007)
Training (on-the-job)[1]→Job satisfaction	.020 (.006)***	.035 (.022)	.024 (.012)*	.013 (.007)
Indirect effects (via Meaningfulness)				
Skill use[1]→Job satisfaction	-.002 (.002)	.012 (.006)	.001 (.003)	-.007 (.002)***
Career opp→Job satisfaction	.052 (.002)***	.085 (.010)***	.060 (.005)***	.049 (.002)***
Training (paid for)[1]→Job satisfaction	.008 (.002)***	.004 (006)	.005 (.003)	.007 (.002)***
Training (on-the-job)[1]→Job satisfaction	-.011 (.002)***	-.012 (.006)*	-.007 (.003)*	-.008 (.002)***
Control variables				
Female→Meaningfulness	.008 (.006)	.028 (.021)	.039 (.012)***	-.006 (.007)
Education→Meaningfulness	.070 (.006)***	.091 (.020)***	.056 (.013)***	.063 (.008)***
Job security→Meaningfulness	.164 (.006)***	.124 (.022)***	.147 (.013)***	.161 (.007)***
Female→Job satisfaction	.039 (.005)***	.040 (.019)*	.040 (.011)***	.040 (.006)***
Education→Job satisfaction	-.009 (.006)	-.016 (.021)	-.015 (.012)	.001 (.007)
Job Security→Job satisfaction	.166 (.006)***	.182 (.021)***	.163 (.013)	.163 (.007)***
Model fit				
χ2/df	8609.87/15	887.11/45	887.11/45	887.11/45
RMSEA	.000	.000	.000	.000
CFI	1.000	1.000	1.000	1.000
TLI	1.000	1.000	1.000	1.000

Direct effects	H3 (EU27 & age 16–24)			H4 (EU27 & age 16–24 & postrecession)	
	2005	2010	2015	Social Democratic	Liberal
Skill Use[1]→Meaningfulness	.054 (.037)	.010 (.038)	.046 (.042)	.005 (.071)	-.002 (.072)
Career opp→Meaningfulness	.373 (.033)***	.256 (.034)***	.332 (.040)***	.273 (.063)***	.402 (.055)***
Training (paid for)[1]→Meaningfulness	-.010 (.037)	.036 (.036)	.016 (.041)	.065 (.059)	.084 (.072)
Training (on-the-job) →Meaningfulness	-.036 (.038)	.008 (.035)	-.121 (.039)***	-.033 (.060)	-.009 (.073)
Meaningfulness→Job satisfaction	.297 (.043)***	.221 (.037)***	.225 (.043)***	.263 (.081)***	.303 (.083)***
Skill Use[1]→Job satisfaction	.057 (.035)	.052 (.034)	-.070 (.039)	.145 (.063)*	.028 (.070)
Career opp→Job satisfaction	.248 (.041)***	.256 (.033)***	.226 (.043)***	.118 (.065)	.117 (.077)
Training (paid for)[1]→Job satisfaction	.033 (.031)	.033 (.035)	-.050 (.040)	-.248 (.060)***	-.035 (.078)
Training (on-the-job)[1]→ Job satisfaction	.042 (.036)	-.017 (.033)	.041 (.038)	.112 (.058)	-.012 (.070)
Indirect effects (via Meaningfulness)					
Skill use[1]→Job satisfaction	.016 (.012)	.002 (.008)	.010 (.009)	.001 (.019)	-.001 (.022)
Career opp→Job satisfaction	.111 (.017)***	.056 (.012)***	.074 (.017)***	.072 (.027)**	.122 (.040)**
Training (paid for)[1]→Job satisfaction	-.003 (.011)	.008 (.008)	.004 (.009)	.017 (.016)	.025 (.022)
Training (on-the-job)[1]→Job satisfaction	-.011 (.012)	.002 (.008)	-.027 (.010)**	-.009 (.015)	-.003 (.022)
Control variables					
Female→Meaningfulness	.027 (.034)	.013 (.035)	.043 (.036)	.100 (.058)	-.054 (.067)
Education→Meaningfulness	.065 (.032)*	.043 (.034)	.160 (.038)***	.007 (.040)	.150 (.055)**
Job Security→Meaningfulness	.158 (.036)***	.158 (.036)***	.048 (.038)	.236 (.058)***	.051 (.059)
Female→Job satisfaction	.061 (.031)*	.022 (.032)	.011 (.037)	-.048 (.055)	.016 (.069)
Education→Job satisfaction	.009 (.030)	-.046 (.037)	-.049 (.043)	.002 (.044)	-.083 (.075)
Job Security→Job satisfaction	.212 (.036)***	.176 (.033)***	.140 (.038)***	.157 (.060)***	.174 (.067)**
Model fit					
χ2/df	912.01/45	912.01/45	912.01/45	189.60/30	189.60/30
RMSEA	.000	.000	.000	.000	.000
CFI	1.000	1.000	1.000	1.000	1.000
TLI	1.000	1.000	1.000	1.000	1.000

[1]0 = No, 1 = Yes; coefficients reflect nonstandardized Beta coefficients with standard errors in parentheses
* p < .05; ** p < .01; *** p < .001.

all age categories, career opportunities and on-the-job training directly and indirectly predict job satisfaction. Moreover, the strength of indirect effects of career opportunities in predicting young workers' job satisfaction ($\beta = .09$, SE = .010, p < .001) was greater than that for the older workforce (35–65; $\beta = .05$, SE = .002, p < .001). The strength of on-the-job training for predicting job satisfaction via work meaningfulness was stronger for the latter ($\beta = -.01$, SE = .002, p < .001), in comparison to the younger workforce (both 16–24 and 25–35). Predictors of young workers' job satisfaction were similar to those aged between 25 and 34. By comparison, the pattern of relationships observed among the 35–65 age category were similar to those reported above under the baseline model. The only exception to this pattern was the negative and indirect association between skill utilisation and job satisfaction via meaningfulness ($\beta = -.01$, SE = .002, p < .001) for this age category. These findings only partially support Hypothesis 2.

Table 9.2 (column H3) shows multigroup analyses examining the strength of relationships predicting young workers' job satisfaction across prerecession (2005) and postrecession (2010 and 2015) data. Young workers' job satisfaction was directly and indirectly, via meaningfulness, associated with career opportunities. Moreover, the strength of the indirect relationship is lower after the recession (2010: $\beta = .06$, SE = .01, p < .001 and 2015: $\beta = .07$, SE = .02, p < .001) in comparison to the prerecession coefficient (2005; $\beta = .11$, SE = .02, p < .001). A similar pattern is observed for the direct relationships between career opportunities and meaningfulness, and meaningfulness and job satisfaction where the strength of the relationship is lower postrecession. In 2015, we also observe on-the-job training to have a negative indirect effect on job satisfaction ($\beta = -.03$, SE = .01, p < .01) and a negative direct effect on meaningfulness ($\beta = -.12$, SE = .04, p < .001). These findings do not support Hypothesis 3.

Young people's postrecession job satisfaction is presented for Social Democratic and Liberal employment regimes in Table 9.2 (column H4). As above, significant direct and indirect relationships were observed between career opportunities (via meaningfulness for the latter) and job satisfaction. The strength of these relationships was stronger for young workers in Liberal, in comparison to Social Democratic, regimes. Moreover, among young workers in Social Democratic regimes, job satisfaction was negatively associated with employer-paid training ($\beta = -.25$, SE = .06, p < .001) and positively associated with skill use ($\beta = .15$, SE = .06, p < .05).

Discussion

This chapter examines the role of skill use and development in shaping meaningful work and job satisfaction for young people. Given the pervasive issue of underemployment of young people across Europe, skills play a vital role in young people's work attitudes and represent a key aspect of job quality and career success. In addition, by taking into account the socioeconomic context of recession and national country characteristics represented by employment regime, the chapter extends understanding of some of the boundary conditions influencing young workers' work attitudes.

We set out three aims designed to assess the changing importance of skills as a source of work meaningfulness and job satisfaction for young people. The test of a baseline model with the working population across the EU27 countries (H1) confirmed the importance of career opportunities as expected; however, the effects of other aspects of how organisations deliver skill use and development showed mixed results. Workers' perceived skill utilisation was not a significant predictor of job satisfaction. On-the-job training was positively associated with job satisfaction but negatively with meaningfulness, implying that the overall indirect effect on job satisfaction was negative, contrary to expectation. In the case of employer-paid training, there was no direct relationship to job satisfaction but an overall positive indirect effect via meaningfulness.

These baseline findings indicate the importance of career development opportunities and some types of training for job satisfaction across the working population, thus supporting previous evidence promoting job prospects which impact job quality and in turn work attitudes (Felstead et al. 2016; Boxall, Hutchison and Wassenaar 2015; Fujishiro and Heaney 2017). Moreover, the confirmed role of meaningfulness as an explanatory mechanism demonstrates the continued applicability of Hackman and Oldham's (1976) job characteristics model across European workers and supports the link between work which is experienced as meaningful and well-being more generally (Steger, Dik and Duffy 2012; Arnold et al. 2007; Lysova et al. 2019).

Building on this baseline model, our first aim was to examine whether this model holds for younger workers and is in fact stronger than for older workers (H2). Patterns predicting job satisfaction for 16–24 year olds were similar to the 24–34 age group but different from older workers (aged 35–65). We observed more reported career development opportunities in their jobs by the younger workers (Table 9.1), and these have a stronger indirect impact on young workers' job satisfaction. This finding indicates a greater relevance of work meaningfulness for youth job satisfaction, a point which was confirmed also by the stronger significant direct relationship between meaningfulness and satisfaction found for the 16–24 age group. Considering the prevalence of precarity among young entrants to European labour markets (regardless of educational attainment) (Lodovici and Semenza 2012), jobs that provide career opportunities may satisfy both growth and security needs at work. There is support across European data, therefore, that younger workers are more likely to gain meaning from work which provides employability and that jobs which provide skill development are more important for youth job satisfaction than for older workers (Kooij et al. 2010).

We also found that employer-paid training was indirectly related to job satisfaction through meaningfulness only for the 35–65 age category, indicating that this means of skill development was not important for younger workers. Younger workers also reported lower provision of such training (Table 9.1). Such a finding may indicate that older workers attach greater importance to 'maintenance' HRM practices (as opposed to 'developmental' HRM). The former are more likely to help people avoid skill obsolescence and hence are more directly related to performance outcomes (Kooij et al. 2013). Employer-paid training may fall into this category. On-the-job training was most common among young workers (Table 9.1). Contrary to expectation, the direct and indirect effect of on-the-job training with job satisfaction was negative across all age groups; this effect was strongest for the older workers. Moreover, negative indirect effects of skill use, via work meaningfulness, on job satisfaction were also observed among older workers. Nevertheless, no differences were observed between age categories with respect to skill use. Together, these unexpected findings may point to the conflicting effects of HRM (Ogbonnaya and Messersmith 2018), where not all HRM practices may be perceived and experienced positively by employees (Schmidt, Pohler and Willness 2018).

The second aim of this chapter was to examine the changing importance of skill utilisation and development on job satisfaction for Europe's young workers, pre- and postrecession. We expected the importance of skill utilisation and development to increase for young workers following the recession. We observe provision of all measures of skill use and development included in this analysis to show an upward trend from prerecession (2005) to postrecession for young worker cohorts (2010 and 2015). Findings show organisational career opportunities to play a pivotal role. Most notably, postrecession the importance of career opportunities on meaningfulness and indirectly on job satisfaction lessens. Alongside this, the importance of job security on job satisfaction has been declining across the three time points. Hence, although career opportunities are consistently significantly related to job satisfaction, their importance may fluctuate with the macroeconomic context. This may indicate that in today's postrecessionary context, young people may value career opportunities less as relevant for job satisfaction, as the labour markets they enter require that they show greater flexibility in seizing employment opportunities (O'Higgins 2012). Moreover, the 2015 data set also shows that meaningfulness is not associated with job security (although the relationship was significant and showed comparable levels in the 2005 and 2010 data sets) and that those with higher levels of education experience more meaningfulness at work. We may interpret these findings as young workers' internalisation of the 'new economy discourse' that they should be more reliant on their proactive behaviours (e.g., networking) and less so on organisational management of career. Both prerecession (King 2003) and postrecession (Guillot-Soulez and Soulez 2014) evidence shows that young workers do have a preference for traditional organisational careers and more specifically for job security at work. Moreover, although the recession has been shown to lower young workers' optimism, little change has been reported in expectations for job content—for example, training, career development and financial rewards (De Hauw and De Vos 2010). Nevertheless, proactive career behaviours, especially during early career, positively impact career success (De Vos, De Clippeleer and Dewilde 2009). For instance, Agut, Peiro and Grau (2009) show that for young Spanish workers, personal initiative buffers the negative work-related effects of underemployment.

Our final aim in this chapter was to examine the impact of skill utilisation and development on job satisfaction for young workers in Social Democratic and Liberal regimes in postrecession Europe. Based on employment regimes theory, we expected young workers in Liberal regimes to benefit less from skill use and development at work, as they suffer greater insecurity and precarity in the labour market. Confirming previous research on job quality (Holman 2013), descriptive findings (Table 9.1) show that young workers in Liberal regimes are afforded poorer skill use and development, with the exception of the measure of career development opportunities. Our findings show that the key distinction relevant for predicting young workers' job satisfaction was, as above, on career opportunities. Contrary to how we formulated the hypothesis here, we find that career development opportunities have stronger direct and indirect effect on job satisfaction for youth in Liberal, in comparison to Social Democratic, regimes. Perhaps due to the relatively compressed wage structure in the latter, compared to the UK at least (Berglund and Esser 2014), career advancement is not as salient for young workers' job satisfaction. Supporting this speculation, job security was significantly associated with work meaningfulness for youth in the Social Democratic, but not in Liberal, regimes. Nevertheless, job security was significantly associated with job satisfaction for young workers across both regimes. Although the European Commission recommends 'flexicurity'—simultaneously increasing labour market flexibility and security by enhancing employability—for improving productivity, evidence on training investments in postrecessionary Denmark and Sweden shows declining investment in employer-provided training (Bengtsson, de la Porte and Jacobsson 2017). Our findings show that in Social Democratic regimes skill use and employer-provided training have positive and negative direct effects on job satisfaction, respectively. For explaining the negative relationship, we can speculate based on Bengtsson, de la Porte and Jacobsson's (2017) findings that perhaps the content of employer-provided training does not necessarily lead to growth and development through work for young people, as postrecessionary organisations feel less pressure to invest in employee skills and knowledge, similar to UK employers' preference for 'training smarter' (i.e., for maximum impact) (Jewson, Felstead and Green 2015). The lack of a significant relationship between skill use and job satisfaction among youth in Liberal regimes may be explained by the prevalence of overskilling. For instance, as high as 58.8% of university leavers have been reported to be working in nongraduate jobs in the UK (Holmes and Mayhew 2015), and the evidence of job upskilling for better use of these high skills remains limited (Okay-Somerville and Scholarios 2013).

Conclusion

The findings highlight the importance of jobs which provide career development opportunities and work meaningfulness for youth job satisfaction across Europe, especially postrecession and for those in Liberal employment regimes. The analysis reaffirms concerns for young people's employability, and whether employers/governments are providing adequate skill utilisation and development. Such concerns are also reflected in the Europe 2020 strategy. Moreover, the confirmed role of meaningfulness as an explanatory mechanism demonstrates the continued applicability of Hackman and Oldham's (1976) job characteristics model across European workers, and supports the link between work which is experienced as meaningful and well-being more generally (Arnold et al. 2007; Lysova et al. 2019; Steger, Dik and Duffy 2012).

The approach taken in this chapter acknowledges the importance of a macroeconomic and institutional context for a nuanced understanding of job satisfaction for young workers, especially for those without tertiary education, and confirms the importance of skills and career development for young people in the period following the Great Recession, despite increased precariousness in work opportunities.

References

Abel, J. R. and R. Deitz (2017) 'Underemployment in the Early Careers of College Graduates Following the Great Recession', in C. H. Hulten and V. A. Ramey (eds) *Education, Skills, and Technical Change: Implications for Future US GDP Growth*. London: University of Chicago Press.

Agut, S., J. M. Peiro and R. Grau (2009) 'The Effect of Overeducation on Job Content Innovation and Career-Enhancing Strategies Among Young Spanish Employees.' *Journal of Career Development* 36(2): 159–182.

Alba-Ramírez, A. and M. Blázquez (2003) 'Types of Job Match, Overeducation and Labour Mobility in Spain', 65–92, in F. Buchel, A. De Grip and A. Mertens (eds) *Overeducation in Europe: Current Issues in Theory and Practice*. Cheltenham, UK: Edward Elgar Publishing Limited.

Amable, B (2003) *The Diversity of Modern Capitalism*. Oxford: Oxford University Press.

Anderson, P (2010) 'The Utility of Operationalising the Concept of Skill Ecosystems: The Case of Intermediate Occupations in Scotland.' *Employee Relations* 32(4): 435–452.

Arnold, K. A., N. Turner, J. Barling, E. K. Kelloway and M. C. McKee (2007) 'Transformational Leadership and Psychological Well-being: The Mediating Role of Meaningful Work.' *Journal of Occupational Health Psychology* 12(3): 193–203.

Bandura, A (1995) 'Exercise of Personal and Collective Agency in Changing Societies', 1–45, in A. Bandura (ed.) *Self-Efficacy in Changing Societies*. Cambridge: Cambridge University Press.

Bashshur, M. R., A. Hernández and J. M. Peiró (2011) 'The Impact of Underemployment on Individual and Team Performance', 187–213, in D. C. Maynard and D. C. Feldman (eds) *Underemployment: Pyschological, Economic and Social Challenges*. New York: Springer.

Baumeister, R. F. and K. D. Vohs (2002) 'The Pursuit of Meaningfulness in Life', 608–618, in C. R. Snyder and S. J. Lopez (eds) *Handbook of Positive Psychology*. Oxford: Oxford University Press.

Bell, D. N. F. and D. G. Blanchflower (2011) 'Young People and the Great Recession.' *Oxford Review of Economic Policy* 27(2): 241–267.

Bell, D. N. F. and D. G. Blanchflower (2018) 'Underemployment in the US and Europe.' *NBER Working Paper No. 24927*, National Bureau of Economic Research. www.nber.org/papers/w24927.pdf.

Bengtsson, M., C. de la Porte and K. Jacobsson (2017) 'Labour Market Policy Under Conditions of Permanent Austerity: Any Sign of Social Investment?' *Social Policy & Administration* 51(2): 367–388.

Berglund, T. and I. Esser (2014) *Modell i förändring. Landrapport om Sverige (Model in Change: Country Report on Sweden: NordMod2030. Interim Report 8)*. Oslo: Fafo.

Boxall, P., A. Hutchison and B. Wassenaar (2015) 'How do High-Involvement Work Processes Influence Employee Outcomes? An Examination of the Mediating Roles of Skill Utilisation and Intrinsic Motivation.' *The International Journal of Human Resource Management* 26(13): 1737–1752.

Britt, T. W, A. B. Adler and P. T. Bartone (2001) 'Deriving Benefits From Stressful Events: The Role of Engagement in Meaningful Work and Hardiness.' *Journal of Occupational Health Psychology* 6(1): 53–63.

Buchanan, J., L. Scott, S. Yu, H. Schutz and M. Jakubauskas (2010) *Skills Demand and Utilisation: An International Review of Approaches to Measurement and Policy Development*. OECD Local Economic and Employment Development (LEED). Working Papers 2010/4. París: OECD Publishing.

Chung, H., S. Bekker and H. Houwing (2012) 'Young People and the Post-Recession Labour Market in the Context of Europe 2020.' *Transfer: European Review of Labour and Research* 18(3): 301–317.

Chung, H. and W. Van Oorschot (2011) 'Institutions Versus Market Forces: Explaining the Employment Insecurity of European Individuals During (the Beginning of) the Financial Crisis.' *Journal of European Social Policy* 21(4): 287–301.

Clark, A., A. Oswald and P. Warr (1996) 'Is Job Satisfaction U-Shaped in Age?' *Journal of Occupational and Organizational Psychology* 69(1): 57–81.

Costanza, D.P, J. B. Darrow, A. B. Yost and J. B. Severt (2017) 'A Review of Analytical Methods Used to Study Generational Differences: Strengths and Limitations.' *Work, Aging and Retirement* 3(2): 149–165.

De Hauw, S. and A. De Vos (2010) 'Millennials' Career Perspective and Psychological Contract Expectations: Does the Recession Lead to Lowered Expectations?' *Journal of Business and Psychology* 25(2): 293–302.

Demerouti, E., A. B. Bakker, F. Nachreiner and W. B. Schaufeli (2001) 'The Job Demands-Resources Model of Burnout.' *Journal of Applied Psychology* 86(3): 499–512.

De Moura, G. R., D. Abrams, C. Retter, S. Gunnarsdottir and K. Ando (2009) 'Identification as an Organizational Anchor: How Identification and Job Satisfaction Combine to Predict Turnover Intention.' *European Journal of Social Psychology* 39(4): 540–557.

De Vos, A., I. De Clippeleer and T. Dewilde (2009) 'Proactive Career Behaviours and Career Success During the Early Career.' *Journal of Occupational and Organizational Psychology* 82(4): 761–777.

De Witte, H., E. Verhofstadt and E. Omey (2007) 'Testing Karasek's Learning and Strain Hypotheses on Young Workers in Their First Job.' *Work & Stress* 21(2): 131–141.

Edwards, R., P. Garonna and P. Ryan (2016) *The Problem of Youth: The Regulation of Youth Employment and Training in Advanced Economies*. London: Springer.

Egdell, V. and R. McQuaid (2016) 'Supporting Disadvantaged Young People Into Work: Insights from the Capability Approach.' *Social Policy & Administration* 50(1): 1–18.

Esping-Andersen, G. (1990) 'The Three Political Economies of the Welfare State.' *International Journal of Sociology* 20(3): 92–123.

European Commission (2010) *Europe 2020: A Strategy for Smart, Sustainable and Inclusive Growth: Communication from the Commission*. Luxembourg: Publications Office of the European Union.

Eurofound (2013) *Working Conditions of Young Entrants to the Labour Market*. European Foundation for the Improvement of Living Working Conditions. Dublin: Eurofound. http://ketlib.lib.unipi.gr/xmlui/bitstream/handle/ket/950/tn1306013s.pdf?sequence=2&isAllowed=y.

Eurostat (2018a) *Education and Training in the EU—Facts and Figures*. https://ec.europa.eu/eurostat/statistics-explained/index.php/Education_and_training_in_the_EU_-_facts_and_figures.

Eurostat (2018b) *Unemployment Statistics*. https://ec.europa.eu/eurostat/statistics-explained/index.php?title=Unemployment_statistics#Youth_unemployment: Eurostat.

Feldman, D. C., C. R Leana and M. C Bolino (2002) 'Underemployment and Relative Deprivation Among Re-Employed Executives.' *Journal of Occupational and Organizational Psychology* 75(4): 453–471.

Felstead, A., D. Gallie, F. Green and G. Henseke (2016) 'The Determinants of Skills Use and Work Pressure: A Longitudinal Analysis.' *Economic and Industrial Democracy* (Online first).

Felstead, A., F. Green and N. Jewson (2012) 'An Analysis of the Impact of the 2008–9 Recession on the Provision of Training in the UK.' *Work, Employment and Society* 26(6): 968–986.

Freund, A. M. (2006) 'Age-Differential Motivational Consequences of Optimization Versus Compensation Focus in Younger and Older Adults.' *Psychology and Aging* 21(2): 240–252.

Fujishiro, K. and C. A. Heaney (2017) ' "Doing What I Do Best": The Association Between Skill Utilization and Employee Health with Healthy Behavior as a Mediator.' *Social Science & Medicine* 175: 235–243.

Gallie, D. (2007) 'Production Regimes and the Quality of Employment in Europe.' *Annual Review of Sociology.* 33(1): 85–104.

Gallie, D. (2009a) *Employment Regimes and the Quality of Work.* Oxford: Oxford University Press.

Gallie, D. (2009b) 'Institutional Regimes and Employee Influence at Work: A European Comparison.' *Cambridge Journal of Regions, Economy and Society* 2(3): 379–393.

Gazioglu, S. and A. Tansel (2006) 'Job Satisfaction in Britain: Individual and Job Related Factors.' *Applied Economics* 38(10): 1163–1171.

Grant, A. M. (2008) 'Designing Jobs to Do Good: Dimensions and Psychological Consequences of Prosocial Job Characteristics.' *The Journal of Positive Psychology* 3(1): 19–39.

Grant, A. M. and S. K. Parker (2009) 'Redesigning Work Design Theories: The Rise of Relational and Proactive Perspectives.' *The Academy of Management Annals* 3(1): 317–375.

Guillot-Soulez, C. and S. Soulez (2014) 'On the Heterogeneity of Generation Y Job Preferences.' *Employee Relations* 36(4): 319–332.

Hackman, J. R. and G. R. Oldham (1976) 'Motivation Through the Design of Work: Test of a Theory.' *Organizational Behavior & Human Performance* 16(2): 250–279.

Hall, P. A. and D. Soskice (2003) 'Varieties of Capitalism and Institutional Complementarities', 43–76, in R. Franzese, P. Mooslechner and M. Schürz (eds) *Institutional Conflicts and Complementarities*, London: Springer.

Hall, P. A. and K. Thelen (2009) 'Institutional Change in Varieties of Capitalism.' *Socio-economic Review* 7(1): 7–34.

Helyer, R. and D. Lee (2014) 'The Role of Work Experience in the Future Employability of Higher Education Graduates.' *Higher Education Quarterly* 68(3): 348–372.

Henseke, G. and F. Green (2017) 'Cross-National Deployment of "Graduate Jobs": Analysis Using a New Indicator Based on High Skills Use', 41–79, in S. W. Polachek, K. Pouliakas, G. Russo and K. Tatsiramos (eds) *Skill Mismatch in Labor Markets*. Bingley: Emerald Publishing Limited.

Herzberg, F. (1966) *Work and the Nature of Man.* Cleveland: World.

Holman, D. (2013) 'Job Types and Job Quality in Europe.' *Human Relations* 66(4): 475–502.

Holman, D. and A. Rafferty (2017) 'The Convergence and Divergence of Job Discretion Between Occupations and Institutional Regimes in Europe from 1995 to 2010.' *Journal of Management Studies.* 55(4): 619–647.

Holmes, C. and K. Mayhew (2015) *Over-Qualification and Skills Mismatch in the Graduate Labour Market.* London: Chartered Institute of Personnel and Development.

Hu, J., B. Erdogan, T. N. Bauer, K. Jiang, S. Liu and Y. Li (2015) 'There are Lots of Big Fish in this Pond: The Role of Peer Overqualification on Task Significance, Perceived Fit, and Performance for Overqualified Employees.' *Journal of Applied Psychology* 100(4): 1228–1238.

Hu, L. and B. M. Bentler (1999) 'Cutoff Criteria for Fit Indexes in Covariance Structure Analysis: Conventional Criteria Versus New Alternatives.' *Structural Equation Modeling: A Multidisciplinary Journal* 6(1): 1–55.

IPSOS (2016) *6th European Working Conditions Survey: Technical Report.* Dublin: Eurofound. www.eurofound.europa.eu/sites/default/files/ef_survey/field_ ef_documents/6th_ewcs_-_technical_report.pdf: EUROFOUND.

Jewson, N., A. Felstead and F. Green (2015) 'Training in the Public Sector in a Period of Austerity: The Case of the UK.' *Journal of Education and Work* 28(3): 228–249.

Judge, T. A. and R. Klinger (2008) 'Job Satisfaction: Subjective Well-Being at Work', 393–413, in M. Eid and R. J. Larsen (eds) *The Science of Subjective Well-being.* New York: Guilford Press.

Judge, T. A., C. J. Thoresen, J. E. Bono and G. K. Patton (2001) 'The Job Satisfaction—Job Performance Relationship: A Qualitative and Quantitative Review.' *Psychological Bulletin* 127(3): 376–407.

Kalleberg, A. L. (2018) 'Precarious Work and Young Workers in the United States', 35–55, in Y. S. Chancer, M. Sánchez-Jankowski and C. Trost (eds) *Youth, Jobs, and the Future: Problems and Prospects* Oxford: Oxford University Press.

Kalleberg, A. L. and K. A. Loscocco (1983) 'Aging, Values, and Rewards: Explaining Age Differences in Job Satisfaction.' *American Sociological Review* 48(1): 78–90.

Kanfer, R. and P. L. Ackerman (2004) 'Aging, Adult Development, and Work Motivation.' *Academy of Management Review* 2(3): 440–458.

Kanfer, R., M. E. Beier and P. L. Ackerman (2013) 'Goals and Motivation Related to Work in Later Adulthood: An Organizing Framework.' *European Journal of Work and Organizational Psychology* 22(3): 253–264.

Karasek, R. A. (1979) 'Job Demands, Job Decision Latitude, and Mental Strain: Implications for Job Redesign.' *Administrative Science Quarterly* 24(2): 285–308.

Karasek, R. A. and T. Theorell (1990) *Healthy Work: Stress, Productivity, and the Reconstruction of Working Life.* New York: Basic Books.

Kifle, T., P. Kler and S. Shankar (2018) 'The Underemployment-Job Satisfaction Nexus: A Study of Part-Time Employment in Australia.' *Social Indicators Research* 1–17 (Online first). https://doi.org/10.1007/s11205-018-1976-2.

King, Z. (2003) 'New or Traditional Careers? A Study of UK Graduates' Preferences.' *Human Resource Management Journal* 13(1): 5–26.

Kooij, D. T. A. M., P. G. W. Jansen, J. S. E. Dikkers and A. H. De Lange (2010) 'The Influence of Age on the Associations Between HR Practices and Both Affective Commitment and Job Satisfaction: A Meta-Analysis.' *Journal of Organizational Behavior* 31(8): 1111–1136.

Kooij, D. T., D. E. Guest, M. Clinton, T. Knight, P. G. Jansen and J. S. Dikkers (2013) 'How the Impact of HR Practices on Employee Well-being and Performance Changes With Age.' *Human Resource Management Journal* 23(1): 18–35.

Krumm, S., A. Grube and G. Hertel (2013) 'No Time for Compromises: Age as a Moderator of the Relation Between Needs—Supply Fit and Job Satisfaction.' *European Journal of Work and Organizational Psychology* 22(5): 547–562.

Locke, E. A. (1969) 'What is Job Satisfaction?' *Organizational Behavior and Human Performance* 4(4): 309–336.

Lodovici, M. S. and R. Semenza (2012) 'Precarious Work and High-Skilled Youth in Europe', 11–23, in M. S. Lodovici and R. Semenza (eds) *Precarious Work and High Skilled Youth in Europe*. Milan: FrancoAngeli.

Lysova, E. I., B. A. Allan, B. J. Dik, R. D. Duffy and M. F. Steger (2019) 'Fostering Meaningful Work in Organizations: A Multi-Level Review and Integration.' *Journal of Vocational Behavior* 110(Part B): 374–389.

Marsh, H. W., K. Hau and Z. Wen (2004) 'In Search of Golden Rules: Comment on Hypothesis-Testing Approaches to Setting Cutoff Values for Fit Indexes and Dangers in Overgeneralizing Hu and Bentler's (1999) Findings.' *Structural Equation Modeling* 11(3): 320–341.

McKee-Ryan, F. M. and J. Harvey (2011) ' "I Have a Job, But . . .": A Review of Underemployment.' *Journal of Management* 37(4): 962–996.

Morrison, D., J. Cordery, A. Girardi and R. Payne (2005) 'Job Design, Opportunities for Skill Utilization, and Intrinsic Job Satisfaction.' *European Journal of Work and Organizational Psychology* 14(1): 59–79.

O'Brien, G. E (1983) 'Skill-Utilization, Skill-Variety and the Job Characteristics Model.' *Australian Journal of Psychology* 35(3): 461–468.

OECD (2013) *Education at a Glance 2014: OECD Indicators*. París: OECD Publishing.

Ogbonnaya, C. and J. Messersmith (2018) 'Employee Performance, Well-Being and Differential Effects of HRM Sub-Dimensions: Mutual Gains or Conflicting Outcomes?' *Human Resource Management Journal* (Online first).

O'Higgins, N. (2012) 'This Time It's Different? Youth Labour Markets During "The Great Recession".' *Comparative Economic Studies* 54(2): 395–412.

O'Higgins, N. (2017) *Rising to the Youth Employment Challenge: New Evidence on Key Policy Issues*. Geneva: International Labour Organisation.

Okay-Somerville, B. and D. Scholarios (2013) 'Shades of Grey: Understanding Job Quality in Emerging Graduate Occupations.' *Human Relations* 66(4): 555–585.

Okay-Somerville, B. and D. Scholarios (2019) 'A Multilevel Examination of Skills-Oriented Human Resource Management and Perceived Skill Utilization During Recession: Implications for the Well-being of All Workers.' *Human Resource Management* 58(2): 139–154.

Oldham, G. R. and J. R. Hackman (2010) 'Not What It Was and Not What It Will Be: The Future of Job Design Research.' *Journal of Organizational Behavior* 31(2–3): 463–479.

O'Reilly, J., W. Eichhorst, A. Gábos, K. Hadjivassiliou, D. Lain, J. Leschke, S. McGuinness, L. M. Kureková, T. Nazio, R. Ortlieb and H. Russell (2015) 'Five Characteristics of Youth Unemployment in Europe: Flexibility, Education, Migration, Family Legacies, and EU Policy.' *SAGE Open*. https://doi.org/10.1177/2158244015574962.

Oreopoulos, P., T. von Wachter and A. Heisz (2012) 'The Short- and Long-Term Career Effects of Graduating in a Recession.' *American Economic Journal: Applied Economics* 4(1): 1–29.

Payne, J. (2007) *Skill Ecosystems: A New Approach to Vocational Education and Training Policy*. SKOPE Issues Paper No. 14, ESRC Centre on Skills, Knowledge and Organisational Performance (SKOPE).

Peiró, J. M, S. Agut and R. Grau (2010) 'The Relationship Between Overeducation and Job Satisfaction Among Young Spanish Workers: The Role of Salary, Contract of Employment, and Work Experience.' *Journal of Applied Social Psychology* 40(3): 666–689.

Peters, M. A. and T. Besley (2013) Marx and Foucault: Subjectivity, Employability and the Crisis of Youth Unemployment in the Great Global Recession.' *Policy Futures in Education* 11(6): 779–784.

Rosso, B. D., K. H. Dekas and A. Wrzesniewski (2010) 'On the Meaning of Work: A Theoretical Integration and Review.' *Research in Organizational Behavior* 30: 91–127.

Sánchez-Sánchez, N. and S. McGuinness (2015) 'Decomposing the Impacts of Overeducation and Overskilling on Earnings and Job Satisfaction: An Analysis Using REFLEX Data.' *Education Economics* 23(4): 419–432.

Schmidt, J. A., D. Pohler and C. R. Willness (2018) 'Strategic HR System Differentiation Between Jobs: The Effects on Firm Performance and Employee Outcomes.' *Human Resource Management* 57(1): 65–81.

Semeijn, J. H., K. Van Dam, T. Van Vuuren and B. I. J. M. Van der Heijden (2015) 'Sustainable Labour Participation and Sustainable Careers', 146–161, in A. De Vos, B. I. J. M. Van der Heijden (eds) *Handbook of Research on Sustainable Careers*. Cheltenham: Edward Elgar Publishing.

Steger, M. F., B. J. Dik and R. D. Duffy (2012) 'Measuring Meaningful Work: The Work and Meaning Inventory (WAMI).' *Journal of Career Assessment* 20(3): 322–337.

Trist, E. (1981) 'The Evolution of Socio-Technical Systems.' *Occasional Paper* 2. Toronto, ON: Ontario Quality of Working Life Centre.

Twenge, J. M., S. M. Campbell, B. J. Hoffman and C. E. Lance (2010) 'Generational Differences in Work Values: Leisure and Extrinsic Values Increasing, Social and Intrinsic Values Decreasing.' *Journal of Management* 36(5): 1117–1142.

UKCES (2012) *Investing in Youth Employment*. UK Commission for Employment and Skills. www.ukces.org.uk/ourwork/investment/investing-in-youth-employment-investment.

Van Aerden, K., V. Puig-Barrachina, K. Bosmans and C. Vanroelen (2016) 'How Does Employment Quality Relate to Health and Job Satisfaction in Europe? A Typological Approach.' *Social Science & Medicine* 158: 132–140.

Verjans, M., V. De Broeck and L. Eeckelaert (2007) *OSH in Figures: Young Workers: Facts and Figures*, Vol. 4. Luxembourg: Official Publications of the European Communities.

Wanous, J. P., A. E. Reichers and M. J. Hudy (1997) 'Overall Job Satisfaction: How Good are Single-Item Measures?' *Journal of Applied Psychology* 82(2): 247–252.

Wrzesniewski, A. and J. E. Dutton (2001) 'Crafting a Job: Revisioning Employees as Active Crafters of Their Work.' *Academy of Management Review* 26(2): 179–201.

10 Matching Work Values With Job Qualities for Job Satisfaction

A Comparison of 24 OECD Countries in 2015

Tomas Berglund and Ingrid Esser

Introduction

In recent decades, the swerve towards workfare in policies to increase participation and combat unemployment appears to be the norm among politicians and policymakers. Pressure on people to work is high and much of the responsibility and cost is increasingly born by the individual. Concern with increased participation is understandable for its positive effects on the overall economy as well as in line with most people's expectations—having a job is central in most people's lives, allowing independence and the ability to fend for oneself. Yet, people may also carry greater expectations about paid work than only constituting a means for making a living, not least in modern welfare states.

Much research confirms how people associate an array of personal values and expectations with a job. Broad comparisons of modern welfare states have shown how most individuals hold strong job preferences spanning both extrinsic (e.g., security and pay) and intrinsic (e.g., finding one's job interesting and varying) job qualities (Berglund, 2012; Esser and Lindh 2018). Furthermore, persons who have higher quality jobs have been found consistently to have higher job and life satisfaction (e.g., Drobnič et al. 2010; Eurofound 2013) and self-rated health (e.g., Esser 2017; Eurofound 2013). Yet, while matching of individuals' job preferences with the job qualities has been a recurring theme in organizational psychology (e.g., Kristof-Brown et al. 2005), sociological and comparative research remains quite limited (Esser and Olsen 2018).

This chapter addresses the matching of job preferences on eight central extrinsic and intrinsic dimensions of job quality. Three considerations may influence the matching outcome. First, people's values and expectations of working life may differ. For some, fewer specific aspects of work may be important, while others' expectations may span numerous equally central dimensions. Second, jobs will vary in the ways they entail distinct job qualities both within and across countries. This means that the availability of quality jobs on the labour market matters. Third, employees face the challenge of navigating the matching process of finding the specific job that better matches their preferences. Hence, matching outcomes may range from a perfect fit, to the unfortunate sheer mismatch with few or no aspired qualities present.

Psychologists have shown that the congruence/discrepancy between important values and what the situation offers or demands of the individual—the so called person-environment fit—may have important effects on well-being and job satisfaction (see the meta-analysis in Kristof-Brown, Zimmerman and Johnson 2005). As job satisfaction is a highly beneficial factor for both individuals and organizations (Spector 1997), there is strong rationale to further assess the importance of matching for job satisfaction. Furthermore, this body of research draws our attention to the need for assessing several dimensions of job quality for a more appropriate assessment of person-environment fit in matching on job qualities.

This chapter has two aims. First, it describes variation in work values and job qualities and their matching across eight central job quality dimensions. Second, it assesses the importance of matching on job satisfaction. Analyses draw on data from the International Social Survey Programme's (ISSP) 2015 survey on work orientations.

Next, we discuss the central concepts of work values, job qualities and job satisfaction, and set out the theoretical framework for the analyses. Thereafter, the data and method are described, after which we report results. The chapter concludes with a summary of main findings and a discussion.

Work Values

From a general point of view, values are something that help people to orientate in the world and play a role in people's ability to act. Examples of basic values relate to security, self-determination and power (Rokeach 1973; Schwartz 1999). Values are created and transmitted in social interaction with others; in childhood (primary socialization), as well as later in life—for example, in the school system or working life (secondary socialization). According to Schwartz (1999), values vary between cultures and countries. Values of equality have been found to be very widespread in Sweden and Denmark, while the populations of several East Asian countries emphasize hierarchy (differences in power) and traditional values. However, some job preferences seem relatively universal. Vast majorities, more than 90 percent of all employees, value having a secure and interesting job, while there is more variation in other work valuations (Esser and Lindh 2018).

In relation to work values, a central distinction is between intrinsic and extrinsic values of work (Porter and Lawler 1968). Intrinsic values reflect how the work task itself is perceived as valuable—for example, by being interesting and offering opportunity for development. Extrinsic work values include characteristics such as salary, employment security, status and prestige. These features of a job often function as means for other goals outside work life, such as a rich family life and leisure. Another value orientation studied relates to altruistic rewards, such as how a job may help others or contribute to society (Berglund 2012; Twenge et al. 2010). Sometimes this dimension is included as an aspect of intrinsic values (Super 1970).

Why people differ in their work values is disputed. It has been argued that extrinsic work values must first be met—for example, with regard to a sufficiently high salary and employment security—before inherent properties of work become important (Maslow 1954). Others have emphasized how the intrinsic values of work are fundamental and related to basic psychological needs: people need to feel that what they do is important, and not just be motivated by external rewards (Gagné and Deci 2005). Some researchers emphasize instead that the culture surrounding the individual is crucial for whether extrinsic or intrinsic values become central (see Schwartz 1999).

In this comparative context, we do not focus on explaining variation in work values, but simply acknowledge how work values and work preferences in fact vary between individuals and countries. Our goal is instead to study the significance of matching between job values and job qualities, the latter of which is our next focus.

Job Quality

Similarly, as in the case of valuations, job quality is an essentially multidimensional concept spanning extrinsic and intrinsic aspects. In addition to central aspects described above, research has focused on, for example, job variation, social contacts and work-family balance. Job quality has also been shown to correlate strongly with the type of job conducted, positions in the organization and type of employment contract (Esser and Olsen 2012; Gallie 2007; Green et al. 2013; Kalleberg 2009, 2011). In a comparative perspective, large differences in job quality exist between countries (Leschke and Watt 2014), which relates not only to the characteristics of their main industries, but also to institutional factors such as the industrial relations system and the strength of unions (e.g., Esser and Olsen 2012).

Generally, job quality is beneficial to a variety of health and well-being outcomes as well as to job satisfaction. One explanation for this relationship is that several of these qualities are experienced as rewarding by the individual, and in particular, if they correspond to core values and preferences. However, there may also be an indirect effect of job qualities on well-being. According to the so called job demands-resources model (Bakker and Demerouti 2007), several of the qualities in focus may function as resources to handle the demands of the work process—for example, autonomy and social support, which may also be beneficial for well-being outcomes.

While the relationship between job qualities and well-being has been well-established in previous and for the most part national studies, the specific matching perspective remains largely unassessed, especially in comparative research. One study specifically addressed matching to job security and work-family balance among single and coupled parents across 19 European countries. While single parents were generally at a disadvantage, matching was substantially better in northern and western continental Europe. This was extensively related to the availability of higher quality jobs, but also systematically associated with countries' unemployment rate, unions' bargaining power and unemployment insurance generosity (Esser and Olsen 2018). This study did not, however, address to what extent matching is related to individuals' well-being. Hence, the crucial question remains of whether it is the direct effect of job quality that is the main driver of job satisfaction, or whether, and if so, to what extent, matches/mismatches of job preferences and job qualities can add to our understanding of job satisfaction. The analyses below specifically focus on assessing to what extent matching on multiple value dimensions matters for job satisfaction, when also controlling for the independent effect of job qualities.

Matching and Job Satisfaction

How the match/mismatch between the person's preferences and the quality of the person's job affects job satisfaction has been discussed as a person-job fit (Cable and Edwards 2004; Hult 2005; Kristof-Brown, Zimmerman and Johnson 2005). According to psychological theories, the individual has needs and values related to a job—for example, security or independence. Jobs offer these dimensions to a varying degree in relation to the type of business, the profitability of the firm and the institutional setting in which it operates. A fit (or match) is defined as congruence between these needs/values and the characteristics of the job. Usually, the measurement and indicators of these two sides in the matching process are highly subjective—that is, it is the individual who expresses needs and values, as well as assesses the characteristics of the job.

Research, predominantly in the field of organizational psychology, shows how a fit between the person's needs/values and the job is related to job satisfaction (Kristof-Brown, Zimmerman and Johnson 2005). The matching outcome can also be understood by the theory of cognitive dissonance, where a mismatch between preferences and the qualities of the situation/environment may cause stress and anxiousness (Festinger 1957). According to Festinger, there are basically three ways to deal with the dissonance (see also Hirschman 1970). The first is to try to change the situation. For example, if the salary does not correspond to what the employee expects, that employee may try to convince the employer to raise it (voice). Through collective action, such bargaining power may increase, which stresses the importance of unions and collective bargaining. If the situation is still hard to change—for example, if the employer does not accept a wage increase—a second strategy is to leave the situation (exit)—that is, to find another job that better corresponds to the individual's expectations. This possibility emphasizes mobility in the labour market, in particular voluntary mobility, both as reflection of high levels of labour market mismatches and as a mechanism to create better matches.

However, Festinger also stressed a third 'strategy' to avoid dissonance. Situations that are difficult to influence and change, and with limited exit options (e.g., due to high levels of unemployment), may force the individuals instead to alter their preferences and expectations to fit the situation. Psychologically, this is regarded either as a form of rationalization, where the individual suppresses underlying desires, or as a necessary coping strategy. Methodologically, this may have different implications. On the one hand, people may tend to adapt by conforming to the values and expectations expressed in the organization (De Cooman et al. 2009). On the other, we cannot preclude that the work situation and work tasks over time becomes adapted to individuals' preferences, thereby increasing person-job fit. Taking these arguments seriously calls for taking tenure into account, or as the case is here, age when studying job matches.[1]

The central distinction between extrinsic and intrinsic dimensions of valuations and job quality points to the importance of also assessing matching along such job quality dimensions. In the psychological literature on person-environment fit, very few studies make this distinction. A study of employees in Singapore (n=164) finds a positive relationship between intrinsic person-organizational fit and job satisfaction, while not controlling for extrinsic person-organizational fit (Greguras and Diefendorff 2009). A Dutch study (n = 467) focused on interaction effects between extrinsic respective intrinsic work values and corresponding job qualities, revealing only unique effects of job qualities on job satisfaction (Taris and Feij 2001). Another larger Dutch study (n = 4,009) on emotional exhaustion shows how fit between an intrinsic value orientation and job resources (learning opportunities) increased the negative effect of the latter (Van den Broeck et al. 2011). Evidence for different effects of extrinsic and intrinsic job matches on job satisfaction is thus still inconclusive.

Another possible, also debated, perspective is the classical two-factor theory of Frederick Herzberg (1966). This view distinguishes between so-called *motivators* in a job—referring to interesting work tasks, responsibility, learning, etc. —and so-called *hygiene factors*, concerning aspects such as pay, work environment and job security. Conceptually and empirically, these factors are quite similar to intrinsic respectively extrinsic work rewards and work motivations (Sachau 2007). According to Herzberg (1966), the presence of extrinsic (hygiene) job qualities does not result in satisfaction, but only reduces dissatisfaction. For satisfaction to increase, people also need to find more of intrinsic qualities (motivators) in a job—for example, challenging and meaningful work tasks and recognition of achievements. Accordingly, intrinsic job matches may be more strongly related to job satisfaction than extrinsic job matches.

In sum, the analyses below test how matches between valued and actual job qualities affect workers' job satisfaction. This is expected as both theory asserts and previous research shows that person-environment fit is important for both job satisfaction and well-being. However, a competing perspective asserts that the value dimension is less important than the direct effect of job quality—that is, good work environment and working conditions, which provide the means and resources to handle different job demands. Consequently, it is central also to control for the direct effects of job quality in analyses to determine if matching adds anything further to the explanation of job satisfaction. Moreover, we distinguish between intrinsic and extrinsic matching in relation to the theoretically based expectation that intrinsic matching may be more important than extrinsic matching for job satisfaction.

Data and Method

Data for the current study are from the ISSP Work Orientations module of 2015, which is a comparative survey on work valuations, job quality and job satisfaction. The selected subsample contains all employees aged 18–59 years, in total, 14,099 respondents across 24 countries.[2] The countries included are: Austria (AT), Australia (AU), Belgium (BE), Switzerland (CH), Czech Republic (CZ), Germany (DE), Denmark (DK), Estonia (EE), Spain (ES), Finland (FI), France (FR), Great Britain (GB), Hungary (HU), Iceland (IS), Japan (JP), Latvia (LV), Lithuania (LT), Norway (NO), New Zealand (NZ), Poland (PL), Sweden (SE), Slovenia (SI), Slovakia (SK) and the United States (US).

These survey data are analysed with multilevel regressions, appropriate with nested structures of the data (individuals within countries). All specified models are random intercept models, using a STATA-statistical package. Job satisfaction is regressed on matching of job values and job qualities, where the main focus is addressing the question of whether matching adds to our understanding of job satisfaction—that is, in addition to previously studied direct effects of job quality that we expect to be the main driver of job satisfaction.

Measures of Job Preferences and Job Qualities

There were eight corresponding indicators of job preferences and qualities respectively. For job preferences the question was: '*For you personally, how important do you think each of the following would be if you were choosing a job?*', relating to having *secure job, high income,* good opportunities for advancement, interesting job, job that allows one to help other people, job that is useful to society, job that allows one to work independently and job that allows contact with other people. Answers were available on a scale of 1–5, indicating the degree of importance—from 'very important' to 'not important at all'.

For job qualities, the question was: 'To what degree does this apply to your job?', relating to the corresponding eight dimensions as above, with answers on a scale of 1–5 indicating the degree of agreement: from 'strongly agree' to 'strongly disagree'.

Three indicators of matching are calculated. First, we constructed an index called *total matching* including all eight job quality dimensions. Conducting a principal component analysis, two possible subscales were discerned. The first refers to *matching on extrinsic qualities* (security, income and advancement opportunities). The second we term *matching on intrinsic qualities*, based on useful to society, help others and social contact. Notably, these mainly allude to the collective and social aspects of intrinsic matching. Excluded were indicators of independent and interesting work, as the principal component analyses revealed noncongruent factor loadings across countries for these indicators.

Calculation of matching scores is done in two steps. First, each response alternative on job values and job qualities is assigned a 'multiplier score'. After this, each combination is multiplied to reach the matching scores for the 25 possible combinations as presented in the matrix (Table 10.1), resulting in scores ranging from –6 to +6. Two general assumptions motivate the multiplier values and matching scores. The first assumption is that a match is considered more important (afforded higher scores) in relation to how strongly a quality is valued—that is, higher scores in the upper left corner, but decreasing scores along the diagonal towards the lower right corner. This grading is achieved when original response is assigned a 'multiplier score' (both in relation to preferences and qualities), which are multiplied for each combination of job preference and quality to attain final

Table 10.1 Matching scores (higher scores for better matching) as the product of multiplier scores assigned to original survey responses (scales 1–5).

			Job values				
		Original scale	1	2	3	4	5
		Multipliers	2	1	0	–1	–1
Job quality	1	3	6	3	0	–3	–3
	2	2	4	2	0	–2	–2
	3	–1	–2	–1	0	1	1
	4	–2	–4	–2	0	2	2
	5	–3	–6	–3	0	3	3

Note: In original survey scales lower values indicate stronger values/higher job quality.

matching scores shown in the matrix.[3] In this way mismatch in the lower left corner of the matrix (job quality deficit on important values) returns lower match scores as compared to mismatch in the upper right corner of the matrix (job qualities surplus on dimensions *not* aspired to). The second consideration concerns the midpoint of valuations as indicative of 'indifferent' respondents (i.e., *'neither important nor unimportant'*). Here, a 0 multiplier affords 0 scores to all combinations, reflecting indifference. However, for the job quality dimensions, the middle score (*'neither agree nor disagree'*) is assigned –1 as we interpret this answer as not having (or not being sure about having) the quality in focus.

In the second step, the three overall matching scores (total matching, extrinsic and intrinsic matching) are calculated as straightforward means across the separate matching scores.[4] The three corresponding indicators of job quality were also constructed, and calculated as averages of the constituting dimensions: a measure of overall job quality (eight dimensions), extrinsic and intrinsic job quality (albeit reversed so that higher scores indicate higher job quality). For comparability in analyses, the scores for both the matching scales and the job quality scales are transformed to scales with the range 1–5 in multivariate analyses.

The second dependent variable, *job satisfaction*, was measured by the question, *'How satisfied are you in your (main) job?'*, to which respondents gave answers on a 1–7 scale, ranging from *'completely dissatisfied'* to *'completely satisfied'* (higher scores indicating higher job satisfaction).

Individual-Level Variables

Individual characteristics include *gender* (binary distinction between men and women) and *age*, contrasting three age groups (18–29, 30–49 and 50–59) to capture mainly life course–related differences. Household indicators include *cohabitation*, either as married or partnered, compared to being either single or separated/widowed; and *child in household*, comparing households without children to families with 1, 2 or 3 or more children. *Educational level* distinguishes between those with lower levels of education, from those with upper secondary (including postsecondary but not tertiary) and those with tertiary education. *Working hours* separates full-time work ($\geq$ 30 hours/week) from part-time work (< 30 hours/week). Social class is captured by five categories of the EGP-class scheme: unskilled and skilled manual workers, routine non-manual workers, lower and higher service classes. Last, we include a control for whether the respondent's job is in the private or public *sector*.

Finally, no less than 11 additional job quality indicators, besides our job quality scales, were included in our analysis, so as to thoroughly challenge the importance of our matching indicators for job satisfaction. All these indicators were dichotomized to indicate how often work is *physically hard* (always/often), *stressful* (always/often), if work *hours are flexible* (somewhat free/free to decide), if work *interferes with family life* (always/often), if work *schedule is irregular* (regularly changing/employer decides on short notice), if one can *control the organization of work* (not free to decide), the *possibility to take off* from work for short-notice matters (somewhat/very difficult), *relationship to boss* (quite/very bad) or *co-workers* (quite/very bad).

Results

We start by presenting descriptive statistics after which results from multivariate analyses follow. In Figure 10.1, the diamond- and circle-shaped markers indicate how job preferences on average substantially over-trump the availability of quality jobs in all quality dimensions compared. The lines in the figure indicate the range between those countries displaying highest and lowest average valuations and job qualities respectively, hence indicative of variation across countries in values and available job quality. First, we can note how job security on average is valued most strongly, followed by having an interesting job, independent work, high income, usefulness to society, helpful to others and social contacts in the job situation. Finally, the least concern is expressed in relation to jobs offering advancement opportunities. Second, the average availability of quality jobs is decidedly lower, displaying also larger cross-country variation, as indicated by the longer (dashed) lines. In relation to jobs providing independent

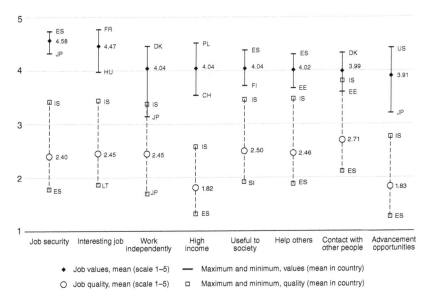

Figure 10.1 Work values and job quality overall means, maximum and minimum country means (scale 1–5, higher scores indicating stronger values/higher job quality), 24 countries 2015

Sources: ISSP 2015, own calculations

work situations and jobs offering social contact, the visible overlaps with work valuations may indicate greater opportunity for matching.

Interestingly, a few countries stand out as representatives of maximum and minimum averages among the 24 compared countries. In Spain (ES), valuations in several dimensions (security, useful to society, helpful to others) are especially strong, while availability of quality jobs in no less than five of the eight respects is especially meagre (security, income, helpful to others, social contact and advancement opportunities). Iceland (IS) stands out as a mirage-country for providing the highest average job quality in every dimension. Noteworthy is how the Japanese (JP) on average hold the lowest valuations of job security, independent work and advancement opportunities, while the Americans (U.S.) on average are highly concerned with advancement opportunities. Perhaps a bit contradictory, the Danes (DK) combine the strongest valuations of both independent work and social contact, while Estonians (EE) are least concerned about both social contact and jobs perceived as helpful to others.

Figure 10.1 is in line with previous comparative research. People simultaneously prefer several job quality dimensions of both the extrinsic and intrinsic kind. A further confirmation of this is provided by results in Figure 10.2, showing how most individuals have strong valuations

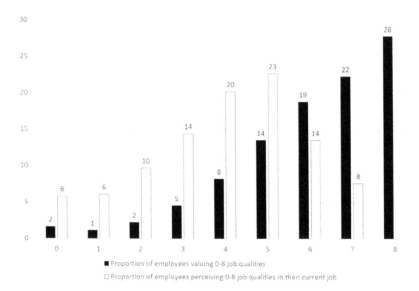

Figure 10.2 Proportions of employees valuing/perceiving 0–8 job qualities. Proportions refer to respondents answering value statements with '*very important*' or '*important*' or job quality statements '*strongly agree*' or '*agree*' about their jobs being characterized by the specific job quality, 24 countries in 2015

Sources: ISSP 2015, own calculations

for multiple job qualities (black bars). More than every fourth (28 percent) employee holds all eight aspects as important or very important, and almost another fourth (22 percent) consider seven out of eight quality dimensions as important. Overall, as many as four of five employees (82 percent) recognize five or more of the eight job quality dimensions as important. The fraction of employees with no concern for job quality, or concern only with one quality dimension, is tiny.

On the contrary, availability of job quality (white bars in Figure 10.2) is much less abundant. In fact, no respondent has a job that fulfils all eight qualities. About every fifth employee (22 percent) has a job presenting 6–7 job qualities, roughly two of five employees are offered 4–5 job qualities (43 percent), while as many as a third of all employees (36 percent) have jobs containing fewer than four qualities.

Next, we may assess graphically the relationship between matching and job satisfaction, shown in Figure 10.3. There is a clear positive correspondence between matching on extrinsic (r =.711) as well as intrinsic (r = .817) job qualities and job satisfaction, thus indicating a stronger association with intrinsic values. Yet, apart from several eastern and central European countries showing lower scores on both job satisfaction and the two matching measures, geographical country groupings are difficult to discern. The Nordic countries display average to slightly higher than average scores in both dimensions. Switzerland (CH) and Austria (AT) stand out with overall highest job satisfaction and matching scores, while Poland (PL) stands out in the opposite position.

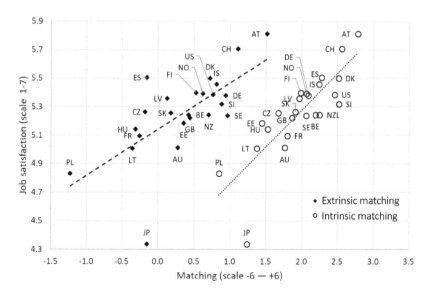

Figure 10.3 Job satisfaction and matching on extrinsic and intrinsic job qualities

Sources: ISSP 2015, own calculations

Results From Multivariate Analyses

In Table 10.2, we evaluate the relationship between matching and job satisfaction. As discussed in the method section, we distinguish between total matching, extrinsic matching and intrinsic matching. Here we seek to establish if matching is a significant factor for job satisfaction when exposing this relationship to the firmest test possible with available data. First, we control for several important background variables (gender, age, family situation, social class, etc.). Second, indices of job quality are included in models. By including these, we test if matching yields any more explanatory power than the direct and strong effect we expect of job quality on job satisfaction. Third, we include a range of additional indicators of working conditions in our analysis.

In models 1–3, we see how the total matching index is significantly related to job satisfaction across all models, indicating higher job satisfaction with better matching. When model 2 includes the direct effect of job quality, the estimate decreases considerably, which is indicative of the strong and direct positive effect of job quality on job satisfaction. Still, however, a substantial effect of total matching remains, indicating a unique effect of matching itself for job satisfaction. When the range of additional working conditions are included in model 3, the effect of total matching does not change substantially, although most working conditions are, as expected, significantly related to job satisfaction. Job satisfaction is generally weaker among employees in jobs that are physically hard, stressful, and interfere with family life. Similarly, job satisfaction is also negatively associated with jobs where the work organization is set (cannot be affected by respondent), taking leave is more difficult, or where the relationship to the boss or workmates is poor.

Models 4–6 show results for extrinsic and intrinsic matching. This specification strengthens the conclusion of the importance of matching. Both estimates of extrinsic and intrinsic matching remain significant in all models. Similarly as with total matching, estimates of extrinsic matching and intrinsic matching are substantially reduced in model 5, which also includes indicators of extrinsic and intrinsic job qualities. Notably the reduction is larger in relation to extrinsic matching. In addition, the use of similar scales (range 1–5) for matching and quality indicates how intrinsic matching matters slightly more than extrinsic matching for job satisfaction—a finding that is rather in line with what can be expected from Herzberg's theory on motivational factors being more important for satisfaction than hygiene factors. Moreover, the impact of intrinsic matching is rather similar to the impact of the intrinsic job quality index. Adding to the importance of working conditions, model 6, like model 3, reconfirms the significance of several additional working conditions, with the addition that employees with flexible work hours are somewhat more satisfied with their jobs. Even still, both the intrinsic and extrinsic

Table 10.2 Job satisfaction regressed on individual and work-place characteristics. Linear random intercept models. Extrinsic dimension: security, income, advancement opportunities; intrinsic dimension: help others, useful to society, social contact.

Model	1	2	3	4	5	6
Constant	1.44	1.19	1.90	2.11	1.94	2.58
Match total	1.10	.35	.36			
Match extrinsic				.55	.12	.10
Match intrinsic				.36	.16	.18
Gender (ref. male) Female	-.08	-.03	.01	-.05	-.01	.02
Age (ref. 18–29) 30–49	-.02	.00	.00	.00	.03	.01
50–59	.03	.08	.05	.07	.12	.08
Cohabitation (ref. single) Separated	.04	.04	.07	.06	.05	.08
Married/partnered	.06	.05	.07	.09	.07	.08
Child (ref. no child) 1 child	-.01	-.03	-.01	-.01	-.02	-.01
2 children	.02	.02	.03	.02	.02	.04
3 or more	.03	.01	.00	.04	.03	.00
Education, level (ref. primary/lower secondary) Upper/postsecondary	-.10	-.11	-.12	-.09	-.11	-.12
Tertiary	-.17	-.19	-.20	-.13	-.16	-.19
Social class (ref. unskilled) Service class 1	.18	.06	.04	.27	.14	.08
Service class 2	.13	.05	.03	.22	.13	.08
Routine nonmanual	.10	.04	.02	.13	.07	.04
Skilled	.13	.07	.06	.20	.14	.11
Work hours (ref. full-time) Part-time	.07	.09	.02	.07	.10	.02
Sector (ref. private) Public	-.07	-.09	-.02	-.06	-.09	-.01
Job quality (8 dimensions) Extrinsic job qualities.		.80	.67		.42	.35
Intrinsic qualities					.24	.21

(Continued)

Table 10.2 (Continued)

Model	1	2	3	4	5	6
Hard physical work			-.07			-.06
Stressful work			**-.27**			**-.28**
Work interfers with family			**-.28**			**-.27**
Flexible work hours			.01			.05
Work schedule irregular			.01			.03
Work organization set (cannot decide)			-.08			**-.15**
Take off from work difficult			**-.14**			**-.16**
Work relation to boss			**-.65**			**-.70**
Work relation to mates			**-.42**			**-.46**
Weekend work*			.04			.06
Work from home possibility*			.01			.04
Variance	Country-level	.03	.02	.02	.04	.03	.02
	Individual-level	.95	.89	.77	1.02	.97	.83
Intraclass correlation coefficient (ICC)	3.1	2.5	2.2	3.7	3.0	2.4
N	14,099	14,099	12,469	14,099	14,099	14,099
Countries	24	24	24	24	24	24

Sources: ISSP 2015, own calculations

Note: significant estimates p < .05 in **bold**. * Estimates refer to subsample, excluding DK (n = 11,852).

matching indices are statistically significant even when these important controls are included.

Last, several sociodemographic indicators are generally significantly related to job satisfaction—in particular, the social class variable shows how employees in the service classes, as well as skilled workers, are more satisfied than unskilled workers. Notably, effects of social class are reduced (and even disappear in the case of extrinsic matching) when job quality and additional working conditions are accounted for in models. There is also a clear indication that older employees are more satisfied with their jobs.

Conclusion

Individuals carry values, preferences and expectations as guiding principles for their choices and actions in life. This also applies to labour markets and working life, where a job and its qualities can be something sought after, or a disappointment with few desirable properties. The matching between a person's work values and the corresponding qualities of a job seems therefore to be a precondition for a satisfying working life and a well-functioning labour market. This has been the focus of this chapter. We have discussed the possible theoretical foundation of this perspective, attempted an efficient operationalization of job matching across multiple central quality dimensions, and assessed the relevance of job matches in relation to job satisfaction.

In seeking improved understanding of factors driving job satisfaction, we see how actual matching of work values to job quality is an additional factor that matters above the sheer presence of job qualities—that is, when the direct effects of job quality are taken into account. This implies that people are more satisfied if they value the specific qualities they find in their present job. While large majorities strongly value most of the here assessed (eight) extrinsic and intrinsic dimensions, there is a general shortage of jobs measuring up to such aspirations, although differences between countries in this regard are substantial. When the independent effects of extrinsic and intrinsic matching on job satisfaction were assessed, both forms of matching were significantly related to job satisfaction. However, the intrinsic aspect emerges as more strongly related to job satisfaction than the extrinsic aspect—at least when job quality dimensions are also accounted for in the analysis. Relating this finding to previous theory and research, this difference is not unexpected. In Herzberg's classical study on hygiene factors and motivators—two dimensions very similar to the extrinsic/intrinsic distinction—only the latter were regarded as contributing to satisfaction. However, in this study, we need to emphasize how the intrinsic dimension reflects more collectively altruistic and social aspects of a job, implying that workers, motivated by the altruistic and social aspects of work, are more satisfied if they find these aspects in their job. Taking this finding seriously, it means that people who, besides extrinsic factors such as pay and job security, are able to realize their valuations of social contacts in their job and striving to do good for others and society, are more likely to experience a higher degree of inner satisfaction of work.

This study indicates how matching of work values with job qualities is important, in addition to the more general significance of beneficial work environment and working conditions. As discussed previously, a labour market with a larger amount of high-quality jobs should be the best precondition to increase the probability for people to find a job that meets their expectations. However, this study draws attention to the importance also of other factors, in particular mobility in the labour market, which conditions the possibilities for people to move and transit into jobs that better fit their work aspirations. Importantly, both these aspects—the availability of high-quality jobs and the preconditions for labour market mobility—are formed by the institutional context of a country, especially the system of industrial relations. This calls for further comparative analyses of the preconditions for matching of work values and job qualities in different types of labour markets.

Notes

1. The data permits only accounting for age since non-response to the survey question on tenure is too high.
2. Employees were selected based on their response to question on their main activity status ('working'). Self-employed people were excluded as they did not answer questions about job quality. The upper age restriction is imposed to avoid bias relating to varying retirement patterns across countries.
3. Several multiplier-alternatives were tested. This measure was selected mainly on theoretical grounds and for its slightly lower correlation with job quality.
4. The total matching score is based on at least five of eight valid scores; extrinsic and intrinsic matching is calculated for respondents with valid scores on all three dimensions.

References

Bakker, A. B. and E. Demerouti (2007) 'The Job Demands-Resources Model: State of the Art.' *Journal of Managerial Psychology* 22(3): 309–328.
Berglund, T. (2012) 'Work Orientations in Western Europe and the United States', 47–66, in B. Furåker, K. Håkansson, and J. C. Karlsson (eds), *Commitment to Work and Job Satisfaction: Studies of Work Orientations*. New York: Routledge.
Cable, D. M. and J. R. Edwards (2004) 'Complementary and Supplementary Fit: A Theoretical and Empirical Integration.' *Journal of Applied Psychology* 89(5): 822–834.
De Cooman, R., S. De Gieter, R. Pepermans, S. Hermans, C. Du Bois, R. Caers and M. Jegers (2009) 'Person—Organization Fit: Testing Socialization and Attraction—Selection—Attrition Hypotheses.' *Journal of Vocational Behavior* 74(1): 102–107.

Drobnič, S., B. Beham and P. Präg (2010) 'Good Job, Good Life? Working Conditions and Quality of Life in Europe.' *Social Indicators Research* 99(2): 205–225.

Esser, I. (2017) 'Lone Parents' Self-rated Health in European Comparative Perspective: Socio-Economic Factors, Job Context and Social Protection', 180–207, in F. Portier (ed.) *Fertility, Health and Lone Parenting: European Contexts*. Oxford: Routledge.

Esser, I. and A. Lindh (2018) 'Job Preferences in Comparative Perspective 1989–2015: A Multi-Dimensional Evaluation of Individual and Contextual Influences.' *International Journal of Sociology* 48(2): 142–169. doi: 10.1080/00207659.2018.1446118.

Esser, I. and K. M. Olsen (2012) 'Perceived Job Quality: Autonomy and Job Security Within a Multi-Level Framework.' *European Sociological Review* 28(4): 443–454.

Esser, I. and K. M. Olsen (2018) 'Single and Coupled Parents' Matching on Job Quality: How Institutions Matter in European Perspective', 285–312, in R. Nieuwenhuis and L. C. Maldonado (eds) *The Triple Bind of Single-Parent Families*. University of Bristol: Policy Press.

Eurofound (2013) *Quality of Life in Europe: Subjective Well-Being*. Authors: S. Abdallah, L. Stoll and F. Eiffe. Luxembourg: Publications Office of the European Union. www.eurofound.europa.eu/sites/default/files/ef_publication/field_ef_document/ef1359en.pdf.

Festinger, L. (1957) *A Theory of Cognitive Dissonance*. Stanford: Stanford University Press.

Gagné, M. and E. L. Deci (2005) 'Self-Determination Theory and Work Motivation.' *Journal of Organizational Behavior* 26(4): 331–362.

Gallie, D. (2007) *Employment Regimes and the Quality of Work*. Oxford: Oxford University Press.

Green, F., T. Mostafa, A. Parent-Thirion, G. Vermeylen, G. V. Houten, I. Biletta and M. Lyly-Yrjanainen (2013) 'Is Job Quality Becoming More Unequal?' *Industrial & Labor Relations Review* 66(4): 753–784.

Greguras, G. J. and J. M. Diefendorff (2009) 'Different Fits Satisfy Different Needs: Linking Person Environment Fit to Employee Commitment and Performance Using Self-Determination Theory.' *Journal of Applied Psychology* 94(2): 465–477.

Herzberg, F. I. (1966) *Work and the Nature of Man*. Cleveland, NY: The World Publishing Company.

Hirschman, A. O. (1970) *Exit, Voice, and Loyalty: Responses to Decline in Firms, Organizations and States*. Cambridge, MA: Harvard University Press.

Hult, C. (2005) 'Organizational Commitment and Person-Environment Fit in Six Western Countries.' *Organization Studies* 26(2): 249–270.

Kalleberg, A. L. (2009) 'Precarious Work, Insecure Workers: Employment Relations in Transitions.' *American Sociological Review* 74(1): 1–22. doi: http://doi.org/10.1177/000312240907400101.

Kalleberg, A. L. (2011) *Good Jobs, Bad Jobs. The Rise of Polarized and Precarious Employment Systems in the United States, 1970s to 2000s*. New York: Russell Sage Foundation.

Kristof-Brown, A. L., R. D. Zimmerman and E. C. Johnson (2005) 'Consequences of Individuals' Fit at Work: A Meta-Analysis of Person-Job,

Person-Organization, Person-Group and Person-Supervisor Fit.' *Personnel Psychology* 58(2): 281–342.

Leschke, J. and A. Watt (2014) 'Challenges in Constructing a Multi-Dimensional European Job Quality Index.' *Social Indicator Research* 118(1): 1–31.

Maslow, A. (1954) *Motivation and Personality*. New York: Harper & Row.

Porter, L. W. and E. E. Lawler (1968) *Managerial Attitudes and Performance*. Homewood, IL: Irwin Inc.

Rokeach, M. (1973) *The Nature of Human Values*. New York: Free Press.

Sachau, D. A. (2007) 'Resurrecting the Motivation-Hygiene Theory: Herzberg and the Positive Psychology Movement.' *Human Resource Development Review* 6(4): 377–393.

Schwartz, S. H. (1999) 'A Theory of Cultural Values and Some Implications for Work.' *Applied Psychology: An International Review* 48(1): 23–47.

Spector, P. E. (1997) *Job Satisfaction. Application, Assessment, Causes, and Consequences*. Thousand Oaks: SAGE Publications.

Super, D. (1970) *Work Values Inventory Manual*. Boston: Houghton Mifflin.

Taris, R. and J. A. Feij (2001) 'Longitudinal Examination of the Relationship Between Supplies—Values Fit and Work Outcomes.' *Applied Psychology: An International Review* 50(1): 52–80.

Twenge, J. M., S. M. Campbell, B. J. Hoffman and C. E. Lance (2010) 'Generational Differences in Work Values: Leisure and Extrinsic Values Increasing, Social and Intrinsic Values Decreasing.' *Journal of Management* 36(5): 1117–1142.

Van den Broeck, A., J. Van Ruysseveldt, P. Smulders and H. De Witte (2011) 'Does an Intrinsic Work Value Orientation Strengthen the Impact of Job Resources? A Perspective From the Job Demands—Resources Model.' *European Journal of Work and Organizational Psychology* 20(5): 581–609.

Contributors

Mattias Bengtsson is Associate Professor of Sociology at the Department of Sociology and Work Science, University of Gothenburg. Bengtsson has among other things published texts on the meaning of work and retirement, the transformation of Swedish welfare and labour market policies, changes in active labour market policies in Europe, conditions and obstacles for transnational trade union cooperation, and social class and ideological orientations.

Tomas Berglund is Professor of Sociology, University of Gothenburg, Sweden. His areas of research are working life and labour markets in a comparative perspective. He has conducted extensive research on attitudes to work, job insecurity, atypical employment and labour market mobility.

Ann Bergman is Professor of Working Life Science at Karlstad University, Sweden. Her research interest lies within the fields of gender and work, segregation, inequality and futures studies. Currently she is doing research on digitalization and work-life boundaries.

Tómas Bjarnason has a doctoral degree in sociology from University of Gothenburg, Sweden. He is a management consultant at Gallup Iceland with a focus on employee motivation, organizational commitment, employee turnover, employee engagement and social recognition. He has written articles on work centrality, work attitudes, trust and work—life balance.

Ingrid Esser is Associate Professor of Sociology, Swedish Institute for Social Research at Stockholm University, Sweden. Her areas of research have concerned work orientations, health and well-being in comparative perspective, including studies on work values, job quality, self-rated health and well-being, social policy, and labour market organisation.

Marita Flisbäck is Associate Professor of Sociology at the Department of Sociology and Work Science, University of Gothenburg, Sweden.

Flisbäck's research has focused on careers in the arts and culture sector, creative entrepreneurship, questions of recognition and meaning-making in low status occupations and in the retirement process.

Bengt Furåker is Professor at the Department of Sociology and Work Science, University of Gothenburg, Sweden. His research mainly focuses on labour market and working life issues and the relationship between the labour market and the welfare state. Among his books are *Sociological Perspectives on Labor Markets* and two co-edited volumes: *Flexibility and Stability in Working Life* and *Commitment to Work and Job Satisfaction. Studies of Work Orientations.*

Kristina Håkansson is Professor at the Department of Sociology and Work Science, University of Gothenburg, Sweden. Her main research interest is oriented towards work organization issues. In particular, she focuses on examining the consequences of flexibility for individuals, organizations and the labour market. She was co-editor for the publications *Flexibility and Stability in Working Life* and *Commitment to Work and Job Satisfaction.*

Tommy Isidorsson is Associate Professor of Work Science at the Department of Sociology and Work Science, University of Gothenburg, Sweden. His main interest is how firms and organizations adapt to changes in demand—that is, the different strategies utilized for handling changes in production volume, including working-time, functional and numerical flexibility. He has also conducted several studies on temporary agency work and its consequences at societal, workplace and individual levels.

Jan Ch. Karlsson is Professor Emeritus of Sociology at Working Life Science, Karlstad University, Sweden. He has published widely within the areas of working life and methodology of social science. Among his books are *Organizational Misbehavior in the Workplace*, *Methods for Social Theory* (with Ann Bergman), *Explaining Society* (with Berth Danermark and Mats Ekström) and *Collective Mobilization in Changing Conditions* (with Jonas Axelsson and Egil J. Skorstad).

Belgin Okay-Somerville is Lecturer (Assistant Professor) in Human Resource Management at the Adam Smith Business School, University of Glasgow, Scotland. Her research interests focus broadly on skill utilisation, strategic HRM, employability, career development and employee well-being, particularly within the graduate labour market.

Dora Scholarios is Professor of Work Psychology at the University of Strathclyde Business School in Glasgow, Scotland. Her recent research has focused on job quality (e.g., skill utilisation, underemployment), graduate career transitions and employee well-being, including the effects of shift work and human resource management. She is currently Co-Editor-in-Chief of the *Human Resource Management Journal.*

Edward Sosu is Senior Lecturer in the School of Education at University of Strathclyde, Glasgow, Scotland. He has a strong interest in quantitative methods and in addressing issues from a psychological perspective. His current research is predominantly focused on understanding how experiences of socioeconomic disadvantage in childhood influence educational, psychological and labour market outcomes for individuals.

Index

For Product Safety Concerns and Information please contact our EU
representative GPSR@taylorandfrancis.com
Taylor & Francis Verlag GmbH, Kaufingerstraße 24, 80331 München, Germany